A
HEART LIKE
HIS

BETH MOORE

A
HEART LIKE
HIS

INTIMATE REFLECTIONS *on the*

LIFE OF DAVID

INTERNATIONAL

NASHVILLE, TENNESSEE

ISBN: 978-0-6331-5242-0

© 2002 International Edition

Not For Sale in the USA

Published by B&H Publishing Group, Nashville, Tennessee

Dewey Decimal Classification: 222
Subject Heading: DAVID, KING OF ISRAEL: MEDITATIONS / BIBLE STUDY
Library of Congress Card Catalog Number: 99-24850

Original 1999 edition published with same title but different cover.

Unless otherwise stated all Scripture citation is from the NIV, the Holy Bible,
New International Version, copyright © 1973, 1978, 1984 by International Bible Society.
Other versions cited are the NKJV, New King James Version, copyright © 1979, 1980, 1982,
Thomas Nelson, Inc., Publishers; NASB, the New American Standard Bible,
© the Lockman Foundation, 1960, 1962, 1963, 1968, 1971, 1972, 1973, 1975, 1977;
used by permission; RSV, Revised Standard Version of the Bible, copyrighted
1946, 1952, © 1971, 1973; used by permission; KJV, the King James Version.

Library of Congress Cataloging-in-Publication Data
Moore, Beth, 1957–
    A heart like his : intimate reflections on the life of David / Beth Moore, with
    Dale McCleskey.
       p.   cm.
    ISBN 0-8054-2035-5
    1. David, King of Israel Meditations.   I. McCleskey, Dale.   II. Title.
BS580.D3M58   1999
    222'.4092—dc21

                                                                    99-24850
                                                                    CIP

2 3 4 5 6 7 8 9   13 12 11 10 09 08

DEDICATION

*To those willing to walk any road on feet of clay
to have a heart like His.*

CONTENTS

PREFACE

Beth Moore and I met as writer and editor doing the workbook version of *A Heart Like His*. When we finished the workbook in the spring of 1996, it was a part of a women's enrichment ministry. Beth immediately said she wanted me to do a version of the study for men because David should not be restricted to women's ministry. We agreed to pray and see what God would do. In October 1998 Broadman & Holman asked us to do the present volume. We are tremendously excited about what God has done—exceeding abundantly above all that we asked or thought (Eph. 3:20).

We pray that this volume will be an enrichment resource for those doing in-depth Bible study and that it will reach thousands who have not yet done the workbook. We encourage you to do the additional study in the workbook.

Beth: I am indebted to my editor and dear friend, Dale McCleskey, for taking the in-depth study I wrote by the same title and reformatting it into this book. His partnership in this work and many others is invaluable to me. Our earnest prayer is not so much that you meet David but that you meet David's God. His refuge. His fortress. His strength. His deliverer. And share his passion. May God delve a little deeper into your heart with every turn of the page . . . and create within you a heart like His.

Dale: Beth Moore is a Bible teacher God has been using to reach vast numbers of women and men. I serve as an editor for LifeWay Christian Resources. One of the joys of studying the life of David appears in the relationship between Jonathan and David. They were two men who developed

XII A Heart Like His

a special friendship because they shared a common commitment to God. From the moment we began to work together, Beth and I discovered a similar commitment. We share a passion for the Word of God and for people—especially for people with hurts.

We both believe deeply in the message of this book. We believe God is the author, so we have made no distinction between human authors— no "he said, she said." We commend to you the wonderful message of David—the man who had a heart like His.

PREPARATION FOR THE JOURNEY

"As for me, this is my covenant with you: You will be the father of many nations." (Gen. 17:4)

I am so excited that you are coming along on this excursion. The journey has all the romance, mystery, intrigue, love, betrayal, and majesty of the greatest epic. As you read, I believe your spirit will soar and your heart will break. You will climb to the heights of the most noble human emotions and behavior, and you will plummet with us to the depths of our sin nature. Pack your backpack, throw in a jar of peanut butter, and let's go.

Maybe it was the fact that David was his father's last choice. Maybe it was his uncanny way with a harp . . . and a slingshot. Maybe it was his unwillingness to kill a madman because he feared God even more. Or surely it was his ability to dance down the streets of Jerusalem. Then again, perhaps it was his shocking humanity and the resulting suggestion that we cannot out-sin God's ability to forgive. I can't quite put my finger on why an ancient shepherd boy-king so captured my imagination over and over. I simply like him. His story gives me hope and terrifies me into fresh reverence. I see so many things in him I wish I had—and so many others I'm scared to death I do have.

All you need to relate to David is a membership to the human race. No matter how familiar you are with the biblical account of his life, I believe you'll be stirred, shocked, amazed, and forced to think a few hard thoughts all over again. His story is proof once again that truth is far more intriguing than fiction.

Why study David? I believe he is extremely important for several reasons.

First, he was a man with a tremendous relationship with God—called a man after God's own heart. His songs and poetry inspire us to worship. Since we believe that an intimate love relationship with God is the highest blessing possible in this life or the next, David is a worthy subject for our study.

Second, David simply merits our attention. He was a wondrously complex man. A musician and a warrior. He was capable of both the highest loyalty and the most base sin. In David we see the very best and the very worst in the human species. Getting to know David allows us to get to know ourselves.

A third reason to study David involves his relationship to Jesus Christ, the Messiah. In many ways David prefigures Christ. As we study David, we will come both to understand and to appreciate our Savior in new ways.

I believe strongly in a fourth reason to study David. Simply stated, he's in the Bible. You see, Bible study saved my life. I believe studying God's Word has enormous life-enhancing value. In many different ways I have benefitted from spending time in God's Word. As you read *A Heart Like His,* you will accomplish a detailed study of the books of 1 and 2 Samuel. You will also read portions of Psalms, 1 and 2 Chronicles, and many verses from other Old and New Testament books. I have written this book so that you can read it by itself, but I would encourage you to read the Scripture passages from your own Bible. The Scripture references for reading appear at the beginning of each chapter.

We will devote our entire study to answering practical questions about being a person after God's own heart:

:: How can a person be forgiven and restored after sin?

:: How can a person continue to be faithful to God when nothing seems to be going his or her way?

:: How can a person find God when he or she feels all alone?

:: How important is God's influence on the family?

On our journey, we will certainly discover insights into these and other questions. Until then, let's allow God to use our curiosity to keep us committed to our excursion through His Word.

So turn the page; it's too good to miss.

PART I

SUMMONED FROM THE SHEEPFOLD

Psalm 23

A psalm of David.

1 The LORD is my shepherd, I shall not be in want.

2   He makes me lie down in green pastures,

he leads me beside quiet waters,

3   he restores my soul.

He guides me in paths of righteousness

for his name's sake.

4 Even though I walk

through the valley of the shadow of death,

I will fear no evil,

for you are with me;

your rod and your staff,

they comfort me.

5 You prepare a table before me

in the presence of my enemies.

You anoint my head with oil;

my cup overflows.

6 Surely goodness and love will follow me

all the days of my life,

and I will dwell in the house of the LORD

forever.

Chapter 1

A LOOK
AT THE HEART

1 Samuel 16:1–13

The Lord said to Samuel, "Do not consider his appearance
or his height, for I have rejected him. The Lord does not look at
the things man looks at. Man looks at the outward appearance,
but the Lord looks at the heart." (1 Sam. 16:7)

We begin with Scripture's first mention of David; we will end with his last breath. From our first glimpses of David, you will begin to wonder how one person could be so utterly typical in some ways and so completely atypical in others. That question will bless and haunt us intermittently throughout our study of David. We look first to David's youth and the relationships that shaped his future.

I love to discover new truths through Scripture, but I also love wrapping the familiar passages around me like a security blanket and feeling their warmth. Perhaps we'll have the joy of experiencing the best of both worlds in these pages.

David appears first in 1 Samuel 16, in turbulent circumstances. The opening words of the chapter ring with change:

The LORD said to Samuel, "How long will you mourn for Saul,
since I have rejected him as king over Israel? Fill your horn with
oil and be on your way; I am sending you to Jesse of Bethlehem.
I have chosen one of his sons to be king." (1 Sam. 16:1)

The verse supplies interesting facts to file away. Saul had been rejected as king of Israel. Samuel the prophet had been grieving over Saul. Samuel, uncharacteristically, argued with God. He said "How can I go? Saul will hear about it and kill me" (v. 2).

The plot thickens.

Samuel the prophet took a heifer for a sacrifice (when engaging in matters of espionage, it always pays to have a good cover story) and set out for the Bethlehem home of a man named Jesse. Jesse had six of the finest sons in all Israel, and—did I mention?—those six had a kid brother.

Have you noticed how much you can learn about a person by the reaction others have in his or her presence? When Samuel arrived in Bethlehem, the town council trembled with fear. Nobody to trifle with, that Samuel. He announced his peaceful intentions and invited the village to attend the sacrifice. When Jesse arrived, Samuel's heart leaped at the sight. The eldest son, Eliab, was certainly king material, but God gave a clear no. Each of the sons of Jesse followed—each with the same result.

A slightly puzzled Samuel inquired, "Are these all the sons you have?"

Have you ever felt like the youngest son, the consummate "little brother?" You don't have to be male and you don't have to have siblings to feel that way. In fact, I don't think anyone escapes the feeling completely. Sometime, somewhere, you've probably been treated as if you didn't exist, weren't wanted, didn't matter.

For example, when a friend was about four years old, his two older brothers had company, and he wanted to tag along. Probably he annoyed his older siblings into a brilliant idea. They took him to an anthill, and with a couple of serving spoons and a coffee can, soon had his pants filled with very angry insects.

The few glimpses we see of David and his brothers suggest that he too knew the "sting" of being left out. I believe his wisdom and meditative nature got their start in the loneliness of a little brother accustomed to being put down and ostracized. Did he inherit the duties of keeping sheep, or were the woolly creatures preferable to the company of taunting brothers?

When Samuel asked Jesse if he had any other sons, Jesse answered, "There is still the youngest . . . but he is tending the sheep."

Samuel's stubbornness amuses me. Notice his response to Jesse once he learned that Jesse had one more son: "Send for him; we will not sit down until he arrives." He certainly knew how to get them moving! Don't forget how everyone trembled when he arrived in Bethlehem.

David, a young teenager, arrived on the scene with no idea what awaited him. He was handsome, with a reddish complexion, and no doubt smelled like sheep. He obviously was not his own father's first choice, nor Samuel's. But God taught Samuel a very important lesson: "Man looks at the outward appearance, but the LORD looks at the heart." God reminded Samuel that the human mind has an overwhelming tendency to make assumptions based on appearances. God's choices don't always make sense to us, but they are never haphazard or random. A few considerations about David shed light on why God may have chosen him.

The genealogy David and Christ shared was of obvious importance. In Matthew 1:3, we see that both David and Christ were descendants of Judah, one of the sons of Jacob. In the prophecy Jacob spoke over Judah, he said, "The scepter will not depart from Judah, nor the ruler's staff from between his feet" (Gen. 49:10). You see, David was not a random choice. He was one of the most important figures in the genealogy of Christ, "the Lion of the tribe of Judah" (Rev. 5:5).

I never fail to be encouraged by Christ's heritage. How do you respond to the fact that the only perfect person in Christ's genealogy is Christ Himself?

To me, Christ's flawed family history serves as a continual reminder of the grace of God in my life. In my human desire for perfection, I want to be so good that I need no one and no thing. It may surprise you to know that that desire grows from a biblical base: the tower of Babel. The tower pictures graphically our human drive to take God's place. Whenever my perfectionism kicks in, I run back to Scripture—to the only source of perfection:

> *For all have sinned and fall short of the glory of God, and are justified freely by his grace through the redemption that came by Christ Jesus.* (Rom. 3:23–24)

God chose David. On the surface, the choice made no sense. But God doesn't work on sense; He works on grace. God called you, and God called me. He knew what He was doing.

In many ways David's life foreshadowed or pictured details of Christ's life. God illustrated the unknown about the Messiah through the known about David. David was not divine or perfect, as we will quickly discover, but God has used him to teach us truths about the One who is. I think you'll enjoy knowing that the name *Jesse* is a "personal name meaning, 'man.'"[1] Christ referred to Himself as the "Son of Man" more than any other title. Isn't it interesting that the King of Israel who often prefigured Jesus was technically also the "son of man"?

David's occupation also made him a candidate for kingship. Do you find God's activity as fascinating as I do? He loves us, calls us, redeems us, and uses us totally because of who He is. We might be tempted to go overboard and believe only His grace matters—that we are the hole in the proverbial doughnut. Of David we might think, "God called him in spite of the fact that he was a common shepherd." The facts prove otherwise. God was working in David's life from the beginning.

David received invaluable experience keeping sheep. Psalm 78:70–72 states, "He chose David his servant / and took him from the sheep pens; / from tending the sheep he brought him / to be the shepherd of his people Jacob, / of Israel his inheritance. / And David shepherded them with integrity of heart; / with skillful hands he led them."

The God who prepared David has been preparing you throughout your life also. What are your skills? Your life experiences? I believe God usually takes the building blocks of our lives and uses them to His glory. Have you ever felt that your occupational skills were useless in areas of service to God? He may have great plans to use who you are in unique and powerful ways. Never assume that to follow Him means to throw away who He has made you to be. Few things seem less spiritual than keeping a bunch of smelly sheep, yet God used David's skills for eternal purposes.

When David arrived at home, Samuel saw that he was "ruddy, with a fine appearance and handsome features" (1 Sam. 16:12). Still, Samuel did not move. He had already made a mistake based on appearances. Then God said, "Rise and anoint him; he is the one" (v. 12). The next few words send chills up my spine.

> So Samuel took the horn of oil and anointed him in the presence
> of his brothers, and from that day on the Spirit of the LORD came
> upon David in power. (1 Sam. 16:13)

The Holy Spirit just can't seem to arrive without power, can He? As we study the life of a shepherd boy, we will no doubt see testimony of that power again and again. Samuel stood before a young lad and with awe and reverence poured the oil on his head. Although the oil surely blurred the vision of the one whose eyes it bathed, God's vision was crystal clear. He had said, "I will send thee to Jesse the Bethlehemite: for

I have provided me a king among his sons" (1 Sam. 16:1b, KJV). The Hebrew word for *provided* is *ra'ah*. It means "to see, to look at, view, inspect, regard, to perceive; . . . to feel; to experience."[2] Second Chronicles 16:9 says, "For the eyes of the LORD run to and fro throughout the whole earth, to show Himself strong on behalf of those whose heart is loyal to Him" (NKJV).

That day so many years ago, the eyes of the Lord looked throughout the whole earth and fell upon an obscure little village called Bethlehem. There He found a heart—one like unto His own. He found a heart tender to little lost sheep, and He showed Himself strong on behalf of that heart, just as He promised.

Chapter 2

DAVID'S BACK STORY

1 Samuel 1–3

*O Lord Almighty, if you will only look upon your servant's misery and
remember me. (1 Sam. 1:11)*

One of the blessed gifts God has given our ministry is Lee Sizemore,
who produces our videos for LifeWay Christian Resources. Lee intro-
duced me to a new term. We were talking about David and the forces
that shaped his life, the time in which he lived, and the people who
preceded him. Lee said, "In video production terms, that is David's
'back story.'" What a wonderful term. We all come with a "back story."
Some of us come with a heritage of faith and faithfulness. Some of us
come with the testimony of God's ability to rescue us from terrible
circumstances.

To understand and appreciate David, we need to venture into his
back story. In David's back story we get to meet some heroic characters
and some despicable ones. We begin with one of the high points. We
read about Samuel's anointing David to be the king, but we would have
no Samuel without a brave and obedient mother named Hannah. As
1 Samuel begins, we meet Elkanah and his two wives, Hannah and
Peninnah. Peninnah had children, but Hannah was childless. They had
gone up to the tabernacle at Shiloh to offer sacrifices.

Because the LORD had closed her [Hannah's] womb, her rival kept provoking her in order to irritate her. This went on year after year. Whenever Hannah went up to the house of the LORD, her rival provoked her till she wept and would not eat. Elkanah her husband would say to her, "Hannah, why are you weeping? Why don't you eat? Why are you downhearted? Don't I mean more to you than ten sons?" (1 Sam. 1:6–8)

I'm sorry to report that Elkanah reminds me of one of the thinly developed characters in a TV sitcom. To his credit we read of his making the appropriate sacrifices with his family, but we also find he is married to two wives. Ultimately the word *clueless* comes to mind to describe Elkanah. There he is, married to two wives, one of them childless in a society where childbearing is everything, and the wife with children torturing the wife without. In that situation he said, "Hannah, why are you weeping? Why don't you eat? Why are you downhearted? Don't I mean more to you than ten sons?"

Does this guy deserve the "I just don't get it" award, or what? I'm jumping ahead, but when Hannah gave birth to Samuel and later prepared to give him up to be reared by the priests, Elkanah said: "Do what seems best to you" (1 Sam. 1:23).

Guys, don't follow Elkanah's example. Get involved at home. If God has given you a wife, put the effort into understanding her. Is it an impossible task? Most assuredly. But sometimes the challenging jobs are the most rewarding. Wives need men who engage and participate, not abdicate as parent and spouse. For too many husbands the lights are on, but nobody is home.

A serious problem arises in this section of Scripture. The situation certainly adds to Elkanah's inability to understand or meet his wife's needs. Simply stated, he had too many wives!

Let's take a look at where polygamy first crawled into history. Genesis 4:19 tells us: "Lamech married two women, one named Adah and the other Zillah." Lamech disobeyed God's very specific directive in Genesis 2:24: "A man will leave his father and mother and be united to his wife, and they will become one flesh." Tough assignment becoming one flesh when three or more get involved.

We need to nail solidly into our lives two important precepts that come from comparing these Scriptures. First, prevalence does not equal acceptance. Just because polygamy became a common practice, God did not change the rules. Polygamy did not become acceptable with God because it became common with man any more than statistics cause Him to change His mind about any other sin. Our God is incredibly "public opinion resistant."

Second, a man cannot be one flesh with two women. Nor can a woman be one flesh with two men. According to God's math, only two can become one. Both of Elkanah's wives suffered because of his disobedience to God.

As we have all discovered in our individual lives, one problem unchecked invariably leads to plenty of others. "Year after year" the mother of Elkanah's children baited Hannah, and "year after year" the woman of Elkanah's heart bit the bait. Small wonder Hannah felt "bitterness of soul."

What constitutes the most bitter pill you've ever had to swallow? All of us have them. Compared to each other they may seem major or minor, but just as the only minor surgery is one that happens to someone else, the bitterness we feel is never minor. Hannah's situation certainly involved no small pain. Childless. Tormented. Alone. A plight many have faced, but company proves small solace for misery.

Hannah made the right choices about what to do with her bitterness. She "wept much and prayed to the LORD" (1 Sam. 1:10). In her prayer, she made two almost unimaginable commitments. One was by far the easiest of the pair. She promised no razor would be used on his head. This meant the child would be a Nazirite, especially consecrated to the Lord. The other promise was to give him to the Lord for all the days of his life.

We could accuse her of bargaining with God, who does not bargain, but our God does search the earth for those with a heart toward Him so He can bless them (2 Chron. 16:9). Chronicles had not yet been written, but somehow Hannah sought in God what David later learned to be true: "The LORD searches every heart and understands every motive behind the thoughts. If you seek him, he will be found by you" (1 Chron. 28:9). In her bitterness she sought her Lord.

I believe God responded to Hannah's prayer for two reasons. First, He is gracious. He longs to pour His love on us. Second, He knew her heart. He knew that what she said, she would do.

Verses 12–14 never cease to make me grin. Only God would give us all sides to a story. Had man written the Bible, he surely would have extolled only his virtues. Eli saw Hannah praying fervently, and he misunderstood badly. He said to her, "How long will you keep on getting drunk? Get rid of your wine" (1 Sam. 1:14).

When you were a child, did you ever get blamed for something you didn't do? It must be close to a universal experience. Imagine how Hannah felt when Eli added insult to her injuries. Yet this scene reveals Hannah's character. As the saying goes: "You never really know what's inside until someone bumps you." For Hannah to respond in anger, or at least indignation, would have been so easy, but she said:

> "Not so, my lord," Hannah replied, "I am a woman who is deeply troubled. I have not been drinking wine or beer; I was pouring out my soul to the LORD. Do not take your servant for a wicked woman; I have been praying here out of my great anguish and grief." (1 Sam. 1:15–16)

Eli responded to Hannah's gentle spirit with a blessing: "Go in peace, and may the God of Israel grant you what you have asked of him" (v. 17).

Hannah promptly responded to Eli's prophetic blessing. She "went her way and ate something, and her face was no longer downcast." Verses 19 and 20 tell us what Hannah and Elkanah did before they left Shiloh, what they did when they got home, and what God did for them.

> *Early the next morning they arose and worshiped before the LORD and then went back to their home at Ramah. Elkanah lay with Hannah his wife, and the LORD remembered her. So in the course of time Hannah conceived and gave birth to a son. She named him Samuel, saying, "Because I asked the LORD for him."* (1 Sam. 1:19–20)

By the very choice of a name, Hannah demonstrated that she took her vow to God seriously. For three years she would hold and love this child. Then she would fulfill her vow and love him as she gave him to the one who gave him to her.

"She named him Samuel." So precious. So prayed for. So deeply loved. And so very important to the Hebrew nation. Hannah vowed to the Lord that she would give the son she asked for to the Lord and that the child would be a Nazirite. Can you imagine how much easier it would be to say the words about a hypothetical baby, before you held the child in your arms—before your heart became so wrapped up in his that you could hardly keep them separate? Imagine the emotion that filled Hannah's heart. Elkanah went up to make the annual sacrifice. Hannah did not go along, but she told him, "After the boy is weaned, I will take him and present him before the LORD, and he will live there always" (1 Sam. 1:22). After Samuel was weaned, she took him to Eli and said,

"I prayed for this child, and the LORD has granted me what I asked of him. So now I give him to the LORD. For his whole life he will be given over to the LORD." And he worshiped the LORD there. (1 Sam.1:27–28)

I never fail to be moved by this account in Scripture. How deeply this woman wanted a child. How easy to promise anything to get what we want, but Hannah did not voice empty words. Even in her bitterness of soul and great weeping, she made her vow to God with the steadfast determination to fulfill it.

Hebrew mothers, according to the accounts recorded in the Apocrypha (2 Mac. 7:27), customarily nursed their children until they were about three years old. I cannot imagine a more difficult age to tear myself away from a child. Still young enough to be such a baby! Old enough to question why. I cried the first time I let mine go to Mother's Day Out for half a day!

If Hannah mustered up the strength to take him there, you would never expect that she could walk away and leave him. In fact, these days we would question such a mother's love for her child.

Oh, but God had a plan. A marvelous plan. He allowed Hannah to be childless so that she would petition God for a child instead of assuming it would be the normal result of marital relations. He also allowed Hannah to be deeply desirous of a child so she would dedicate him entirely to the Lord. He sovereignly planned for His word to come through Eli at the temple so that she would return him to the exact place where she made the vow. Why? Because God had a plan for Samuel that was far more significant than even the most loving set of parents could devise.

Surely while nursing him, Hannah looked into the face of her precious son, and with love overflowing, rehearsed the faithfulness of God in his tiny ears. No doubt he was weaned to know he was appointed to grow up in the house of the Lord. What did the child do when she took him there? "He worshiped the LORD" (v. 28). The Hebrew word is *shachah*. The *Complete Word Study Old Testament* tells us that "*shachah* was not used in the general sense of worship, but specifically to bow down, to prostrate oneself as an act of respect before a superior being."[3]

I recall a scene, engraved in many of our memories, of a tiny boy stepping forward from his grieving mother, saluting the flag-draped coffin of a man who was not only his daddy but the President of the United States. Imagine another scene: A tiny three-year-old boy, still with creases of satiny baby skin around his plump little thighs, bending his knee and bowing before El Elyon, the sovereign God of all creation. How precious this child must have been to God. How in the world could a child that age have such respect for the God of the universe? We get a clue from Hannah's prayer of praise, found in 1 Samuel 2:1–10.

Samuel learned faith from his mother—a woman whose faithfulness evidenced her faith, a woman with compulsory praise on her lips. She met painful sacrifice with a song.

God does not ask of us that we take our children to the temple and leave them there to be reared by priests, but we must give them to God in other, equally important ways.

Remember the faith of Hannah. She sought God in her deep need. She made a vow that, by its very nature, was either a deep commitment or a hollow mockery. Then she fulfilled her vow with a mother's sacrifice.

What a wonderful addendum to the story of Hannah in 1 Samuel 2:21:

> *The LORD was gracious to Hannah; she conceived and gave birth to three sons and two daughters. Meanwhile, the boy Samuel grew up in the presence of the LORD.*

That God gave Hannah other children warms our heart, but, as any parent who has ever lost a child can tell you, all the children in the world cannot replace the one who is lost. Hannah's circumstances were made even more difficult due to the presence of evil men in the temple. When faced with evil and loss, trusting God doesn't come easy.

Eli was the priest in charge of the tabernacle at Shiloh. At the time of our story, he was an old man. His two sons, Hophni and Phinehas, had followed him as priests in charge. Worshipers came to Shiloh from all the tribes of Israel, bringing with them offerings. We read that "Eli's sons were wicked men; they had no regard for the LORD" (1 Sam. 2:12). They abused worshipers, flaunted the sacrificial laws and customs, and even committed adultery with the women who served at the tabernacle.

At first look, the situation with Eli, his sons, and Samuel seems unfathomable. As credentials for effective parenting, Eli's sons would get him expelled from any waiting list for adoptive parents. Why would God entrust Samuel to a man who had two such sons? One friend of mine observed that Eli demonstrated God's willingness to recommission us. No matter how badly we've messed up in the past, God can still use us. What an expression of His grace to Eli, to give him another chance at fathering!

As we see the unbending character of the man that Samuel became, remember the influences that shaped his life. Possibly he chose to learn from the negative example of Hophni and Phinehas. Most certainly he learned from his mother's respect for God and her commitment to obedience. From Samuel's example we can conclude at least the following truths:

- We cannot use even the worst of our leaders' failures as excuses before God for lives of negligence and compromise. Despite the example of Eli's sons, Samuel chose a life of unparalleled faithfulness to God.
- Parents, like Hannah, do a tremendous service to their children when they rear them to worship and adore God and God alone. Hannah could not train Samuel to depend on her because she

knew she wouldn't be there. As we witness his life, we will never see Samuel confuse God and man.

First Samuel, chapter 3, tells one of those wonderful human-interest, God-at-work stories. Apparently Samuel served daily in the tabernacle and slept there at night as well. The story contains two interesting tidbits. "In those days the word of the LORD was rare" (v. 1) and Samuel "was lying down in the temple of the LORD, where the ark of God was" (v. 3).

Knowing what we do about Eli and his sons, we would expect the Word of the Lord to be rare. As the prophet Amos wrote later concerning a similar circumstance, God had sent on them "a famine of hearing the words of the LORD" (Amos 8:11b). They did not hear from God because they did not honor God. God did not speak because they did not listen.

Samuel appears in stark contrast to the disobedience of the people around him. Samuel was where he was supposed to be. Before the Lord. Where the ark of God was.

The young boy heard a voice calling "Samuel" and responded by running to Eli. Samuel said, "Here I am; you called me," but Eli sent him back to bed. The scene repeated itself.

Don't you see the humor in the situation? Most of us know how annoying and persistent a small child can be at bedtime. Eli probably felt like we feel when a child calls for the fourth drink of water.

Then Eli realized what was going on. Did the realization come with a stab of conscience? Did he recognize that God was speaking to the only person in the household who had not dishonored Him?

There was plenty to criticize about Eli, but when push came to shove, he did come through. "Go and lie down, and if he calls you, say 'Speak, LORD, for your servant is listening' " (v. 9).

Samuel obeyed.

God spoke.

Again, Samuel obeyed.

Just that simply, God initiated one of the great prophets of Scripture and of history. That initial experience presents an overview of the life of Samuel—a man who obeyed God.

We see in Samuel one of the great turning-point figures of the Bible. Abraham signaled the beginning of the covenant and the age of the patriarchs. Moses marked the birth of the nation and the giving of the law. Samuel marked the end of the judges and the birth of the Hebrew monarchy. He was the greatest and last of the judges.

When God first revealed Himself to Samuel, we read some dramatic words: "The LORD came and stood there, calling as at the other times, 'Samuel! Samuel!'" (1 Sam. 3:10). How incredible. The Lord came and stood there, calling out to Samuel. The Lord revealed Himself through His spoken word to a little boy. What is equally amazing, He comes today and reveals Himself through His written Word to you and to me. Yep, standing right there, right now. What do you think of that?

Chapter 3

TAKING GOD FOR GRANTED

1 Samuel 4–6

When the ark of the Lord's covenant came into the camp, all Israel raised
such a great shout that the ground shook. (1 Sam. 4:5)

What strange and amazing circumstances: Eli the priest was now both old and blind. Samuel the boy prophet was growing toward manhood. The Bible says the Lord was with Samuel as he grew and that Samuel let none of God's words fall to the ground (1 Sam. 3:19). "The LORD continued to appear at Shiloh, and there he revealed himself to Samuel through his word" (1 Sam. 3:21).

As was true through much of the period of the judges, the Israelites were under the heel of a neighboring, but not neighborly, country. This time the Philistines had conquered Israel. So in 1 Samuel 4:1–2 we read that the Israelites went out to fight against the Philistines, but the Israelites met bitter defeat. About four thousand soldiers lost their lives in the battle.

Have you noticed how people who most ignore God are the first to blame Him in time of tragedy? The Israelites had rejected and ignored God for a generation; now they met defeat and their first question was: "Why did the LORD bring defeat upon us today?" (v. 3).

I have noticed something else specific to religious people who do not walk with God. They cannot tell the difference between legitimate faith and superstition. The leaders sent for the ark of the covenant. No doubt their thinking ran that their ancestors had carried the ark when God won great victories, so if they had the ark, they would be victorious.

We can take a great lesson from their presumption. The sovereign God loves deeply, but He will not be disrespected. He will not permit us to take Him for granted. He will not honor our neglect.

Genuinely spiritual people recognize that the trappings of God's presence—such as church buildings, human organizations, even the sacred ark—have no meaning apart from Him. Those who honor Him will respect the symbols of His presence, but they will not worship those symbols. They certainly will not allow them to take His place.

According to the 1 Samuel account, the very ones who despised and disrespected the sacred things of God, Hophni and Phinehas, came with the ark. No way under heaven was God going to give them this victory. They were treating the ark of the covenant as a good-luck charm. The ark had no power to save. Only the God who graced the ark with His presence had that power. Likewise, the cross has no power to save—only the Christ who graced it with His presence. We must be very cautious to avoid ever approaching the Divine as a talisman.

Like pagans calling for the witch doctor, the Israelites called for the ark. Once again the army prepared to fight the Philistines, this time with total confidence. The Israelites went into battle with a mighty shout, certain that God would give victory. Meanwhile, the Philistines assumed their own defeat. Having heard about how God sent the plagues on the Eypgtians, still they went into the battle with the thought that to die would be better than becoming slaves to the Hebrews. Here was a game the network brass would never have chosen to broadcast. The outcome was so certain—until God stepped in.

Fighting the Philistines without God's intervention resulted in four thousand dead. When the disrespected God intervened, the Israelites lost thirty thousand soldiers, the ark of God was captured, and Eli's two sons, Hophni and Phinehas, were dead (vv. 10–11).

A messenger returned from the disaster to Shiloh. He announced,

"Israel fled before the Philistines, and the army has suffered heavy losses. Also your two sons, Hophni and Phinehas, are dead, and the ark of God has been captured." (1Sam. 4:17)

The Scripture then offers one of those curious details. When the messenger mentioned the ark, "Eli fell backward off his chair by the side of the gate. His neck was broken and he died, for he was an old man and heavy. He had led Israel forty years" (1 Sam. 4:18). What a strange epitaph for an important, yet pathetic, priest of God!

After the events surrounding the loss of the battle and the ark, the next phase of the story tickles my funny bone. The Philistines, who a few hours before had considered themselves dead men, returned to their capital of Ashdod. In keeping with the custom of the day, they carried the ark through the city in a great victory celebration. The parade ended at the temple of their god, Dagon.

Let me give you a bit of background. The chief deity of the Canaanite pantheon was Baal. The name *Baal* means "lord." You could compare him to Zeus in Greek mythology, the head god of the non-gods. The goddess often encountered in Canaan was Asherah (also called Ashtoreth). Baal and Asherah often appeared as a couple in the pagan worship. In 1 Kings 18:19, Jezebel had 450 prophets of Baal and 400 prophets of Asherah.

Where does Dagon come in? Dagon was supposed to be the father of Baal. So the temple of Dagon was no small matter to the Philistines. They brought the ark and placed it in the temple of Dagon in a classic show of "my god's bigger than your god." They just didn't know who they were messing with.

The next morning the ark was unmoved, but Dagon had fallen face-down on the floor in a position of worship. Remember Romans 14:11? "'As surely as I live,' says the LORD, / 'every knee will bow before me.'" That includes stone knees.

In the long tradition of slow learners, the Philistines spent the day propping Dagon back up and then went home for supper. The next morning Dagon again appeared on his face, this time with his head and hands broken off. You gotta love it. The Book of Isaiah said it well: "'I am the LORD, and there is none else, there is no God beside me'" (Isa. 45:5, KJV). God taught the Philistines this lesson literally.

God commands us to make Him our absolute priority. Even attempting to place Him beside those other things we reverence most means dishonoring Him.

You can read the rest of the story in 1 Samuel 5 and 6, but here's the short form: God wasn't through showin' He's God. So He sent a plague on the Philistines in Ashdod.

They moved the ark to Gath. God moved the plague to Gath.

To Ekron. To Ekron.

You get the picture? God loved the Philistines, and He knew that the best thing for them, and for us, is to worship Him. He is perfectly willing to "plague" us until we acknowledge Him.

Finally the Philistines cried "uncle." They included an offering to the God of the Hebrews and sent the ark back to Israel . . . sort of.

Any farmer would recognize that the Philistines tried to rig the return of the ark. They put the ark on a cart pulled by two cows that had never pulled a cart, cows with nursing calves penned up at home, and sent the cows on their way with the ark. The Philistine leaders obviously did everything they could to keep the cows from taking the ark away.

Have you ever wanted a certain answer from God so desperately that you consciously or subconsciously tried to "rig" the results? Reading things into the answer that just weren't there? Grabbing the first thing out of someone's mouth as your answer? I think we all have. It's easy to do, but it invariably leads to pain because we end up claiming a promise or a position God never gave us.

Obviously, the cows wouldn't pull the cart together, and certainly they wouldn't leave their calves. Certainly, that is, except for God. The cows obeyed the Creator of cows. I guess this story proves another basic truth. Sin makes you stupid. The cows had better sense than the Philistines. God can appoint even the beasts of the field to do His bidding.

I'd love to report that the people of Israel learned their lesson from the fiasco when they lost the ark. Unfortunately, human hearts seem remarkably resistant to wisdom.

When the cows came to Beth Shemesh, the people rejoiced and offered sacrifices. Unfortunately, seventy of the men looked into the ark, and God killed them on the spot for the gross violation of His commands.

So, in fear, the people of Beth Shemesh sent the ark to the nearby town of Kiriath Jearim. There they took the ark to the house of Abinadab and consecrated his son to guard the ark. For the next twenty years the ark remained at the house of Abinadab.

Waiting.

Waiting for a prophet who was still a boy to become a man.

Waiting for a prophet who would not allow a word from the Lord to fall to the ground.

Samuel the prophet. The prophet who anointed two kings for Israel: Saul, the choice of the people, and David, the choice of God.

All part of David's back story . . .

Chapter 4

CHORDS OF COMFORT

1 Samuel 16:14–23

So Samuel took the horn of oil and anointed him in the presence of his brothers, and from that day on the Spirit of the Lord came upon David in power. Samuel then went to Ramah. (1 Sam. 16:13)

Remember the shepherd boy chosen by the prophet of God? Samuel clandestinely anointed David as the rightful king of Israel, but as so often occurs in life, an obstacle existed. This obstacle stood a head taller than any other man in Israel, was the king, and bore the name Saul.

What do you do when God has commissioned you but you don't know the next step? Listen to what the Bible says about David: "The Spirit of the LORD came upon David in power" from that day.

So David began to do great things for God, right?

Wrong!

The anointed shepherd boy took care of his responsibilities. He returned to caring for his father's sheep. What should you do when God has called you but you don't know what to do next? I certainly can't take the Spirit's job, but here's a good principle: Keep studying God's Word and listening to His voice; but while you're listening, take care of the responsibilities He has given you. Looking back at years of ministry, I see that God often uses that small faithfulness to accomplish more than the great things of which we dream.

Meanwhile, we read a puzzling reference to how God worked in Saul's life.

> *Now the Spirit of the LORD had departed from Saul, and an evil spirit from the LORD tormented him.* (1 Sam. 16:14)

The Holy Spirit had a different relationship with people before Christ died on the cross. His Spirit now lives in all believers (Rom. 8:9). Before Calvary, the Holy Spirit worked to empower specific types of service rather than to bring a new relationship with God through salvation. Less than a hundred people in the Old Testament were characterized by the Holy Spirit being on or in them. The Holy Spirit came on only those who were being empowered for specific tasks or positions.

Although David's anointing did not end Saul's reign as king, it marked the end of the power and favor of God on him. The exit of the Holy Spirit left Saul open to the torment of an evil spirit. If he had been a man of character, Saul might have cooperated with God to add David to his royal ranks through less painful means. But self-centered and rebellious Saul had no such character. Still, God used Saul's selfishness to bring David to the royal courts. Saul's attendants suggested that someone play the harp to soothe their half-mad master. They found "a son of Jesse of Bethlehem who knows how to play the harp. He is a brave man and a warrior. He speaks well and is a fine-looking man. And the LORD is with him" (1 Sam. 16:18).

David used the harp to bring joyful praises to God and relief to the torments of Saul. You may rightly imagine that many of your favorite psalms were first sung by the young voice of David, wavering and cracking somewhere between boyhood and manhood to the accompaniment of a well-worn, deeply loved harp. Surely the very sound of its strings summoned the attention of many a straying sheep. The words that accompanied it still do.

Verse 18 combines two descriptions we would not expect to find together: David played the harp; he was a warrior. In two simple descriptions, God tells us volumes about "the man after His own heart." We find that David had the tenderness and the sensitivity of an artist. He was a musician and a songwriter. David did not simply have talent. Talent alone could not have soothed the torment of Saul. David plucked the strings of his harp with tenderness and sensitivity. He chose melodies that ministered to the aching soul. Yet we are also told he was a warrior, brave and strong. The fingers that gently plucked the strings of a harp could wind fiercely around a sling or a sword. We will see his gentle song turn into a corporate rebuke as he faces the Philistines.

These complementary parts of David's character, recorded in 1 Samuel 16:18, will appear throughout our study. David was a complex man. He could be both passionate and withdrawn; dependable and shocking; righteous and wicked—just like us.

Two qualities I've come to admire most in both men and women are tenderness and strength. I no longer see them as exclusive terms. Quite the contrary; I've come to realize that one without the other leaves an individual lacking wholeness. I deeply desire to be a woman of tenderness and strength because my dearest role model possessed both.

Christ Jesus is the artist. He created the world with colors and textures human artists have tried for thousands of years to imitate. Christ Jesus is the musician. He gave the angels their voices. Christ Jesus is the tenderhearted, ministering to our every need.

Christ Jesus is also the warrior, forever leading us in triumphant procession, if only we will follow (2 Cor. 2:14). In our greatest weakness, He is strong. Christ Jesus is the blessed embodiment of both characteristics. He has set an example before us of true manhood and true womanhood.

No greater man or woman exists than one in whom tenderness and strength can be found. David was such a man.

Father, I pray that You will teach us to value tenderness and strength in all Your children, male or female, even as You teach us to rely upon Your Son, the essence of all strength. Amen.

Oh, you're asking the why questions, aren't you? Why did God take His Spirit from Saul? Why did He reject Saul? That's another chapter in David's back story.

Let me introduce you to Saul, the people's choice.

Chapter 5

THE PEOPLE'S CHOICE

1 Samuel 8–9

So all the elders of Israel gathered together and came to Samuel at Ramah.
They said to him, "You are old, and your sons do not walk in your ways;
now appoint a king to lead us, such as all the other nations have."
(1 Sam. 8:4–5)

Samuel judged Israel all the days of his life. Then, when he grew old, he appointed his two sons to serve in his place. Does this begin to sound familiar? Like Eli before him, his sons dishonored the Lord.

We don't know what went wrong. Maybe Samuel neglected his family in favor of his ministry. Possibly he repeated the ingrained patterns he had seen in the household of Eli, or his sons simply chose to rebel. What we do know is that the people demanded a king.

I believe the request devastated Samuel. Hadn't he loved and sacrificially served these people? Then the Lord told him to grant their request because they had not rejected Samuel as judge, they had rejected God as king. As always, Samuel obeyed.

We can see so many truths in the situation. One lesson speaks of patience. God had already planned a king for the people. Their lack of patience was to cost them dearly. If they had waited for the Lord's choice instead of demanding their way, how different might the story have been?

Another lesson from the story deals with rejection. None of us enjoys rejection, but when we are serving Christ, any rejection falls to His broad shoulders rather than our narrow ones. The next time you feel rejection's sting, remember God's words to Samuel: "It is not you they have rejected, but they have rejected me" (1 Sam. 8:7).

Samuel warned the Israelites about what they were getting into. Often when God does not readily give us what we want, it is because He knows what our desire would cost us. Faith sometimes means forgoing our desires because we trust Christ to have a better plan for our lives.

Samuel told the people of the taxes they would pay, the freedoms they would lose, and ultimately how their sons and daughters would be reduced to virtual slavery by the fulfillment of their request. No matter how Samuel reasoned, however, the people wanted a king. They wanted a king for all the wrong reasons. Ultimately, they wanted a king because the other nations had them.

So the people rejected the sons of Samuel and demanded a king. Because they did, we meet one of the great and tragic figures of the Bible. He stood a head taller than anyone in Israel yet showed all the characteristics of a poor self-concept. We first meet him as he searched for his father's donkeys. His name was Saul, and he would be king. He would become crucial to King David. We learn volumes about the shepherd king, David, from his peculiar relationship with his predecessor, Saul. The story of Saul begins in 1 Samuel 9.

God arranged for Saul to encounter Samuel. You've heard of a wild goose chase; this was a wild donkey chase. Saul and a servant had been searching for three lost donkeys. After three days, they consulted the prophet, who happened to be Samuel. Note this principle: God often uses the practical to lead to the spiritual. Saul and his servant might have considered every stop to be a dead end, but from a heavenly Throne's eye view, each closed door ultimately opened the way to a word from God!

I find it very interesting that God wants us so much that He can bring us to Himself even when we think we're going somewhere else. Never forget that the mundane can lead to the miraculous.

God had already told Samuel that Saul was coming. When he appeared, God said to the prophet, "This is the man I spoke to you about; he will govern my people" (1 Sam. 9:17). Samuel assured Saul that the donkeys were found. Then he added a cryptic word, that the desire of all Israel was turned to Saul.

Don't you find reading the stories in Scripture fascinating? Often we see something common to both mysteries and detective novels. We the readers know that Samuel is looking for the man to be king of Israel. Saul did not. Thus, we read knowing more than the character knew. We do know Saul got a puzzled understanding of Samuel's statement, and the knowing gives us a glimpse of a root problem in Saul's life. The future king replied, "But am I not a Benjamite, from the smallest tribe of Israel, and is not my clan the least of all the clans of the tribe of Benjamin?" (1 Sam. 9:21).

How do we distinguish between godly humility and low self-esteem? Which did Saul display? One key lies in our focus. A person with godly humility looks to the Master. He or she neither exalts nor denigrates self, because to do either is to make self the center of our universe. When we're really serving Christ, our reputations and abilities simply cease to be so important. We must decrease that He may increase.

Saul exhibited the core sin of all self-centered people: he focused on himself. We need to recognize that lack of confidence does not equal humility. In fact, genuinely humble people have enormous confidence because it rests in a great God. Saul's self-centeredness eventually cost him dearly, as a self-focus always does.

Saul's meeting with Samuel did not end up being about donkeys, but kings. Within a few short hours, Saul sat as guest of honor at the sacrificial feast and received the news of his appointment. God still works in some of the same mysterious ways. Don't despair if you feel as if you're chasing after donkeys. You might just run head-on into God!

Oh, that we had an extra hundred pages to devote to the study of King Saul. We can learn much from him of how a life with great potential can go wrong; however, we are looking at David's back story, so let's seek to answer two key questions. First, since David was a man after God's heart, what set him apart from Saul? We can often see godly character in contrast to the ungodly. Thus we will look to Saul to compare him with the man after God's heart. Second, since we have seen Saul rejected as king in favor of David, how did Saul squander his office and calling? In the pages to come we will explore these questions.

Chapter 6

THE SEEDS OF DESTRUCTION

1 Samuel 10–11

"The Spirit of the Lord will come upon you in power,
and you will prophesy with them; and you will be changed
into a different person." (1 Sam. 10:6)

Samuel anointed Saul to be king over Israel. At the same time, the prophet gave the new king several signs to prove the truth of his words. These signs included how he would receive word that the donkeys had been found, the actions of people Saul would meet on the road, and Saul's encounter with a band of prophets (1 Sam. 10:2–11). The encounter with the band of prophets leaves questions we would love answered.

> *As Saul turned to leave Samuel, God changed Saul's heart, and all these signs were fulfilled that day. When they arrived at Gibeah, a procession of prophets met him; the Spirit of God came upon him in power, and he joined in their prophesying.* (1 Sam. 10:9–10)

Though we may wonder what the prophets were prophesying about, we can see one clear principle: "God changed Saul's heart." A changed heart is the absolute requirement for kingdom service.

After all these astounding experiences, Saul returned to his father and awaited the next move by Samuel the prophet. In the process, we glimpse another curious tidbit about Saul. His uncle asked what Samuel had said. Saul told him only about the donkeys. He said nothing of the declaration that he was to be king.

Next Samuel summoned all of Israel so that he could declare Saul king. Samuel led the tribes through a dramatic selection process. Only two people knew the eventual outcome: Samuel and Saul. From all the tribes, Samuel selected Benjamin. From all the clans of Benjamin, he chose Matri. From all the families of Matri, the family of Kish. When the big moment arrived—no Saul. Again we get a glimpse of Saul's root problem: Saul was hiding among the baggage. Self-consciousness constitutes the opposite of God-consciousness. Rather than gratefully rejoicing in the privilege God was freely extending to him, Saul's concern ran to himself and what others would think of him.

Once messengers had retrieved Saul from hiding, Samuel presented the new king. The prophet explained to the people the regulations of their new form of government and then dismissed the people.

We immediately get another hint of Saul's deficiency. Most of the people shouted for joy at the stature of the new king, but a few trouble-makers reacted differently. They despised Saul and publicly insulted him. Another characteristic of Saul's self-consciousness appeared: he kept silent. Possibly he wanted everybody to like him. Another Saul wrote a prescription this one could have used:

> *Am I now trying to win the approval of men, or of God? Or am I trying to please men? If I were still trying to please men, I would not be a servant of Christ.* (Gal. 1:10)

Saul, like all people pleasers, had difficulty standing up for right or righteousness because he desired the approval of men. Instead of confrontation, he looked for the easy way out. Saul didn't deal with the problem before him; maybe he hoped it would go away. However, the greater problem lay in himself: he prioritized self over the God who had chosen him.

We are about to see Saul at his best, but like a mighty oak with a fatal infestation of insects, his blight would continue to eat away at his soul. Saul returned to his father's farm. Events didn't leave him there long. We soon see quite a different portrait of the man who might have been a great king had he consistently placed himself under the authority of God.

Nahash the Ammonite attacked Jabesh Gilead, a city of Israel about twenty-five miles south of the Sea of Galilee. The leaders knew they could not hold out against his superior force, so they began to bargain. Nahash agreed to let them live, but at an awful price. He said, "I will make a treaty with you only on the condition that I gouge out the right eye of every one of you and so bring disgrace on all Israel" (1 Sam. 11:2). The people agreed on the condition that they have one week for their fellow Israelites to come to their rescue.

What happened next revealed some important things about the new king. Saul was a man of considerable character (which made his eventual self-destruction all the more painful). Upon receiving his assignment, Saul did not immediately have a palace built in his honor, nor did he sit on a throne to be waited on. He went back to work, just as he had always done, and waited for his marching orders. Did they ever come!

The messenger from Jabesh Gilead found Saul returning with his oxen after plowing a field. I am encouraged that Saul was touched by the tears of "his" people. Scripture tells us that "the Spirit of God came upon him in power, and he burned with anger" (v. 6). The Israelites were about to receive a "special delivery" from their new king. Saul took a pair

of oxen, cut them to pieces, and sent the pieces throughout Israel, proclaiming, "This is what will be done to the oxen of anyone who does not
follow Saul and Samuel" (1 Sam. 11:7). Samuel had warned the people
that a king would mean forced servitude. Hello selective service!

Saul knew he had troublemakers among the Israelites. He wanted to
make dead sure (poor oxen) that he had their respect, even if their obedience was the result of fear. His approach worked. Verse 7 concludes,
"Then the terror of the LORD fell on the people, and they turned out as
one man."

Saul marched his army to Jabesh Gilead and relieved the siege. In
the process he won two mighty victories: one over the Ammonites and
one over his detractors. The victorious Israelites gathered those who had
slighted Saul and . . . well, read it for yourself:

> The people then said to Samuel, "Who was it that asked, 'Shall
> Saul reign over us?' Bring these men to us and we will put them
> to death." But Saul said, "No one shall be put to death today, for
> this day the LORD has rescued Israel." (1 Sam. 11:12–13)

For Saul's sake I wish I could report that Saul was simply a compassionate king, but something else may have been going on. If indeed he
felt compassion, in the days ahead we will see him lose it. Rather, his
actions seem to be the cry of a people pleaser, desiring to be liked rather
than demanding to be respected.

We await the next act in the tragedy of Israel's first king.

Chapter 7

HOW TO LOSE A KINGDOM

1 Samuel 13

Saul was thirty years old when he became king, and he
reigned over Israel forty-two years. (1 Sam. 13:1)

Any serious student of Israel, or of David, must face why God rejected Saul as king of Israel. To fully comprehend the reason, we need to examine three experiences from Saul's life. The three demonstrate both the fundamental flaws in his character and the progressive deterioration that occurs when we turn from God.

The first experience appears in 1 Samuel 13. Saul mustered an army for war against the Philistines, but the Israelite army was so badly outnumbered that they hid in caves.

God gave Saul a chance to shine. He could have taken his place among the great men and women of faith. We learn a key detail from 1 Samuel 13:8. The verse says Saul "waited seven days, the time set by Samuel." God was teaching his new king to wait on the Lord.

Imagine the strain on the fledgling king as he watched his army melt away before his eyes. The prophet told Saul to wait until he came to offer the sacrifice before battle. By the seventh day, Saul's patience snapped.

He could no longer stand to see his army disintegrate. No doubt he chafed under the criticism of his men. He dared not go into battle without making an offering to God, so he offered the sacrifice himself.

Have you noticed the truth in the old statement that God is seldom in a hurry but He's never late? How often do we give up on God and on obedience just five minutes before deliverance? As Saul made the offering, Samuel arrived. At first glance Saul's infraction may seem minor and Samuel's reaction harsh, but we must remember, Saul was king of God's people. If you aspire to greater authority, you must accept the greater accountability that goes with it.

Samuel demanded to know what Saul had done. The king's response reflected his fear of public opinion, his lack of trust in God, and his cavalier attitude toward obedience. Saul said when he saw the men scattering and Samuel didn't come, he "felt compelled to offer the burnt offering" (1 Sam. 13:12).

The prophet responded to Saul's excuses and blaming with harsh words. He told Saul, "You have not kept the command the LORD your God gave you; if you had, he would have established your kingdom over Israel for all time. But now your kingdom will not endure; the LORD has sought out a man after his own heart and appointed him leader of his people, because you have not kept the LORD's command" (1 Sam. 13:13–14).

We dare not minimize disobedience to God. Saul had a clear command from God. He disobeyed, and it cost him the kingdom.

The second stage of the kingdom being stripped from Saul appears in 1 Samuel 15. Through Samuel, God commanded Saul to utterly destroy the Amalekites, including all the people and all the livestock.

Deuteronomy 25:17–19 tells us that the Amalekites attacked Israel when they were traveling from Egypt to the promised land. They followed the Israelites and attacked the stragglers. God is sovereign. He owes us no explanation as to why He desired for this entire population to be exterminated. However, we can assume they were a vile and god-less people, because God is merciful and compassionate.

We can learn another lesson from the episode: God has a powerful and possessive love for His children. Don't be messin' with a child of God, especially any helpless ones. Take comfort, brother or sister. He may not vindicate you as quickly as you would like, but when He does, all will know. I love the wonderful passage in Revelation 6 where the martyrs cried out to God for justice. He gave them a white robe—demonstrating that He had not forgotten—and told them to wait a little longer (Rev. 6:11).

Whatever the reasons God had for ordering the destruction of the Amalekites, Saul led the Israelite army to victory but then disobeyed. They kept the king and the best of the livestock.

Have you noticed how a small disobedience left unchecked always grows? Saul's actions in chapter 13 grew from fear and concern for public opinion. In chapter 15 he had nothing to fear; his disobedience had become open and self-serving.

When God told Samuel what Saul had done, the prophet cried out all night in grief. Then he proceeded to confront Saul directly. The confrontation speaks to us as we consider our approach to God's instructions. When God speaks, we must learn to follow Him with complete obedience.

Saul made some very serious presumptions. He kept King Agag alive to present him as a trophy—a public exhibit. He did not slaughter the sheep and cattle for the very same reason: he saved the best to make himself look better. Chapter 15, verse 9 ends with a sad commentary on Saul's actions: "These they were unwilling to destroy completely, but everything that was despised and weak they totally destroyed." Saul had the audacity to improve on God's command. Several breaches in Saul's character become evident in this dramatic chapter.

First, Saul was arrogant. Remember that we said he was self-centered? If we needed any further proof of Saul's pride and audacity, verse 12 certainly provides it. Saul went directly to Carmel and built a monument to himself.

Next, note how Saul refused to take responsibility for his actions. He first excused himself for disobeying God by claiming he spared the best of the sheep and cattle for a sacrifice to the Lord. Amazing, isn't it? Believe it or not, we can sometimes use God as our excuse for disobedience too. One woman told me she was certain God's will was for her to leave her husband because she simply wasn't happy. Another woman explained to me that she had found the man God intended her to marry, though she was already married.

Saul not only tried to use God as his excuse for disobedience; he also claimed he was afraid of, and gave in to, the people (v. 24). When we've done something wrong or foolish, we find shouldering the responsibility difficult, don't we? At times we are all tempted to blame someone else when we've blown it. I wonder if the outcome might have been different if Saul simply had admitted that he made a wrong choice.

Saul minimized the seriousness of disobedience. In verse 23, Samuel made a striking statement. He said, "rebellion is like the sin of divination, / and arrogance like the evil of idolatry" (1 Sam. 15:23).

The comparison seems puzzling until we consider that rebellion is a means by which we attempt to set the course of our futures. We try to choose our own futures by our independent actions. Divination attempts to foretell or sway the future. In the same verse, God likens arrogance to the evil of idolatry. When we are arrogant, who becomes God in our lives?

We see the final stage of Saul's disobedience and disintegration in chapter 28. Once again he had to go into battle. By this time Samuel was dead. Saul sought without success to contact God. Since the Lord chose to remain silent, Saul, in an attempt to contact Samuel, consulted a medium known as the witch of Endor. We see the fleshing out of Samuel's earlier statement. Saul's rebellion became literal witchcraft.

How does a man who is the people's choice lose a kingdom? Saul provides a sad object lesson. All his life he focused on himself instead of his God. Therefore, he feared public opinion; he would not trust God but rather had to feel he was in control. He disobeyed, because obedience requires the trust and humility he did not possess.

Saul. The first king of Israel. The people's choice. Not an accident waiting for a place to happen but a train wreck mangling the lives of others. Sad but true. A head taller but a heart shorter.

Chapter 8

A FATHER UNLIKE HIS SON

1 Samuel 14

Jonathan said to his young armor-bearer, "Come, let's go over to the outpost of those uncircumcised fellows. Perhaps the Lord will act in our behalf. Nothing can hinder the Lord from saving, whether by many or by few." (1 Sam. 14:6)

Saul, a man with such potential, squandered the kingdom through his disobedience. Now we meet a character who was as noble as Saul was disappointing. First Samuel 13 introduces us to Jonathan, son of King Saul, a man vastly different from his father. The one who became so dear to David is sure to become dear to us.

Once again Saul, Jonathan, and the Israelite army faced a far superior force of Philistines. The Israelites were literally hiding in fear. Jonathan obviously decided the army of the mighty God need not hide.

In one of the great statements of faith backed by action, Jonathan said to his armor-bearer: "Come, let's go over to the outpost of those uncircumcised fellows. Perhaps the LORD will act in our behalf. Nothing can hinder the LORD from saving, whether by many or by few" (1 Sam. 14:6). They challenged the Philistine detachment holding the pass at

Micmash. God showed them they should attack. So the two climbed up to the soldiers, killed twenty men, and began the battle. Before the day ended, the Israelites won a great victory over the Philistines.

Jonathan and his armor-bearer were impressive and worthy men. I am amazed by them in two ways. First, Jonathan's perception of the Lord's ways impresses me. His keen perception of the Lord certainly did not come from his father, because Jonathan's understanding exceeded that of Saul. Jonathan had his own relationship with the Lord, completely separate from his father's. Jonathan made two profound statements:

1. "Perhaps the Lord will act in our behalf."
2. "Nothing can hinder the Lord from saving, whether by many or by few."

Consider how these statements reveal Jonathan's distinct perception of God's ways: Jonathan knew the Lord could save, no matter who or how many were fighting the battle. In fact, he knew that if God chose to save, nothing could hinder Him! His faith in God's strength and determination stood solidly; God could do anything. Jonathan's only question was whether God would choose to do it through them that day. Whether or not He did, Jonathan understood God's response to be based on sovereignty, not weakness.

I want to have faith like that of Jonathan, don't you? Romans 10:17 tells us that "faith comes by hearing, and hearing by the word of God" (NKJV). The Word of God results in faith.

Jonathan began the battle that quickly turned into a rout. God sent panic on the Philistines until they killed one another. The Israelites merely chased the Philistines in a mopping-up operation.

Then Jonathan's father, the king, entered the picture. Saul saw the Philistine army in disarray and ordered the Israelites into battle. In the process he did an impulsive and stupid thing. Saul "bound the people under an oath, saying, 'Cursed be any man who eats food before evening comes, before I have avenged myself on my enemies!'" (1 Sam. 14:24). He forced the army into an ill-advised and non-God-directed fast.

I believe we need to take a lesson in two ways from Saul's impulsive action. First, we simply need to beware of decisions made on impulse. Saul displayed an excessive capacity for action without consulting either God or good sense.

The second lesson from Saul's action relates specifically to our eating habits. Beware. Like Saul's impulsive command, many people indulge in fasting that does not come from God. Some carry dieting to fatal extremes. I have known friends who have died as a result of depriving their bodies of food. Remember that only God has the right to call a fast.

Hasty self-centered vows can cost us. Since Jonathan was not in the camp, he did not hear his father's command. As the army chased the Philistines, they became exhausted. They came to a place where a beehive had been broken open. Jonathan ate some of the honey.

In this story we encounter an amazing and humbling truth: God expected the people to obey the king even when his edicts made no sense. So the next day when they inquired of God, He remained silent.

Through a process of elimination, they discovered that Jonathan had disobeyed the command of Saul. The king would have put his own son to death, but the men would not allow it.

God tried to teach Saul a very serious lesson that day. Saul's pride could have caused him to keep a foolish vow. Better to repent than to add foolishness to foolishness.

In the account of the battle and its aftermath, we see evidence that God is for us in battle, not against us. He wants us fortified before our enemy with faith like Jonathan's, obedience like the armor-bearer's, and proper fuel like Saul's army should have received.

Chapter 9

ONE SMOOTH STONE

1 Samuel 17

Who is this uncircumcised Philistine that he should defy the
armies of the living God? (1 Sam. 17:26)

We arrive today at an account in Scripture that has captured the imaginations of every little boy and girl who ever sat in a circle of small, wooden chairs in a Sunday school room. This is the story of David and Goliath. May we have the joy of reading it again as if for the very first time.

If you have access to a Bible, read 1 Samuel 17:1–58. A now middle-aged King Saul once again had his army confronting the Philistines. Three of David's brothers were in the army. David apparently had returned to tending sheep after his time of living in Saul's household and playing the harp to soothe the king.

David regularly transported provisions from the family farm to the older brothers in the army. On this occasion when David arrived, he learned that Goliath, a nine-foot-tall Philistine warrior, had been taunting the Israelites every morning and evening for forty days. He challenged one champion to a fight representing the army of Israel. Goliath defied the army of Israel, and Saul and his army were dismayed and terrified.

We have discovered that David, as an artist and a warrior, possessed qualities of tenderness and strength. We saw tenderness in the soothing way he played the harp. Now we see the strength of David as a warrior. When David heard Goliath's taunts and he said, "Who is this uncircumcised Philistine that he should defy the armies of the living God?" (1 Sam. 17:26), David volunteered to fight the giant. As his countrymen cowered in fear, David saw the situation differently. You see, if a person fears God, he or she has no reason to fear anything else. On the other hand, if a person does not fear God, then fear becomes a way of life. David feared God so he did not fear Goliath. Saul did not fear God. Thus he feared the opinions of others, the enemy, and even a loyal young boy who played the harp.

Before we go on with the story, notice two details. First, remember David knew the sting of disapproval by his brothers. When David's oldest brother, Eliab, heard him talking about Goliath, he became angry. Eliab accused David of wrong motives: "Why have you come down here? And with whom did you leave those few sheep in the desert? I know how conceited you are and how wicked your heart is; you came down only to watch the battle" (1 Sam 17:28).

Eliab said everything he could to discourage David. He said David didn't belong, made fun of David's trade, and accused him of conceit and deceit. David's response, "Now what have I done?" evidenced the fact that Eliab and David were not at odds for the first time. David's brothers obviously weren't pleased to see him. I have to wonder if Eliab's response resulted from almost being anointed king. The first drop of oil had almost fallen on his head when God stopped Samuel and chided him for looking on the outward appearance. For whatever reason, Eliab was very critical of David.

I'm not sure anyone can encourage or discourage us like family. The views of our family members toward us are very convincing, aren't they? If people who know us the best encourage us the least, we have few chances to develop confidence.

David remained undaunted by Eliab's criticisms for one reason: David took God's Word over the opinions of others. As a Hebrew lad, David heard the promises of victory God made to the nation that would call upon His name. David believed those promises.

Whenever you feel alone, rejected, or misunderstood, stand your situation up next to David's. The boy had as pure a heart as humanly possible, and his own family blasted him. Ouch. I don't want to minimize your hurts, but in David you can certainly find someone who has been there, done that.

Also, notice another detail of the story. When David volunteered to fight the giant, Saul promptly dressed David in the king's armor. Imagine that picture: a young shepherd boy, dressed in the armor of the middle-aged king who was twice his size. Is it any wonder David could hardly walk, let alone fight?

David made a wise choice that is a lesson for us: "'I cannot go in these,' he said to Saul, 'because I am not used to them'" (1 Sam. 17:39). What wisdom from such a youth. David was comfortable enough with himself to say, "This just isn't me."

I heard a great phrase from Norris Smith, a wonderful man who counsels ministers. He said our attempts to copy somebody else is like "wearing Saul's armor." Have you tried to wear Saul's armor? It is a miserable fit. We can learn from David that God has made us to be who we are, not who somebody else is. What a life lesson!

So David shed the armor of Saul, picked up five smooth stones, took his shepherd's sling, and went out to meet Goliath—in the power of God. You know the rest. No giant will ever be a match for a big God with a little rock.

David's example teaches us some wonderful, practical truths we can use to deal with the giants in our lives. First, he illustrates what God's Word tells us—that we are loved, gifted, and blessed. We can do anything

God calls us to do through Christ who strengthens us (Phil. 4:13). We must develop more confidence in God's Word than in the opinions of others.

Second, David reminds us to measure the size of our obstacles against the size of our God. Goliath was nine feet tall, with 140 pounds of armor shielding him. We tend to measure our obstacles against our own strength. We often feel overwhelmed and defeated before the battle begins. I am not suggesting that if we measure our obstacles against God our battles will be effortless. David still had to face his giant obstacle and use the strength he possessed, but his confidence in God caused a simple pebble to hit like a boulder.

Third, David shows us our need to acknowledge an active and living God in our lives. Look how David referred to God in 1 Samuel 17:26: "Who is this uncircumcised Philistine that he should defy the armies of the living God?"

Do you approach every circumstance and conflict as a member of the army of the living God? Do you continually regard God as able? Do you stand in His name? Our victory rests not on faith in our spirituality. Our victory rests on faith in our God.

We're often intimidated in battle because we are uncertain of our faith. We must remember we don't stand in victory because of our faith. We stand in victory because of our God. Faith in faith is pointless. Faith in a living, active God moves mountains. He is alive. He is active. He wants to make you living proof. Remember, the Cross would have been God's worst defeat had the people not had cause to exclaim, "He's alive!"

Stories don't get any better than David and Goliath, do they? Some stories are worth retelling. A living God is worth believing.

Chapter 10

AN AMAZING COVENANT

1 Samuel 18

Jonathan made a covenant with David because
he loved him as himself. (1 Sam. 18:3)

Saul reigned as king over Israel for forty-two years. David appeared on the scene about halfway through those years. The king, who once possessed such potential, had now come to resemble a half-mad character from a Shakespearean play. David had been in the king's home often. The shepherd boy had played the harp to soothe the king, but obviously Saul was so full of himself that he paid no attention to the boy. When David volunteered to fight Goliath, the cowardly king did not even recognize the lad whose music had soothed his shattered nerves. As David went out to face the giant, Saul asked his general who the boy was.

At least for a moment David received the recognition his character deserved. Soon we will witness a tragic turning point in the relationship between Saul and David, but for now let's behold a tender scene between two young men.

*After David had finished talking with Saul, Jonathan became
one in spirit with David, and he loved him as himself. . . .
Jonathan made a covenant with David because he loved him as
himself. Jonathan took off the robe he was wearing and gave it to
David, along with his tunic, and even his sword, his bow and his
belt. (1 Sam. 18:1–4)*

Who but God can explain the ways of the heart? Sometimes friendships bloom over months or years. At other times someone touches your heart almost instantly, and you seem to have known him or her forever. Have you ever felt an almost instant bond to a new friend? Such was the deep and abiding friendship between Jonathan and David.

Jonathan's expressions of love and friendship toward David paint one of the most beautiful portraits of a covenant in the Word of God. The word *covenant* in 1 Samuel 18:3 derives from the Hebrew term *berith*, which means "determination, stipulation, covenant. It was a treaty, alliance of friendship, a pledge, an obligation between a monarch and his subjects, a constitution. It was a contract which was accompanied by signs, sacrifices and a solemn oath which sealed the relationship with promises of blessing for obedience and curses for disobedience."[4]

According to the definition, three elements accompanied the making of a covenant: signs, sacrifice, and a spoken commitment. Although in the covenant of Jonathan and David the three elements are less obvious than in other covenants in Scripture, their covenant includes each of the parts.

The sign: Jonathan demonstrated his covenant with David by giving him his robe, tunic, and weapons. We will see the greater significance of Jonathan's sign as we consider the sacrifice and the spoken commitment.

The sacrifice: In Jonathan's covenant with David, the sacrifice is less obvious than other examples in Scripture, but it is profound. Clearly Saul intended for Jonathan to become the second king of Israel (1 Sam. 20:30–31), but this son had other plans. In David, Jonathan saw character fit for a king. He was so determined that the throne be occupied by God's chosen instrument that he offered everything he had. In this unique covenant, Jonathan sacrificed himself. Jonathan removed his royal regalia—his robe and tunic—and placed it on David, symbolizing that David would be king instead of him. Can you picture the face of the recipient, whose clothing probably still carried the faint scent of sheep?

Jonathan acknowledged David as prince of the Hebrew nation, a position which he could have jealously and vehemently claimed as his own. Men like Jonathan are a rarity. Few people have "in mind the things of God" at risk of their own favor and position (Matt. 16:23).

Do you have the privilege of knowing someone like Jonathan? Have you known anyone who has given up power or position for God's will? Now is a good time to stop and pray for that person. Give God thanks for providing such examples for us to follow.

The spoken commitment: The oath of Jonathan's covenant with David does not take place in words in chapter 18. Jonathan symbolized the solemn oath by giving David his weapons of protection: his sword, bow, and belt. He symbolically gave all he had to protect David from harm and ensure his position as future king. Jonathan verbalized his solemn oath by pledging in 1 Samuel 20:13 to protect David from harm at great personal risk.

We have examined three elements of covenant, but we have not yet noted the most critical issue: the basis of the covenant.

Deuteronomy makes a staggering assertion about why God chose the nation of Israel. It simply and majestically declares that God redeemed Israel "because the LORD loved you and kept the oath he swore to your forefathers" (Deut. 7:8).

Reconsider Jonathan's covenant with David. You will see that they had the same basis to their covenant. In fact, 1 Samuel 18:1–4 shows something else about the covenant. If you go back and read the passage, you will find no mention of David returning Jonathan's love.

God's covenant with the nation of Israel was based on His love for them—not their love for Him. Amazing! In this same way, Jonathan's covenant with David was based on Jonathan's love, not David's response. We who have accepted Christ as Savior are part of the most wonderful covenant God ever made with man. God loves us for a singular reason—because He chooses to.

Look at a final Scripture as we consider the covenant God has made with us. Examine 1 John 4:10, 15, and reflect on how our covenant compares to Jonathan's covenant with David.

> *This is love: not that we loved God, but that he loved us and sent his Son as an atoning sacrifice for our sins. . . . If anyone acknowledges that Jesus is the Son of God, God lives in him and he in God.* (1 John 4:10–15)

The sign: God sent His only Son.

The sacrifice: He "sent his Son as an atoning sacrifice for our sins" (v. 10).

The spoken commitment: "If anyone acknowledges that Jesus is the Son of God, God lives in him and he in God" (v. 15).

The basis of this covenant is the same as the basis of Jonathan's covenant with David: "not that we loved God, but that he loved us" (v. 10). What greater covenant could possibly exist?

How did you enter into the covenant with God through Christ? When and how did you receive Christ as Savior? If you cannot answer that question, or if you are unsure that you have entered into the covenant of eternal life through the death of Christ, would you consider accepting Christ as Savior right now? The steps to eternal life are very simple, but the results are profound and everlasting:

- Tell God that you are a sinner and you cannot earn eternal life (Rom. 3:10–12, 23).

+ Agree with God that Jesus Christ is the Son of God and He died on the cross for you (Rom. 10:9–10, 13).

+ Ask Jesus to forgive you of your sins and to live in your heart through His Holy Spirit (1 John 1:9; John 1:12; John 14:6).

+ Commit your life to love and serve Him (Matt. 22:37; John 14:15).

+ Thank Him for your new salvation (Luke 17:15–17; 2 Cor. 9:15; Eph. 5:20).

If you have accepted Christ as Savior, please share your decision as soon as possible. Who would be most excited to hear that you have given your life to Christ? If you are already a Christian, take time to pray. Thank God for His salvation, and pray for someone you know who has never accepted Christ as Savior.

PART II

A Friendship Made in Heaven

Psalm 59

When Saul had sent men to watch David's house in order to kill him.

1 *Deliver me from my enemies, O God;*

    protect me from those who rise up against me.

2 *Deliver me from evildoers*

    and save me from bloodthirsty men.

3 *See how they lie in wait for me!*

    Fierce men conspire against me

    for no offense or sin of mine, O LORD.

4 *I have done no wrong, yet they are ready to attack me.*

    Arise to help me; look on my plight!

5 *O LORD God Almighty, the God of Israel,*

    rouse yourself to punish all the nations;

    show no mercy to wicked traitors.

6 *They return at evening,*

    snarling like dogs,

    and prowl about the city.

7 *See what they spew from their mouths—*

    they spew out swords from their lips,

    and they say, "Who can hear us?"

8 *But you, O LORD, laugh at them;*

    you scoff at all those nations.

. . . .

16 *But I will sing of your strength,*
    in the morning I will sing of your love;
    for you are my fortress,
    my refuge in times of trouble.

17 *O my Strength, I sing praise to you;*
    you, O God, are my fortress, my loving God.

Chapter 11

A JEALOUS EYE

1 Samuel 18:5–30

"'They have credited David with tens of thousands,' [Saul] thought, 'but me with only thousands. What more can he get but the kingdom?' And from that time on Saul kept a jealous eye on David." (1 Sam. 18:8–9)

John Dryden, a sixteenth-century philosopher, once called it "the jaundice of the soul."[5] The Song of Solomon says it is as "cruel as the grave" (Song of Sol. 8:6, KJV). Others call it the green-eyed monster. It sends some to jail; others to insanity. It is jealousy.

In stark contrast to Jonathan's self-sacrifice and solemn allegiance, Saul regarded David as the ultimate threat. The praise of the people that was directed at David planted a seed of jealousy in Saul. That seed would express itself with a vengeance over many chapters and years.

Motivated by jealousy, Saul sent David to fight with the army. The king hoped young David would come to harm. In 1 Samuel 18:5–16, we see how effectively young David performed the duties Saul assigned to him: "Whatever Saul sent him to do, David did it so successfully that Saul gave him a high rank in the army. This pleased all the people, and Saul's officers as well" (v. 5).

Unfortunately for David, the people loved him almost too much. As he came in from battle, the women of Israel sang,

Saul has slain his thousands, and David his tens of thousands.
(1 Sam. 18:7)

A man as big in character as Saul stood in stature could have rejoiced with David, but Saul was no such man. The words galled him. He decided it would be only a matter of time until David took his kingdom.

So the next day Saul tried to kill David. As the loyal harpist played for his master, Saul threw a spear in an attempt to pin David to the wall, but David avoided Saul's attacks twice.

In his fear, Saul sent David to command a thousand troops. He probably hoped David would be killed, but David only grew more successful because "the LORD was with him" (v. 14). With each success Saul hated and feared David more.

The Hebrew word for the kind of anger Saul experienced is informative: *Charah*—"to burn, be kindled, glow with anger, be incensed, grow indignant; to be zealous, act zealously." Unlike some of its synonyms, *charah* points to the fire or heat of the anger just after it has been ignited.[6] *Charah* captures the moment a person explodes with anger—the moment anger is ignited before any sense of control takes over, before a rational thought can be processed.

Rarely do we accomplish anything profitable at the moment we become angry. Actions or words immediately following the ignition of anger are almost always regrettable. Moments like the one *charah* describes are exactly the reason I never want to approach a day without praying to be filled with the Holy Spirit. Through the life of Saul, we see a portrait of what our lives might be like if the Holy Spirit either departed or was quenched in us. No thanks!

Saul felt many things toward David, but the most consistent emotion was jealousy. Few experiences are more miserable than being the subject of someone's unleashed jealousy. Perhaps the only thing worse is being the one in whom the jealousy rages. Two men will pay a tremendous price for the jealousy of Saul. We will see some of the suffering that jealousy showered on the lives of both Saul and David.

Is jealousy ever a proper response? Does it ever sow good rather than evil? Believe it or not, the answer is yes! According to 2 Corinthians 11:2, a righteous kind of jealousy does exist. Paul the apostle wrote,

I am jealous for you with a godly jealousy. I promised you to one husband, to Christ, so that I might present you as a pure virgin to him. (2 Cor. 11:2)

Exodus 20:5 tell us that God Himself is a jealous God:

You shall not bow down to them or worship them; for I, the LORD your God, am a jealous God. (Exod. 20:5)

Note the kind of jealousy God possesses:

The LORD will be jealous for his land and take pity on his people. (Joel 2:18)

This is what the LORD Almighty says: "I am very jealous for Jerusalem and Zion." (Zech. 1:14)

This is what the LORD Almighty says: "I am very jealous for Zion; I am burning with jealousy for her." (Zech. 8:2)

Did you see that giant three-letter word modifying each instance of jealousy? A very big difference exists between being jealous *of* someone and being jealous *for* someone. Jealousy *of* someone is a selfish desire for what that person has. Envy motivates such jealousy. Jealousy *for* someone is a selfless desire for that person to have and be the best. Love motivates selfless jealousy. God is jealous on our behalf. He is jealous for us to know the One True God. He is jealous for us to be in a posture of blessing. He is jealous for us to be kept from the evil one. He is jealous for us to be ready for our Bridegroom. Jealousy *for* someone's best is of God. Jealousy *of* someone's best is of the enemy.

Next in 1 Samuel 18 we see an amazing and disgusting picture of what jealousy can do in our hearts. Saul had promised his daughter to the man who would fight Goliath, so he offered his oldest daughter, Merab, to David. If David had been interested in social climbing, he most certainly would have jumped at the chance, but he deferred. So Saul married Merab to another man, but Saul's second daughter, Michal, was in love with David. The king hatched a plan. He thought she could be a "snare" to David (1 Sam. 18:21). Possibly he thought that the Philistines would go to extra lengths to kill David if he was the king's son-in-law.

Saul offered Michal to David in marriage, but David had no dowry. So Saul took his plotting a step further:

> *Saul replied, "Say to David, 'The king wants no other price for the bride than a hundred Philistine foreskins, to take revenge on his enemies.'" Saul's plan was to have David fall by the hands of the Philistines.* (1 Sam. 18:25)

So our David is married. We know little about Michal, but Saul considered the marriage a way to destroy David (v. 21). Can you imagine the evil in the heart of a man who would use his own daughter as a pawn in a personal vendetta? Saul obviously had high hopes that Michal would be the death of David, but David had something much greater than high hopes. He had a Most High God.

Chapter 12

THE GREAT ESCAPE

1 Samuel 19

Saul told his son Jonathan and all the attendants to kill David. But Jonathan was very fond of David. (1 Sam. 19:1)

Once the seed of jealousy was sown in the heart of Saul, fear, anger, and bitterness fueled a jealousy that quickly grew out of control. As I first read 1 Samuel 19, I could almost see the scene unfold on stage. Picture the scene with me.

Saul's jealousy continued to grow. His madness led him through a series of pendulum swings. He would become paranoid and homicidal toward David, then he would temporarily become rational, only to let his madness consume him again. In this instance Jonathan was momentarily able to bring his father back to reality.

Saul told Jonathan and all the attendants to kill David, but Jonathan warned David instead. He told David to hide in the field. Then he brought his father where David could overhear their conversation.

Jonathan spoke well of David to Saul his father and said to him, "Let not the king do wrong to his servant David; he has not wronged you, and what he has done has benefited you greatly. He took his life in his hands when he killed the Philistine. The LORD won a great victory for all Israel, and you saw it and were glad. Why then would you do wrong to an innocent man like David by killing him for no reason?"

Saul listened to Jonathan and took this oath: "As surely as the LORD lives, David will not be put to death." (1 Sam. 19:4–6)

Keep in mind that Jonathan risked his own life in keeping the covenant with David. Saul did not hesitate to order Jonathan's death once before over eating the honey. Again, well-chosen words calmed Saul's jealous rage, but it returned with a vengeance. Without God's intervention, we can offer only a small bandage to someone hemorrhaging from uncontrolled emotions. We may bring calm for a moment, but our efforts will have little lasting effect.

We've probably all been in Saul's place at one time or another. Something makes us furious; then someone tries to "talk some sense into us." We feel a little better and pledge to put our anger away forever. Then, here it comes again with the power of gale-force winds. Our emotions negatively ignited can be more powerful than we are. Our best recourse when negative emotions begin controlling us is to fall before the throne of grace and seek God! Take solace in the fact that Christ knows how it feels to be tempted by feelings (Heb. 4:15; 2:18).

Saul failed to acknowledge his rage and jealousy as evil. His imagination did nothing but further sow the seed within him, and his jealousy became relentless. Our imaginations will also fuel the fires of jealousy if we are not careful.

Jealousy is a powerful emotion, but so is love. When Saul married his daughter Michal to David, he thought she would be a snare to him. When the king discovered his daughter loved David, he became even more afraid (1 Sam. 18:28–29). He was right about love threatening his plans for Michal to bring harm to David. The power of love often exceeds the power of loyalty. Before long, Saul once again sought to kill David. Again Saul threw a spear at the young warrior, but once again he escaped. Again Saul sent soldiers to kill him, but Michal warned her husband. She helped him escape out a window and put an idol in the bed to look like David (1 Sam. 19:11–13).

Saul thought he could trust Michal to make David miserable. He thought she would be a puppet in his hands against the young warrior—until he realized she loved him. Her masterful deception could easily have led to her death. She was spared only because she convinced her father that David would have killed her if she hadn't let him get away.

David went straight to Samuel because he was the one used of God to anoint David as God's chosen leader of Israel. He likely had questions for Samuel, such as "Are you sure God told you to anoint me?" Regardless of his questions, David went to tell on Saul! Samuel received David and no doubt confirmed his calling.

We've seen proof that love can be more powerful than jealousy. Next we will see that the Spirit of God is also more powerful.

First Samuel 19 ends with a humorous account. Saul learned that David was with Samuel, so he sent soldiers to capture the young man. Saul sent one man after another, but every time they entered the presence of Samuel's prophets, the Spirit of God fell on them and they prophesied too! Finally, Saul apparently thought, "Fine. I'll do it myself." The same thing happened to him!

> So Saul went to Naioth at Ramah. But the Spirit of God came even upon him, and he walked along prophesying until he came to Naioth. He stripped off his robes and also prophesied in Samuel's presence. He lay that way all that day and night. (1 Sam. 19:23–24)

When God gets involved, we see real results. Don't miss celebrating that when a group of evil men met a group of godly men, godliness won. How encouraging to remember that the Spirit of God is more powerful than the spirit of wickedness! As 1 John 4:4 reminds us, "You, dear children, are from God and have overcome them, because the one who is in you is greater than the one who is in the world."

In this segment of David's story, we see that love is more powerful than jealousy, godliness is more powerful than wickedness, and the Spirit of God is more powerful than anything! The best laid plans of kings and queens crumble under the mighty Spirit of God. Acts 1:8 tells us that when the Holy Spirit comes on us we will receive power. The Greek word is *dunamis*. We call it "dynamite." That's what it takes to burst the walls of rage and jealousy within us. First John 3:20 says, "God is greater than our hearts."

As children of God, we do not have to be derailed by the way we feel. Our God is greater. Give Him your heart!

Chapter 13

COMMON BONDS, UNCOMMON FRIENDS

1 Samuel 20

*Show me unfailing kindness like that of the Lord as long as I live, so that
I may not be killed, and do not ever cut off your kindness from my
family—not even when the Lord has cut off every one of David's
enemies from the face of the earth. (1 Sam. 20:14–15)*

Chapter 20 describes a comparatively simple scene. Saul's threat of death
gave way to the reaffirmation of Jonathan's covenant. We are going to
talk about friendships, the "once in a lifetime" kind, as we observe the
relationship between Jonathan and David and the events that caused
their separation.

Like a yo-yo, Saul vacillated between moments of appreciating the
loyalty of David and seeking to kill the young man. Imagine the position in
which Saul's madness put his son Jonathan. Any son wants to believe in his
father. After the episode in chapter 19, when the Spirit overcame Saul and he
prophesied all night, the king apparently returned home. Jonathan must have
been at least somewhat blind to the king's murderous intentions.

At that time, David came to Jonathan and demanded to know why
Saul was seeking his life. Though he only partially believed his friend,

Jonathan assured David of his commitment to protect him. Jonathan promised to sound out his father and send David away if his fears were true. They settled on a plan to determine Saul's intentions. David hid during the New Moon Festival. When the shepherd-warrior did not appear at the table for two consecutive days, Saul became furious. In his anger he clearly settled the issue of his hostility toward David.

> *Saul's anger flared up at Jonathan and he said to him, "You son of a perverse and rebellious woman! Don't I know that you have sided with the son of Jesse to your own shame and to the shame of the mother who bore you? As long as the son of Jesse lives on this earth, neither you nor your kingdom will be established. Now send and bring him to me, for he must die!"*
> (1 Sam. 20:30–31)

Rather than turn David over to his father, Jonathan warned David. The two friends parted with much grief.

I wanted to emphasize a special portion of Scripture about the covenant. First Samuel 18:1 tells us, "Jonathan became one in spirit with David, and he loved him as himself." The King James Version helps us draw a more vivid mental image: "The soul of Jonathan was knit with the soul of David." The Hebrew word translated "knit" in the King James Version and "became one" in the New International Version is *qashar*, which means "to tie . . . join together, knit."[7] Jonathan and David are examples of two people knit together by something more powerful than circumstances or preferences.

The Spirit of God sometimes cements two people together as part of His plan. God would never have chosen David to be His future king if He had not planned to sustain him and ultimately deliver him safely to his throne. Jonathan was an important part of God's plan. They were uncommon friends joined by a common bond: the Spirit of God. First

Samuel 18:1 tells us that Jonathan and David were united, but 1 Samuel 20 shows us!

Consider these evidences of an uncommon friendship.

Uncommon friends can speak their minds without fear. Imagine the tone David probably used with Jonathan when he asked, "What have I done? What is my crime? How have I wronged your father, that he is trying to take my life?" (v. 1).

Jonathan replied, "Look, my father doesn't do anything, great or small, without confiding in me. Why would he hide this from me? It's not so!" (v. 2).

David's words suggest nothing less than panic. Jonathan could easily have received David's words as an insult. After all, David practically took his frustration out on Jonathan and asked him to explain his father's actions. As you carefully consider the words they traded, you can almost hear them shouting at each other.

Jonathan responded to David's panic with the words, "Why would he hide this from me? It's not so!" David came very close to holding Jonathan responsible for Saul's actions, and Jonathan came very close to getting defensive.

Their initial words to one another were natural under these circumstances. What is not natural, however, was their freedom to speak their minds and move on to resolution without great incident. At this point Jonathan didn't believe that Saul was really trying to take David's life, yet he acknowledged that David's feelings were authentic by saying, "Whatever you want me to do, I'll do for you" (v. 4). He didn't necessarily agree with David, but he agreed that David was upset and needed his help instead of his doubt.

Allowing others to speak their fears even when we can't understand is characteristic of uncommon friendship. Willingness to listen, then let the potential insults pass is not a sign of weakness. It is a sign of strength. The bonds of uncommon friends are deeper than the width of their differences.

Uncommon friends can share their hearts without shame. The scene between Jonathan and David in 1 Samuel 20:41 touches my heart every time I read it. Jonathan signaled David that he must run for his life. Then Jonathan sent the boy that was with him away and went to David.

> *After the boy had gone, David got up from the south side of the stone and bowed down before Jonathan three times, with his face to the ground. Then they kissed each other and wept together—but David wept the most.* (1 Sam. 20:41)

Something about two men unafraid to share their hearts with one another never fails to move me. Uncommon friends can be vulnerable with one another and still retain their dignity. The friendship between Jonathan and David was far more than emotion, and it was a safe place to trust and show feelings. They shared a common goal: the will of God. Each life complemented the other. They had separate lives but inseparable bonds.

My husband, Keith, runs his family's plumbing business. His best friend, Roger, is a lawyer and judge. They are uncommon friends. They don't talk every day. They don't necessarily talk every week, but their bonds remain firm. They play jokes on one another. They take up for one another. When they see one another, they hug. When they hurt, they sometimes cry. They are "real men" with a rare friendship.

Uncommon friends can stay close even at a distance. Most friendships require time and attention. We saw that Jonathan and David's friendship did not grow out of a lengthy period of time as most friendships do. They were brought together by spiritual ties, not sequences of time. They had "sworn friendship with each other in the name of the LORD" (v. 42). God brought them together. Their friendship was a bond of three.

I am struck by how Ecclesiastes 4:9–12 pictures the friendship of David and Jonathan. We are not sure that Solomon wrote the Book of

Ecclesiastes, but if he did, I wonder if the inspiration from this passage came from the stories of Jonathan he heard at his father David's knee.

> *Two are better than one,*
>> *because they have a good return for their work:*
> *If one falls down,*
>> *his friend can help him up.*
> *But pity the man who falls*
>> *and has no one to help him up!*
>
> . . . .
>
> *A cord of three strands is not quickly broken.*
> (Eccles. 4:9–10, 12b)

This Scripture applies perfectly to Jonathan and David, but especially the last line. Doesn't this statement picture God's part in Jonathan and David's friendship?

If God is not an active part in your friendships, you are missing one of life's most important treasures.

Chapter 14

THE BLESSED REMINDER

1 Samuel 21

*The priest gave him the consecrated bread, since there was no bread
there except the bread of the Presence that had been removed from
before the Lord and replaced by hot bread on the day it
was taken away. (1 Sam. 21:6)*

We now begin a significant season in David's life. He was scarcely twenty years old when he was forced to leave his home, his livelihood, and his beloved friend Jonathan as he fled from the madman who happened to be king of Israel.

I've had the opportunity to work with college students a few times. I always come away thinking how young they seem and how old and savvy I felt at that same age. I suffered enough trauma just leaving home to go to college even though I had a secure room in the dorm, a guaranteed meal in the cafeteria, and more company than I could stand. I certainly have nothing with which to compare this season of David's young life. He was on the run with a madman on his heels. Saul had alerted half the country to take David's life. David faced a terrifying prospect for a person twice his age. Let's take a look at David's initiation to life on the run.

When David resigned to live as a fugitive, he first went to Nob, to Ahimelech the priest. In the first verse of chapter 21, we see that Ahimelech "trembled" when he met David. Ahimelech probably was not aware of the warrant out for David's life. If he had known Saul was seeking to kill David, he would not have asked why David was alone. Perhaps the priest's reference to Goliath's sword provides a little insight. Ahimelech knew of Goliath's demise at the hands of David. He also may have remembered David sporting through Jerusalem swinging Goliath's head in his hand. No doubt, David was rather intimidating. The priests certainly would have wanted no trouble from the Philistine army seeking revenge. Whatever the reasons, the sight of David struck fear in the priest's heart.

David did not haphazardly end up in Nob. He sought relief in the "city of priests." Nob, a village between Jerusalem and Gibeah, was the venue where the tabernacle was relocated after the destruction of Shiloh. Like many of us in times of crisis, David may have desired to draw closest to those who seem closest to God—not a bad idea.

When was the last time you reached out to your pastor, Sunday school teacher, or someone you regard as being "close to God"? Why did you reach out to that particular person in your time of need? If you've never sought such help, you might consider it.

When Ahimelech asked David's reason for coming, David responded to the priest with a lie. Through our study we will be witness to more than a few compromises in David's character. In this case the compromise was David's willingness to lie. He was probably attempting to spare the priest's life, hoping that Saul would not hold Ahimelech responsible for helping David.

Famished from his flight, David asked the priest for bread. He asked for five loaves. The request strikes a familiar chord to those schooled in the Scriptures. Christ fed the multitudes with five loaves of bread in Matthew 14:19. In 1 Samuel 21:3, David requested of Ahimelech, "Give me five loaves of bread, or whatever you can find." In all four of the Gospels, as Christ sent the disciples to search for food, five loaves were all they could find. For David, no bread could be found except the bread of the Presence.

Perhaps God had a point to make with the five loaves. The bread of the Presence has always been connected to God's covenant. The regulation concerning the bread of the Presence appears in Leviticus 24:5–9. Verse 8 says, "This bread is to be set out before the LORD regularly, Sabbath after Sabbath, on behalf of the Israelites, as a lasting covenant."

Isaiah 55:3 tells us about a further extension of the covenant. It speaks of God's "everlasting covenant."

> *Give ear and come to me;*
> * hear me, that your soul may live.*
> *I will make an everlasting covenant with you,*
> * my faithful love promised to David.*

Consider two possible reasons why God might have purposely used the bread of the Presence to feed David. First, the bread of the Presence might have symbolized God's everlasting covenant with David. Somewhat like the stars of the sky symbolized the offspring of Abram (Gen. 15:5), the bread of the Presence was placed before God as a reminder, or symbol, of the everlasting covenant. God may have used the bread of the Presence to remind David of the everlasting covenant He had made with David's kingdom.

Second, the bread of the Presence might have symbolized the provision of God's presence in the life of David. Just as the first possible reason was a corporate symbol for a kingdom covenant, the second reason might have been a private symbol for a personal covenant. The Hebrew term for *presence* is *paneh,* which means "countenance, presence, or face."[8] The everlasting covenant symbolized by the bread of the Presence was a reminder of the pledge of God's presence to His people. As He offered bread to David through Ahimelech the priest, I believe God pledged His presence to David throughout his exile. Might God's promise have inspired David to write the following two verses?

> *For he has not despised or disdained*
> *the suffering of the afflicted one;*
> *he has not hidden his face from him*
> *but has listened to his cry for help.* (Ps. 22:24)

> *Let your face shine on your servant;*
> *save me in your unfailing love.* (Ps. 31:16)

The word for "face" in both the above verses is *paneh*, the exact word for "presence" in the phrase "the bread of the Presence." God was doing more in this moment in Nob than feeding David's hungry stomach. I believe God pledged His presence to David and promised to be his complete sustainer. God also extends His presence to you as your sustaining provision. Note the name Christ calls Himself in the Gospel of John: "I tell you the truth, he who believes has everlasting life. I am the bread of life" (John 6:47–48).

Did you notice how Jesus combined the bread of life with everlasting life? Christ is the bread of God's presence to us. His scars are placed before God as a perpetual memorial that the wages of our sins have been paid. Christ said, "This bread is my flesh, which I will give for the life of the world" (John 6:51b). Those who have eaten the bread of His presence enjoy the same everlasting covenant He made with David thousands of years ago. He renews His promise to us in Hebrews 13:5: "Never will I leave you; / never will I forsake you."

God reminded David of His presence and provision not just through the priest of Nob; God reminded David in another way. Does it seem coincidental that when David asked for a weapon, the only one in the city of Nob was Goliath's sword? Is it possible God was trying to remind David that he had overcome a greater enemy than Saul with God's help? None of these reminders seemed to help, because David had forgotten to measure his obstacle against his God rather than against his own strength (as he had Goliath)! At least his relentless search for refuge led to a rather humorous scene as we see next.

David fled to Achish the king of Gath, but the Philistine king quickly recognized David. In his depleted state, the situation frightened David, but the Israelite was a quick thinker. David pretended to be insane, acting like a madman with "saliva running down his beard" (1 Sam. 21:13).

Had David been auditioning for a theatrical production, he would no doubt have gotten the part! We see a new, creative, and shrewd side of our protagonist in this situation. Not only was he a harpist and a warrior, he could have won an Oscar for best actor! Some people act for pleasure. Others act for money. David was acting for his life. He pulled it off too. You may be wondering why the men of Gath didn't kill him on the spot. David knew the pagan people of his day. They were terrified of a mad-man and far too superstitious to harm one. They feared he was a danger-ous demon who had the power to cause them havoc from the next life. Apparently, David wasn't just sheep-smart, he was street-smart.

The Philistine king delivered one of those wonderful lines that show Scripture is not only the Word of God but the greatest literature you can find. Achish said: "Am I so short of madmen that you have to bring this fellow here to carry on like this in front of me?" (v. 15). (I confess that though good manners have precluded my using the line, the action of some people have made me think of it.)

David may have been short on patience and short on perceiving God's constant reminders, but he certainly wasn't short on personality, was he? Patience and perception might have helped him a little more than personality. Ask God to make you aware of the constant reminders of His presence in your life so that you can have His assurance, no matter your circumstances.

In the chapters ahead we are going to see David as he negotiates some pretty tough times. We'll begin to peek a little deeper into the heart that God saw and loved. Studying God's Word is habit-forming. Keep praying for a hunger and thirst for His Word. Like David, God doesn't want you feeding from common loaves. He desires to feed you with the bread of His Presence. His table is always set.

David wrested food and a weapon from Ahimelech and received significant responses. For food, the priest gave David the bread of the Presence that had been offered to the Lord. For a weapon David took the sword of Goliath.

The narrative also contains an ominous clue. Doeg the Edomite, Saul's chief shepherd, overheard the exchange between David and the priest of Nob. As we read the passage, we suspect we have not seen the last of this sinister figure.

Chapter 15

FOR CRYING OUT LOUD

Psalm 142

*I pour out my complaint before him; before him I tell my
trouble. When my spirit grows faint within me, it is you
who know my way. (Ps. 142:2–3)*

We now begin to consider a vital season that provided painful preparation for the throne God had promised. David responded to life on the run as he fled a wildly jealous king. Can you imagine the devastation David must have experienced having all his hopes dashed to pieces? He probably had never been away from home before he was summoned to Saul's service. Filled with dreams and wonderful expectations, young David was met by a nightmare. He had not only left his home, now he'd run from his "home away from home." He was separated from his new wife and his best friend, and forced to beg bread from the priest of Nob.

First Samuel 22:1 tells us that "David left Gath and escaped to the cave of Adullam." The cave of Adullam, a word meaning "sealed off place," was about twenty miles southwest of Jerusalem.⁹ David had traveled approximately ten miles by foot from Gath to the place of strange refuge he found in the crevice of a mountain.

Cave-pierced mountains are prevalent in the area of Palestine where David's exile took place. Evidence exists that many continued to find refuge in these caves up until the time of Roman rule, when they were common hideaways for Jews fleeing Roman persecution. I wonder how many of those Jews found solace in knowing their beloved King David had also escaped persecution in a similar refuge centuries earlier.

Obviously David's brothers were at least beginning to change their tunes about their younger sibling because his brothers and his father's household joined him in the cave and "those who were in distress or in debt or discontented gathered around him, and he became their leader" (1 Sam. 22:1–2). David asked the king of Moab if his parents could stay with him for awhile. No doubt David feared for the lives of his parents when Saul found that his brothers had joined him.

Can you imagine the mixture of fear, rage, abandonment, and bewilderment David must have felt hiding in that cave? Had 1 Samuel 22 been our only text, we would never have known some of what David experienced. Thankfully, God inspired David to write his feelings and engraved them forever in holy writ. David wrote Psalm 142 after entering this dismal cave, checking all earthly securities at the door. The New International Version identifies Psalm 142 as a prayer when David was in the cave.

> *I cry aloud to the LORD;*
> *I lift up my voice to the LORD for mercy.*
> *I pour out my complaint before him;*
> *before him I tell my trouble.*
> *When my spirit grows faint within me,*
> *it is you who know my way.*
> *In the path where I walk*
> *men have hidden a snare for me.*

Look to my right and see;
  no one is concerned for me.
I have no refuge;
  no one cares for my life.
I cry to you, O LORD;
  I say, "You are my refuge,
  my portion in the land of the living."
Listen to my cry,
  for I am in desperate need;
rescue me from those who pursue me,
  for they are too strong for me. (Ps. 142:1–6)

Few of us have been forced to find refuge in a cave, but all of us have felt some of the same emotions David experienced. Psalm 142 offers a number of insights into David's heart. His responses provide a worthy example for us.

Note what David did when he was overwhelmed with unfair treatment and difficult circumstances.

First and foremost, David *prayed.* The psalm provides an unquestionable testament that David responded to his difficulty with prayer. Few of us would argue about prayer being the proper response in our crises, but we often don't perceive prayer as being the most practical response. We think, *God can save me from my sins but not from my situation.*

Next we notice that David *cried aloud.* The scene touches my heart as I imagine this young man sobbing in the cave. I was nearby when a teenage boy slammed his hand in a car door. He was in immense pain. I watched him as he struggled between his need to be reduced to a bawling baby and his external need to keep his dignity. I watched him try to control his quivering lip. David was probably no different from that young man. I wonder how much he wished for the old days when he was unimportant, unimpressive, and contentedly keeping sheep. He had not asked for God's anointing, yet he had met nothing but trouble since that day. We can only begin to imagine the thoughts, fears, and losses that brought him to tears.

I believe that crying "aloud" helped David maintain sound emotional, mental, and spiritual health. Sometimes there's just nothing like a good cry. It clears the air, doesn't it? David was a real man by anyone's standards, yet he knew no better outlet than crying aloud to his God. "Cry aloud to the Lord" when you feel overwhelmed. He can take it!

A third detail stands out: David *poured out his complaint to God.* He told God his troubles. Tell Him your trouble. Tell Him what's hurting you. You can even tell Him what's bugging you! I am convinced this is one of the major contributors to David's godlike heart: He viewed his heart as a pitcher, and he poured everything in it on his God, whether it was joy or sadness, bitterness or fear. David not only poured out his heart as a personal practice, he urged others to do the same. Note David's words from Psalm 62:8: "Trust in him at all times, O people; / pour out your hearts to him, / for God is our refuge."

David did not just pour out his emotion, he also *rehearsed his trust in God.* In Psalm 142:3, he said, "When my spirit grows faint within me, / it is you who know my way." David was so exhausted that he feared he would become negligent in his alertness to the snares his enemies set for him. His prayer to God also became a reminder to himself: "God knows my way." Prayer is for our sake as much as it is for God's pleasure. When I see the words I've written in my journal extolling the mighty virtues of God, I am reminded of His constant activity on my behalf, and my faith is strengthened.

The text yields a fifth observation; did you notice how David *longed for God's presence?* Because we need God's presence, our feelings are worth sharing with Him whether or not they accurately describe the truth. In verse 4, David said, "Look to my right and see; / no one is concerned for me." (Guards often stood to the right of their appointees, ready to take an arrow in their defense.) David was reminding God that he had no guard. He surmised from his aloneness that no one was concerned for him. His next words were, "I have no refuge; / no one cares for my life." Although he had found a cave in which to hide, he felt he had no refuge because no one was there who cared personally for him.

Certainly many people cared for David, but because they were not in his presence, he felt forsaken. His feelings were not an accurate assessment of the truth, but they were worthy to share with God. Feelings can be a little like our laundry. Sometimes we can't sort them until we dump them out. We can see that God honored David's telling Him exactly how he felt because He brought David's brothers and his father's household to be with him.

In my freshman year in college, I fell head over heels in love with a young man. Every time he broke my heart, I wanted to go home. Home was three-and-a-half hours away, and I had no car. I must have called my daddy a dozen times during that fretful courtship. Each time, no matter what time of the day or night, he got in the car and drove seven hours round-trip to pick me up. In the same way, God knew David needed his daddy. Later, God would mature David and teach him to stand alone. He wouldn't always send David's father to him. He doesn't send my father to rescue me much anymore. But God always responded to David's cry for help.

For a sixth principle from the passage, notice that David *confessed his desperate need.* In Psalm 142:6, he said, "Listen to my cry, / for I am in desperate need; / rescue me from those who pursue me, / for they are too strong for me." A wise man knows when those who stand against him are mightier than he! David had killed both a lion and a bear; then Goliath became "like one of them" (1 Sam. 17:36). So why did David feel overwhelmed on this occasion? It may have been because he had never battled a secret enemy. This time he had members of Saul's entourage pursuing him with secret schemes.

Does David's plight sound familiar? According to Ephesians 6, we also fight an entire assembly of unseen powers and principalities. Without the intervention of God and His holy armor, we are mud on the bottom of the enemy's boots. How wise to humbly seek God's aid by admitting, "rescue me . . . for they are too strong for me"!

David's example certainly demonstrates to us that our prayer lives need to be very specific and personal. I need constant encouragement to remain specific in my prayer life. You probably do too. We often get far more specific sharing our hearts with a friend than we do with our God who can truly intervene and help us! "Pour out your hearts to him, / for God is our refuge" (Ps. 62:8).

Look at our original text in 1 Samuel 22:2: "All those who were in distress or in debt or discontented gathered around him, and he became their leader." Don't forget that this was David's first taste of independent leadership! What could be less appealing than leading a group made up of the three D's: the distressed, the debtors, and the discontented? Ultimately, David would rise to the throne as the forerunner of the King of kings. His kingdom would be known throughout the world. He would be favored by the living Lord as His chosen, His anointed. God had to bring David down to a lowly position before He could raise him up to stand on solid ground.

PART III

SURVIVAL SKILLS AND HE WHO WILLS

Psalm 54

When the Ziphites had gone to Saul and said, "Is not David hiding among us?"

1 Save me, O God, by your name;
    vindicate me by your might.

2 Hear my prayer, O God;
    listen to the words of my mouth.

3 Strangers are attacking me;
    ruthless men seek my life—
    men without regard for God.

4 Surely God is my help;
    the Lord is the one who sustains me.

5 Let evil recoil on those who slander me;
    in your faithfulness destroy them.

6 I will sacrifice a freewill offering to you;
    I will praise your name, O LORD,
    for it is good.

7 For he has delivered me from all my troubles,
    and my eyes have looked in triumph on my foes.

Chapter 16

THE INHUMANITY OF HUMANITY

1 Samuel 22

I will praise you forever for what you have done; in your name
I will hope, for your name is good. I will praise you in
the presence of your saints. (Ps. 52:9)

We are about to see the depth of Saul's irreverence toward God and the breadth of his madness toward David. The account shows how far the once potentially noble Saul had fallen. Remember the hinted reference to Doeg the Edomite? He tattled to Saul about Ahimelech's helping David.

On the word of Doeg, Saul sent for Ahimelech and all his family. The priest nobly and bravely testified to the king that David was loyal to Saul. Enraged, Saul ordered the murder of all the priests, but his guards refused to carry out the order. Doeg the Edomite then volunteered and murdered eighty-five priests plus all the family members—including women, infants, and children. Only one priest—Abiathar, the son of Ahimelech—escaped.

Abiathar fled to join David. He told David that Saul had killed the priests of the Lord. David replied, "That day, when Doeg the Edomite was there, I knew he would be sure to tell Saul. I am responsible for the death of your father's whole family. Stay with me; don't be afraid; the man who is seeking your life is seeking mine also. You will be safe with me" (1 Sam. 22:22–23).

I'll never forget seeing this scene in the movie *King David*. I ran to God's Word to see if the events portrayed were accurate, and to my horror, they were. At that moment, I ceased to feel pity for Saul. In my opinion, David gave him far too much credit. David gambled on the hope that Saul would never put to death an innocent priest. He was wrong.

Once again, we have the great privilege of seeing the words God inspired from David's pen after he learned of the tragic slaughter. The NIV note with Psalm 52 reads: "When Doeg the Edomite had gone to Saul and told him: 'David has gone to the house of Ahimelech.'"

Why do you boast of evil, you mighty man?
Why do you boast all day long,
you who are a disgrace in the eyes of God?
Your tongue plots destruction;
it is like a sharpened razor,
you who practice deceit.
You love evil rather than good,
falsehood rather than speaking the truth.
You love every harmful word,
O you deceitful tongue!
Surely God will bring you down to everlasting ruin:
He will snatch you up and tear you from your tent;
he will uproot you from the land of the living.
(Ps. 52:1–5)

At first glance, it may seem that David was referring to Doeg,
but the seventh verse pinpoints Saul.

Here now is the man

    who did not make God his stronghold

but trusted in his great wealth

    and grew strong by destroying others! (Ps. 52:7)

The great wealth applied to the jealous king. Assuming David is addressing Saul, verse 1 strongly suggests that Saul not only had a multitude of innocent people put to death, many of them priests, but he also bragged about it.

Psalm 52:7 tells us something vile about the ego of King Saul. It says he "grew strong" by destroying others. Have you ever known anyone who made him- or herself feel bigger or better by putting others down? Putting others down to build ourselves up is perhaps the ultimate sign of gross insecurity. Thankfully, most people with such insecurity don't have the kind of power Saul had to destroy people physically. However, if we allow our insecurities to govern our lives, we become destroyers just as certainly.

Don't miss a wonderful lesson in verse 8 of Psalm 52. Remember, David was still on the run in the forest of Hereth (1 Sam. 22:5), but even on the run, not knowing where his next meal would come from, David knew that in comparison to Saul, he was "like an olive tree flourishing in the house of God." Do you see what David did in the face of unimaginable horror? When he received the news of the slaughter of innocent people, David responded in four ways to the tragedy.

1. He placed blame where it should have been: on Saul, on evil (vv. 1–4).
2. He reminded himself that God will repay evil (v. 5).
3. He placed his hope solely in God (v. 9).
4. He reminded himself that God is good (v. 9)!

Think of a time when you were stunned by the depravity of humanity. How did you sort through your feelings about the situation?

I will never forget seeing the first film clips on television from the bombing of the federal building in Oklahoma City. I could not fathom how anyone could be so heartless and depraved. I cried for the children who had been lost or injured; then I tossed and turned most of the night. The day following the bombing I was scheduled to speak at a conference of 4,500 women from the Oklahoma City area—a commitment I had made two years prior to the time. I kept thinking that perhaps we would cancel the event; or perhaps many would not attend. The event was not canceled. Only one person who registered did not come; she was unaccounted for in the rubble of the federal building. Never have I been more frightened that I might give the wrong message. I begged God to be clear with me and not let me say a word on my own. My text was different from Psalm 52, yet the points He sent me to make were almost identical to the ones we've noted above:

1. God is not the author of destruction.
2. God will repay evil.
3. Our hope must be in God.
4. No matter how bad things look, God is good.

In the face of unimaginable horror, we must cast our imaginations on Christ, our only hope. His Word will be our anchor when our faith is tossed like the waves.

David could not have survived the guilt or the pain of Saul's horrendous actions had he not cast himself on God and His Word. We must do the same. Keep having faith even in the face of unexplainable evil or disaster. You will be richly rewarded for your faith even when others have scorned you for still believing. God is the only hope in this depraved world. He is faithful who promised.

Chapter 17

COUNT YOUR BLESSINGS

1 Samuel 23

I will sacrifice a freewill offering to you; I will praise your name,
O Lord, for it is good. (Ps. 54:6)

Have you ever noticed that the colors of God's faithfulness appear brighter when the backdrop of our lives looks bleak and gray? This chapter shows God's faithfulness shining brightly against the bleak backdrop of David's life. David continued to evade the crazed King Saul, but he did more than hide. David took every possible opportunity to defend his people, even when he was repaid with betrayal.

In chapter 23, David faced a dilemma. The Philistines were attacking the Israelite town of Keilah. What was David to do? Should he defend fellow Israelites and thereby put himself and his men at greater risk? In that difficult situation David did something characteristic of a man after God's heart. He inquired of the Lord.

"The Lord answered him, 'Go, attack the Philistines and save Keilah'" (1 Sam. 23:2).

Not surprisingly, David's men greeted the news with less than enthusiasm. They said, "Here in Judah we are afraid. How much more, then, if we go to Keilah against the Philistine forces!" (1 Sam. 23:3).

David responded to them in an interesting way. He returned to ask God once again. Once again God told him to go attack the Philistines and save Keilah. So David and his men fought the Philistines and saved the people of Keilah (1 Sam. 23:4–6).

Have you ever moved too quickly in a direction you believed God was sending you and later realized you were hasty and might have misunderstood? David's example reminds us that doubting God and doubting we understood God are two different things.

I find it interesting that rather than shame his men for questioning the word he had received from God, David went back to God and reconfirmed His direction. God rebuked neither David nor his men. God knew David felt great responsibility to his men. If he misunderstood God, many lives could be lost. David did not ask God a second time because he doubted God, but because he needed to be certain. In the same way, you or I might ask God to reconfirm His direction—not because we doubt God's Word, but because we question our understanding. To doubt God in the face of clear direction is disobedience, but to double-check our understanding and interpretation of God's will is prudent.

When Saul heard that David had rescued the inhabitants of Keilah, the king thought he had trapped his prey in a walled city. When David learned that Saul was gathering his forces, however, David consulted God and asked two questions. He wanted to know if Saul would pursue him and if the people of Keilah would defend him.

David received both answers from God: Saul would pursue him, and the citizens of Keilah would give him over to Saul. So David again fled, this time to the Desert of Ziph. While he was there, two significant events occurred. Saul came in pursuit, and Jonathan came to strengthen his friend.

Jonathan went to David at Horesh and helped him find strength in God. "Don't be afraid," he said. "My father Saul will not lay a hand on you. You will be king over Israel, and I will be second

*to you. Even my father Saul knows this." The two of them made
a covenant before the LORD. Then Jonathan went home, but
David remained at Horesh.* (1 Sam. 23:16–18)

God sent David a minister of encouragement. God used Jonathan to
reconfirm His calling on David's life. David had been betrayed by the
people he tried to help. When we have been betrayed repeatedly, we risk
becoming paranoid and cynical. We can convince ourselves that no one
can be trusted. God was reminding David not to turn his back on trust.
In effect, God was saying, "You can trust Me to fulfill what I promised
you, and you can trust Jonathan not to turn his back on you."

We have the blessing of studying several psalms that coincide with
David's experiences. I wish I could invite you to expect a coinciding psalm
at every venture, but God's Word only tells us the occasions of a few of the
psalms. I invite you to relish the ones we have. God inspired David to
write Psalm 54 (see p. 85) after the Ziphites told Saul his whereabouts.

David began the psalm with the words, "Save me, O God, by your
name." Before David had drawn his final breath, he called on God with
a multitude of names. David seemed to have as many names for God as
he had needs! Why? Because God was everything to him! One of my
favorite ways David referred to God is the little word *my.* In Psalm 62:6–7,
he said, "He alone is my rock and my salvation; / he is my fortress / . . .
my mighty rock, my refuge." Aren't you glad his God can be yours and
mine as well?

No wonder, in spite of his human frailties, David was a man after
God's own heart! The psalm concludes with David's vowing to sacrifice
a freewill offering to the Lord. According to Deuteronomy 16:10, the
freewill offering was to be "in proportion to the blessings the LORD your
God has given you."

Growing up, I often sang a well-loved hymn called "Count Your
Many Blessings." The familiar words and melody flood my memory:

Count your many blessings, name them one by one.
Count your many blessings, see what God has done.

Counting our blessings when we are betrayed, wrongly accused, and hunted by ruthless men is a different kind of worship than counting our blessings in the safety of Sunday worship. David responded to his helpless estate by giving a freewill offering to God in proportion to His blessings.

He left us a wonderful example.

PART IV

IN THE DESERT OF JUDAH

Psalm 63

A psalm of David. When he was in the Desert of Judah.

1   O God, you are my God,
      earnestly I seek you;
      my soul thirsts for you,
      my body longs for you,
      in a dry and weary land
      where there is no water.

2   I have seen you in the sanctuary
      and beheld your power and your glory.

3   Because your love is better than life,
      my lips will glorify you.
4   I will praise you as long as I live,
      and in your name I will lift up my hands.
5   My soul will be satisfied as with the richest of foods;
      with singing lips my mouth will praise you.

6   On my bed I remember you;
      I think of you through the watches of the night.
7   Because you are my help,
      I sing in the shadow of your wings.

Chapter 18

A CHANCE FOR REVENGE

1 Samuel 24

*The Lord forbid that I should do such a thing to my master, the Lord's
anointed, or lift my hand against him; for he is the anointed of the Lord.*
(1 Sam. 24:6)

We have already considered God's unwavering devotion to prepare His children for His service. Now we will see some of the fruit of God's preparation in David. In those caves, God chiseled character into the heart of His king.

Once again the mad Saul came after David, this time with three thousand men. David and his men were hiding in a cave when the king came in to relieve himself. David could easily have killed Saul, but instead he crept up and cut off a piece of Saul's robe.

Amazing! David resisted revenge after all Saul had done to him! After all the lives he had taken! David wasn't even sure Saul had the sense to spare the life of his own son Jonathan or daughter Michal. In this strange circumstance David had an odd reaction to his own action. He became conscience-stricken for cutting the king's robe. He said to his men, "The LORD forbid that I should do such a thing to my master, the LORD's anointed, or lift my hand against him; for he is the anointed of the LORD" (1 Sam. 24:6).

In spite of all that Saul had done, David continued to have a tenacious belief that he must respect God's anointed king. After Saul left the cave, David called to him from a safe distance. He offered the fact that he had just spared Saul's life as proof of his loyalty.

David's men must have thought he was crazy! David apparently chose to risk man's disapproval over God's, regardless of the consequences. David's change of heart offers four evidences that He was greatly influenced by the Holy Spirit:

1. *David's conscience was immediately stricken.* The Holy Spirit convicts of sin (John 16:8). When the Holy Spirit dwells in a person, He uses the individual's conscience as the striking ground for conviction. David evidenced the work of God by saying, "The Lord forbid that I should do such a thing." He was suddenly aware that his actions were displeasing to God. You and I may want to minimize David's sin against Saul because Saul's offense against David seems so much worse. We tend to view sin in relative terms. David's standard for measuring sin was not the wickedness of Saul, but the holiness of God.

2. *David met conviction with a change in behavior.* The Holy Spirit always does His job, but we don't always do ours! If we do not fully yield to the Spirit's influence, we will often fight conviction. One sure measurement of our proximity to God, whether near or far, is the length of time between conviction and repentance. David responded to his Spirit-stricken conscience with an immediate change of behavior. His immediate response to conviction proves David was intimate with God at this point in his life. Remember, the same Holy Spirit who anointed David with His presence also dwells in New Testament believers. As we draw nearer to God, our sensitivity to conviction and our discernment of wrongdoing will increase. If we are filled by His Spirit, conviction will be met with a change in behavior.

3. *David exercised great restraint.* He must have been influenced by the Spirit. He had the perfect chance to get revenge and he didn't take it!

No one would have blamed him. He easily could have argued that his actions were in self-defense.

Such a level of restraint could only have been supernatural! Second Thessalonians 2:6–7 refers to the restraining work of the Holy Spirit. The Holy Spirit works restraint in us when we are tempted toward revenge; if we are fully yielded to the Spirit, we will obey. A moment's revenge is not worth the cost of alienation from God, not even the revenge we've been waiting for and feel so justified to seize!

4. *David respected God more than he desired revenge.* Consider David's words in 1 Samuel 24:6: "The LORD forbid that I should do such a thing to my master, the LORD's anointed." David withdrew from taking the life of Saul out of respect for God, not Saul. David's incomparable respect for God kept him from making a tragic and costly mistake.

If you are willing to honor a person out of respect for God, you can be assured that God will honor you. Several times I've been required to honor a person out of honor to God. A very strange thing has happened almost every time I've been obedient to God in this area: He has restored my respect for the person I had come to resent. God is always faithful. The results of your obedience may differ, but the blessing of your obedience is guaranteed. No doubt the time will come when you will face a window of opportunity to get back at a person who has wronged you. The only way to get through a window God doesn't open is to break it yourself. This is one window sure to leave you injured. Don't do it. Let the Holy Spirit perform His restraining work. Someday you'll be glad you did.

Chapter 19

A SURLY MAN AND A SMART WOMAN

1 Samuel 25

Even though someone is pursuing you to take your life, the life of
my master will be bound securely in the bundle of the living
by the Lord your God. But the lives of your enemies he will hurl
away as from the pocket of a sling. (1 Sam. 25:29)

What a wonderful verse! "Bound securely in the bundle of the living. . . .
hurl away as from the pocket of a sling." I not only love what is inside God's
Word, I love the way He says it. Don't you? Let's study the context of this
marvelous verse. We just saw David in the stronghold while the king whose
life he spared returned home. Now we get to enjoy a brief respite from the
tormented King Saul and meet some new figures in the life of David.

First Samuel 25:1 records a very significant event: the death of
Samuel. The remainder of the chapter makes no further mention of
him. Under the worst of circumstances, Samuel was the best of men. He
was a rare gem, faithful to the end. I cannot express how much I want to
be faithful like Samuel, to my very last breath.

The chapter proceeds with a description of a character who was
nothing like Samuel the prophet. Nabal was a wealthy landowner, surly

and mean in his dealings. His wife Abigail was an intelligent and beautiful woman.

David and his men always made it a practice to protect their fellow Israelites. They had protected Nabal's animals and herdsmen, so, in keeping with the customs of the day, at harvesttime David sent his men to request provisions from Nabal. To David's surprise the surly rancher insulted David, treated his men discourteously, and sent them away empty-handed (1 Sam. 25:10–11).

David obviously did not have the same patience with Nabal that he had with "the LORD's anointed." He had many good character traits, but a high tolerance for insult was not among them. He said, "Put on your swords" (v. 13), and four hundred of his men prepared to "visit" Nabal. All he really had to have was a sling and a few smooth stones!

If Abigail had been like her husband, the result would have been a tragedy. Fortunately, the servants knew their mistress had more sense than Nabal. A servant warned Abigail about what Nabal had done. He said David's men had protected them in the fields. He said, "Night and day they were a wall around us" (v. 16). The servant asked Abigail, "See what you can do, because disaster is hanging over our master and his whole household. He is such a wicked man that no one can talk to him" (1 Sam. 25:16–17).

Not all mates are perfectly suited for one another, are they? Scripture certainly proved that Nabal was indeed "surly and mean" and Abigail was a wise woman. (Before we have too much fun applying this lesson to the couples we know, the Word of God also records several instances of faithful husbands and fretful wives! We might not want to tally the scores of men versus women!)

Abigail prepared gifts for David and his men. Then she hurried to intercept them before they brought retribution to her husband and household. When she reached David, she bowed before him and asked him to forgive her wicked husband. Abigail continued by praising David and making her case for him to spare her household. She asked him to accept her gift of thanks.

> *Please forgive your servant's offense, for the LORD will certainly make a lasting dynasty for my master, because he fights the LORD's battles. Let no wrongdoing be found in you as long as you live. Even though someone is pursuing you to take your life, the life of my master will be bound securely in the bundle of the living by the LORD your God. But the lives of your enemies he will hurl away as from the pocket of a sling. When the LORD has done for my master every good thing he promised concerning him and has appointed him leader over Israel, my master will not have on his conscience the staggering burden of needless bloodshed or of having avenged himself. And when the LORD has brought my master success, remember your servant.* (1 Sam. 25:28–31)

I think we see another glimpse of David's heart in his reply. He quickly agreed to spare Nabal and praised God both for Abigail's good judgment and for keeping him from bloodshed. While David was certainly capable of great violence, he did not harbor grudges or hang on to resentments.

Abigail returned home after rescuing Nabal to find her drunken husband throwing a party. Imagine how she must have felt at that moment.

The Bible teaches the incontrovertible law of sowing and reaping (Gal. 6:7). For Nabal, harvest had arrived. After his night of revelry, Abigail told him about her trip to see David. Apparently the news was too much for his blood pressure. He "became like a stone," and he died after ten days.

In verse 39, David records a wonderful lesson for any of us dealing with wicked, dreadful people, whether in business or in personal relationships. Take the verse to heart in case you ever have to deal with anyone who is "surly and mean."

When David heard that Nabal was dead, he said, "Praise be to the LORD, who has upheld my cause against Nabal for treating me with contempt. He has kept his servant from doing wrong and has brought Nabal's wrongdoing down on his own head." (1 Sam. 25:39)

Not all stories have happy endings, but this one certainly does! David sent Abigail a proposal of marriage, and she became his wife.

Abigail quickly got on a donkey and, attended by her five maids, went with David's messengers and became his wife. David had also married Ahinoam of Jezreel, and they both were his wives. But Saul had given his daughter Michal, David's wife, to Paltiel son of Laish, who was from Gallim. (1 Sam. 25:42–44)

I do love a good romance! Isn't God's Word better than any novel? I see just one little problem. David went a bit overboard in the marriage department. We could be understanding about his broken vows to Michal; after all, Saul had given his wife away to "Paltiel son of Laish." The hopeless romantic in us could say, "Bless his heart" on that one and could be thrilled he had a new bride. But then, who is Ahinoam? I thought we had been with David every minute! When did he come up with her? Sometimes we can thank God not only for what He wrote in His Word, but also for what He did not. We'll just try to celebrate Abigail's good fortune, although I'm not sure how happy you can be sharing your man with another wife! Some things we may never understand, but one principle is definitely clear: polygamy has never been God's will (Gen. 2:24).

I found myself wondering, *Did God tolerate David's actions? Did God make exceptions to His first commands regarding marriage in the lives of his kings?* Our dilemma calls for a brief consideration of some other Scripture.

Deuteronomy 17 contains regulations for the time when the Israelites would have kings. Kings were told not to multiply wives, or their heart "will be led astray" (v. 17). The passage also specifies that "when he takes the throne of his kingdom, he is to write for himself on a scroll a copy of this law, taken from that of the priests, who are Levites. It is to be with him, and he is to read it all the days of his life so that he may learn to revere the Lord his God and follow carefully all the words of this law" (Deut. 17:18–19).

Don't you think God had an interesting approach to ensure that each king would consider His specific commands? If you were required to copy God's Word by hand, you could hardly claim ignorance of the laws it contained.

David knew that God intended him to be the next king of Israel. Already he had disobeyed one of God's specific commands for kings: he had taken more than one wife. As always, God's commands are for our sake, not for His. Kings had been commanded by God not to take "many wives." The word *many* was the Hebrew word *rabah*. It means to "increase, multiply, have more."[10] The Word of God is clear from the second chapter of Genesis that two wives is "more" than God planned. God's reason was clear: Those who multiply wives would have hearts led astray.

We can take a moment to inhale deeply and smell trouble brewing. God's Word will once again prove authentic. Eventually David's heart will be led astray. God presented the consequence as a promise, not a possibility. We will unfortunately be witnesses when David's straying heart ruptures like a volcano. Until then, we'll praise the God of David who still has a fresh supply of mercy every morning, prompting hearts to ache when they are prone to stray. May we take God at His Word and not have to learn everything the hard way!

PART V

THE LONG-AWAITED THRONE

Psalm 56

Of David. When the Philistines had seized him in Gath.

1 *Be merciful to me, O God, for men hotly pursue me;*
   all day long they press their attack.
2 *My slanderers pursue me all day long;*
   many are attacking me in their pride.

3 *When I am afraid,*
   I will trust in you.
4 *In God, whose word I praise,*
   in God I trust; I will not be afraid.
   What can mortal man do to me?

5 *All day long they twist my words;*
   they are always plotting to harm me.
6 *They conspire, they lurk,*
   they watch my steps,
   eager to take my life.

7 *On no account let them escape;*
   in your anger, O God, bring down the nations.

   . . . .

10 *In God, whose word I praise,*
   in the LORD, whose word I praise—

11 in God I trust; I will not be afraid.
       What can man do to me?

12 I am under vows to you, O God;
       I will present my thank offerings to you.
13 For you have delivered me from death
           and my feet from stumbling,
       that I may walk before God
           in the light of life.

Chapter 20

A CASE OF OVERKILL

1 Samuel 26–27

*David thought to himself, "One of these days I will be destroyed by the hand
of Saul. The best thing I can do is to escape to the land of the Philistines."*
(1 Sam. 27:1)

We must now take a difficult look at the life of David; a situation we
probably can't relate to as well. Chapter 26 of 1 Samuel tells one of the
classic David stories. Again Saul came after David. While Saul and his
men were asleep, David and Abishai crept into the camp and took Saul's
spear and water jug.

The next morning David called to Saul and his general, Abner. David
taunted Abner for failing to protect Saul and offered the purloined articles
as evidence that David meant Saul no harm. Once again, the homicidal
king recognized his error, apologized, and returned home. The event seems
another clear victory for David, but his next action seems out of character.
David thought to himself, *One of these days I will be destroyed by the hand
of Saul.* So they fled to the land of the Philistines (1 Sam. 27:1). With his
men, David went to king Achish of Gath as political refugees.

In retrospect, Achish does not seem to have been the sharpest knife
in the drawer, but we could see how he chose to receive David. Achish
saw Saul as his greatest threat. In politics "the enemy of my enemy is my

friend." So Achish gave David the town of Ziklag on the frontier with Judah. Finally David had a reasonably safe place. They lived in Ziklag a year and four months.

I am frankly somewhat at a loss to understand what happened next. David and his men became raiders attacking neighboring cities, and "he did not leave a man or woman alive" (1 Sam. 27:9).

My mind filled with questions when I first saw 1 Samuel 27. What has happened to David? Why was he taking up an alliance with the Philistines? Why was he on a rampage with every surrounding village? I believe two verses hold the keys for understanding David's uncharacteristic actions. In 1 Samuel 27:1, he thought, "One of these days I will be destroyed by the hand of Saul." Then in verse 11 we read that David "did not leave a man or woman alive to be brought to Gath, for he thought, 'They might inform on us and say, "This is what David did." ' "

Life on the run obviously had taken its toll. Fear, frustration, and exhaustion apparently caused David to feel hopeless. Possibly he was driven to the point of paranoia. The result was a literal case of overkill. You can hear the downward spiral of his mood in his thought: *One of these days I will be destroyed by the hand of Saul.* David became convinced he would be destroyed.

David believed his only option was to escape to the land of the Philistines. He knew Saul was afraid of them. David surmised he would at least be safe for awhile. He felt like giving up, but he couldn't because everyone had become an enemy in his eyes! Therefore, he fought everyone with a vengeance—everyone except his two clear enemies: Saul and the Philistines. We have no way of knowing how God responded to his alliance with the Philistines. To be sure, God had an opinion, but He kept the matter between Himself and David. Note, however, that God did not command David to kill all the inhabitants of the villages.

Scholars believe David penned Psalm 10 at this time in his life. Perhaps we will gain some insight into the feelings he was experiencing.

Obviously David felt that God was far away and hidden. In the first verse, he asked God: "Why do you hide yourself in times of trouble?" In verse 2, David characterized his enemy as arrogant and himself as weak: "In his arrogance the wicked man hunts down the weak." At this point David serves as an example of what happens when we focus more on our battles than on God. Our enemy appears bigger, we appear weaker, and our God appears smaller. Beware! Long-term battle can cause vision impairment if eyes focus anywhere but up!

Notice what David apparently believed Saul was saying to himself in verses 6 and 11: "Nothing will shake me; / I'll always be happy and never have trouble" and "God has forgotten; / he covers his face and never sees." In verse 13, David says the wicked man reviles God because he tells himself that he will not have to answer for his actions. But even in his despair, David never lost sight of God. In verse 14, he wrote his conviction that God remained the "helper of the fatherless."

In verse 17, David cited three actions God takes in behalf of His children: "You hear, O LORD, the desire of the afflicted; / you encourage them, and you listen to their cry."

We may have a difficult time relating to David's exact dilemma and his outrageous responses recorded in 1 Samuel 27, but we can certainly relate to his feelings. So the next time you battle an enemy so hard and so long that you feel like giving up or doing something rash, remember David. When you feel powerless over your real enemy and lash out at someone who is innocent, remember Psalm 10.

God has not forgotten. He has seen your battles. He has gathered your tears and blotted your brow. He knows those who have treated you unfairly. He knows when you're almost ready to give up or give in. Keep telling Him. Stay in His Word. Keep claiming His promises.

Chapter 21

THE LIVING DEAD

1 Samuel 28

Samuel said to Saul, "Why have you disturbed me by
bringing me up?" (1 Sam. 28:15)

We are about to study a very peculiar encounter in Scripture and one without precedent. We may share some puzzling moments, some difficult moments, and some humorous moments. God is sovereign. He is Lord over the living and the dead.

The Philistines gathered their forces to attack Israel (1 Sam. 28). David had so fooled Achish that the Philistine king wanted him as his personal bodyguard.

I love the turn of a phrase in Scripture. You've probably seen statements with double meanings, like the job reference from a former employer that read, "You'll be very lucky if you can get this person to work for you." When Achish told David that he would be expected to fight the Israelites, David replied in a similar manner: "Then you will see for yourself what your servant can do" (v. 2). The other Philistines didn't trust David, and so he and his men were sent home before the battle. I've always considered that something of a shame, because I think Achish really would have seen what David and his men could do.

In verse 3, we learn one of those tidbits of information that we suspect will come back to haunt somebody. Saul had expelled the mediums and spiritists from the land. When Saul learned that the Philistines were preparing for war, he was terrified. He sought God to learn the outcome of the battle. When the Lord did not answer Saul, he sent his attendants to find a medium.

God's occasional refusal to respond to the pleas of someone in His Word often strikes a humanitarian chord in us. At first we may wonder why God would not answer Saul since Saul first inquired of Him before he sought a spiritist. Does God seem a little unfair to you at first in His lack of response to Saul?

God never responds haphazardly, nor does He withhold an answer without regard. Why is God silent at times? Isaiah 59:1–3 gives us one very valid explanation for God's occasional silence, and one which certainly applied to Saul at this time. Isaiah wrote, "Your sins have hidden his face from you, / so that he will not hear." Remember, Saul continued in disobedience to God. He relentlessly sought the life of an innocent man and even attempted to spear his own son! He had the priests of the Lord slaughtered and gave approval to an entire town being wiped out. We've seen some regrets, but we've never seen him truly turn from wickedness to righteousness. Notice that Isaiah 59:2 does not say God can't hear but that He won't.

I can vividly remember times in my life when God seemed silent, and I realized He was waiting on me to confront and confess certain sins in my life. His silence suggested, "I will not go on to another matter in your life, my child, until we deal with this one."

One prayer God will surely hear even when we've been rebellious and sought our own way is the prayer of sincere repentance. The prayer for deliverance from sin must precede the prayer for deliverance from our enemies.

When God refused to answer Saul, he asked where to find a spiritist. Isn't it interesting that Saul set out on a journey to seek that which he himself had expelled? He didn't have much difficulty finding a spiritist because he hadn't really made much of an effort to rid the land of them. The fact that his officials hadn't actually followed his orders suggests a practical truth for us. When we don't take God too seriously, others don't take our leadership too seriously! Taking a few steps backward in our Christian walk is not very difficult. Christians used to call it "backsliding." I wish the only direction for a Christian was onward to maturity, but unfortunately some of our footprints in the sand look a lot like figure eights!

Deuteronomy 18:10–12 specifically forbids spiritists and mediums. Saul knew God's Word. Early in his reign as king he did what God's Word commanded. After his regard for God shrank and his flesh abounded, he sought the very thing he once had considered wrong. We've done the same from time to time. We've felt convicted to get rid of something or to cease a certain practice; then, when our regard for God began to shrink and our regard for our own flesh began to grow, we were out the door hunting it down. Can you think of any personal examples? Let me suggest a few: Have you ever given up R-rated movies and found yourself at a later date with a ticket and popcorn in your hand, heading into a movie you formerly wouldn't have watched? Have you ever given up gossip magazines because God convicted you toward purity of mind, but you found yourself throwing one into your grocery basket again? At one time were you very sensitive about saying hurtful things to or about others, but now it doesn't bother you much anymore?

Saul's henchmen knew where to find a medium, so Saul disguised himself and traveled to Endor to consult her. He asked her to bring up the spirit of Samuel. What happened next shows that God has a sense of humor. "When the woman saw Samuel, she cried out at the top of her voice and said to Saul, 'Why have you deceived me? You are Saul!'" (1 Sam. 28:12).

You have to chuckle as the witch almost jumped out of her skin at the sight of Samuel! Either she was an imposter and she was shocked that her incantation worked, or she was expecting a demonic imitation. She not only knew that God alone could have stirred Samuel from the dead, but she also knew that God probably would have done it only for the king himself! God had a point to make, to be sure!

After the woman recovered from the shock of seeing Samuel, Saul assured her she would not be harmed. Then he asked what she saw. She said a spirit was coming up from the ground, "an old man wearing a robe. . . . Then Saul knew it was Samuel, and he bowed down and prostrated himself with his face to the ground" (1 Sam. 28:14).

Admittedly, the vision of Samuel was not for the simple intent of humor, but it never fails to afford me a snicker. I have to smile over the way Saul knew it was Samuel. No doubt Saul had seen Samuel in that same old garb a thousand times! Among Samuel's many wonderful attributes, we never discovered an eye for fashion. Yes, Samuel's robe rang a familiar bell in Saul's mind with good reason! You may remember back in 1 Samuel 15:27, Saul grabbed and tore that robe. Saul might have asked the spiritist, "Do you happen to see a tiny little tear in the robe?"

Neither Samuel's clothing nor his mood had changed. "Why have you disturbed me by bringing me up?" (v. 15). I didn't get the feeling this was a joyful reunion, did you? I think what Samuel wanted to say was, "Now what?"

Let's be careful how much application we draw from this lesson about the dearly departed. God did something very rare that day. He gave Saul a vision of Samuel raised momentarily from the dead so He could smack Saul in the face with His sovereignty. I don't want to mislead you. We cannot conclude from this encounter that we'll be wearing the same clothes eternally (Hallelujah!), that our loved ones can ask God to let us appear to them after we're dead, or that it's OK for us to seek to talk to the dead.

We arrive at God's sovereign purpose for supernaturally intervening. The encounter ended with the harsh news of the imminent death of Saul and his sons. Samuel said,

> *The LORD has torn the kingdom out of your hands and given it*
> *to one of your neighbors—to David. Because you did not obey the*
> *LORD or carry out his fierce wrath against the Amalekites, the*
> *LORD has done this to you today. The LORD will hand over both*
> *Israel and you to the Philistines, and tomorrow you and your sons*
> *will be with me.* (1 Sam. 28:17–19)

I find myself hoping even Saul's life had an ultimately happy ending. When Samuel said, "Tomorrow you and your sons will be with me," we do not know what Samuel meant. He may simply have meant, "You are about to die." Or he may have meant Saul and his sons would join Samuel among the redeemed. I'd like to think that Saul and his sons took the opportunity to settle business with God, knowing of their imminent demise. Sometimes the most merciful thing God can do in a rebellious person's life is let him know he is going to die so he can beg for mercy.

Chapter 22

ALONE WITH GOD

1 Samuel 30

David was greatly distressed because the men were talking of stoning him;
each one was bitter in spirit because of his sons and daughters. But David
found strength in the Lord his God. (1 Sam. 30:6)

We now turn from Saul back to David. When we last saw him, he had entered an alliance with Achish. Now the Philistine armies were preparing to battle King Saul and the Israelites. Achish trusted David, but the other Philistine commanders had a more objective view of the situation. They demanded that David be sent away lest he help the Israelites. They had not forgotten the little ditty the women of Israel had sung about Saul who had slain his thousands and David his tens of thousands. They had no intention of becoming ten thousand and one.

So David and his men returned to Ziklag after a three-day journey. When they arrived, they found that Ziklag had been raided, burned, and their wives and children had been taken captive.

When the men saw what had happened to their families, "David and his men wept aloud until they had no strength left to weep" (1 Sam. 30:4). In their grief David's men even began to discuss stoning him.

David was greatly distressed over the blame his men cast on him, but the circumstance yielded one of the great glimpses of a man after

God's own heart. David was distressed . . . but he found strength in the Lord his God. I'd like to draw a few points from those statements. The passage paints perfect portraits of human nature.

1. *Hurting people often find someone to blame.* When we've suffered a loss, just like David's men we often look for stones to throw—and someone at whom to throw them. Notice that David also suffered the loss of his family. He did not know if he would ever see them again. He had taken many lives. I'm sure he assumed his enemy would not blink an eye at taking the lives of his wives and children. David cried the same tears the other men cried, but because they needed someone to blame, they focused their anger on him.

2. *Nothing hurts more than our children in jeopardy.* Many things hurt and cause us to search for stones to throw, but, as in verse 6, nothing has the potential to cause bitterness in spirit like matters involving our children. They are our Achilles' heel, aren't they? Someone can treat our child unfairly, and we're ready to pounce. We almost can't help living by the philosophy "If you want to make an enemy out of me, just mess with my kid." Can you imagine how many poor decisions have been made when parents have hastily thrown the stones of retaliation on behalf of their children?

David's men ultimately arrived at a place of reason. They chose not to act at the peak of their emotions—a wise response for all of us.

3. *Nothing helps more than finding strength in our God.* Sometimes no one offers us encouragement or helps us find strength. We'd better be prepared to strengthen ourselves in the Lord. Others can help and be encouraging, but this kind of strength comes only from the Lord.

Without a doubt, the most precious and painful times I have had in this Christian experience were times when I realized I was all alone with God. Such times forge an unforgettable, inseparable bond. Don't miss the opportunity. I am convinced that God sometimes stays the encouragement of others purposely so we will learn to find it in Him.

After David and his men had poured out their initial cup of grief, they turned to find a solution. David inquired of the Lord if he should pursue the raiding party. God answered: "Pursue them . . . You will certainly overtake them and succeed in the rescue" (1 Sam. 30:8).

David set out with his six hundred men. At Besor Ravine, two hundred of David's men were too exhausted to continue, so David left them and went on with the remaining four hundred. They overtook the Amalekites, who were celebrating prematurely. The ensuing battle lasted from dusk until the following evening, but David and his men recaptured all they had lost and much more plunder. Only four hundred young Amalekites escaped from David.

When the battle-weary group returned to the two hundred who had stayed behind, some of the men did not want to share the plunder, but David issued a decree that the "share of the man who stayed with the supplies is to be the same as that of him who went down to the battle. All will share alike" (1 Sam. 30:24).

We can make some important life applications from the experiences of David and his men:

1. *Assured victory does not mean easy wins.* God told David in advance that he would "certainly overtake them and succeed in the rescue," yet we see references to exhaustion (v. 10), hard work (v. 17), a nonstop, twenty-four-hour battle (v. 17), and four hundred escapees (v. 17). God was absolutely true to His Word. The end was exactly as God had promised, but what we often don't count on is the means. Many times God gives us a victory that requires blood, sweat, and tears. Why? Because He is practical. When He can bring about a victory and strengthen and mature us all at the same time, He's likely to do it!

God revels in overcoming and undergirding all at once. You see, God's idea of victory has virtually nothing to do with plunder. It has to do with people. What comes out of a battle isn't nearly as important as *who* comes out of a battle. That day God not only worked a victory through David, He worked one *in* David. The man after God's own heart came out of battle with grace and mercy and a little better grasp of God's sovereignty.

2. *We don't have to "win big" to win.* No wholesale slaughter resulted. Quite the contrary. Four hundred men got away, yet God called it a victory! David could have been furious with himself because he let some guys get away. Instead, he chose to focus on the ones he brought home: their families, his family. If your family has come out of a serious battle intact, fall on your face and praise your faithful God. The victory is yours.

We constantly fight an unseen enemy. God has assured us the victory, but He has told us to take an aggressive stand against the evil one, covering ourselves in His armor. We're going to win, but victory is going to take blood, sweat, and tears—His blood, our sweat, and tears from us both.

Chapter 23

THE DEATH OF
ISRAEL'S GIANT

1 Samuel 31

When the armor-bearer saw that Saul was dead, he too fell on his sword and died with him. (1 Sam. 31:5)

With this chapter we close the portion of our study of King David recorded in the Book of 1 Samuel. Some Scripture lessons are hard to swallow, while others make us laugh. God, in His infinite wisdom, tucked something to learn inside every one. We must come to a place of important closure today before we proceed to our next book of the Bible.

First Samuel 31:1 records the victory of the Philistines over Israel. Anytime God's people experience defeat, we should be concerned. God's promise to Israel in Deuteronomy 11:22–25 contains the clear reason Israel lost the battle. God said He would drive out the other nations before Israel, but only if they would "carefully observe all [His] commands." They didn't; now He wouldn't.

As the ghostly Samuel had predicted, Saul saw Israel defeated and his own sons killed. "They killed his sons Jonathan, Abinadab and Malki-Shua. The fighting grew fierce around Saul, and when the archers overtook him, they wounded him critically" (1 Sam. 31:2–3).

The passage is especially difficult because we feel we've come to know the people who perished. We feel we've come face-to-face with the good, the bad, and the ugly in Saul and with the tender and beloved in Jonathan. My heart aches at their difficult end. I wonder if Jonathan had heard that David was on the other side. Did Jonathan look for David's face before he threw his spear for fear he'd harm his friend? Did Jonathan wonder if David intended to keep the covenant they had made even if Jonathan perished that day? Was he afraid? Did tears blur the sight of his brothers' bodies nearby? I find myself wanting to know more, not ready to find his name missing from the page. He was the kind of friend we all want—the kind of friend David needed.

And what about Saul? Critically wounded and hardly able to move, Saul urged his armor-bearer to take his life, but the armor-bearer would not do it. "So Saul took his own sword and fell on it" (1 Sam. 31:4).

Saul knew the history of the Philistines. He knew they made sport of their prize captives. The armor-bearer must have stood frozen as he watched the wounded and bleeding king muster his last bit of strength to fall on his sword.

"When the armor-bearer saw that Saul was dead, he too fell on his sword and died with him." He had pledged to protect his king to the death. He had done it. His job was over, and for one armor-bearer, there would be no other. He would die with his king.

The Philistines did not need Saul alive to mock him. They cut off his head, surely in memory of their slain giant, and impaled his body on the wall of Beth Shan.

Sometimes the worst of events bring out the best in people. When the men of Jabesh Gilead heard of the death of Saul and his sons, they traveled all night and risked their lives to retrieve the bodies. They burned the bodies and buried the bones under a tamarisk tree at Jabesh (1 Sam. 31:11–13).

The men of Jabesh Gilead performed a brave and loving act. Certainly the bodies were well guarded. They could have ended up impaled right beside the bodies they came to rescue. Why would they take such a chance? Remember Saul's first act as king, recorded in 1 Samuel 11:1–11? I am encouraged to think that across forty-two years the people of the village never forgot their debt of gratitude to a young king. The men of Jabesh Gilead paid a tribute to a king who started well.

May we accept and imitate their example. May our memories of kindness be long and of offenses be short. It's not too late to say thanks. Owe somebody a favor? How much better to repay it before you stand with them under the shade of a tamarisk tree.

In the midst of a tragic scene, a group of heroes emerged, all because they had good memories. No doubt God's heroes are those who never forget His faithfulness.

May we be counted among them.

Chapter 24

A FALLEN FRIEND

2 Samuel 1

*Saul and Jonathan—in life they were loved and gracious, and
in death they were not parted. They were swifter than
eagles, they were stronger than lions. (2 Sam. 1:23)*

Second Samuel begins with David and his men's return from rescuing
their families from the Amalekites. A young man who happened to be
an Amalekite living in Israel arrived from the battle scene on Mount
Gilboa. In his hands he carried the crown and armband of Saul. In his
heart he carried dreams of reward. If he had known the heart and character of the man to whom he spoke, he would have behaved differently.

The young man told David that Saul and his sons were dead. He
went on to claim that he had seen the wounded Saul and finished him
off personally. He offered the articles from Saul as proof.

Have you ever heard the saying, "He lies when the truth would fit
better"? If a literal example of this expression ever existed, this is it. The
messenger didn't get the result he had imagined.

> *Then David and all the men with him took hold of their clothes and
> tore them. They mourned and wept and fasted till evening for Saul
> and his son Jonathan, and for the army of the LORD and the house
> of Israel, because they had fallen by the sword. (2 Sam. 1:11–12)*

The passage does not tell us how quickly David dealt with the messenger, but I wonder: *If David grieved until evening before he responded, did the man begin to have misgivings?*

Few people living in the Middle East would have failed to hear rumors of Saul's pursuit of David. Many must have followed them as closely as a faithful watcher of a modern soap opera. People love conflict. We love reading about it and hearing about it.

When the men were returning home after David had killed the Philistine giant, the women met King Saul singing: "Saul has slain his thousands, and David his tens of thousands" (1 Sam. 18:7). Those women started a jealousy that cost both men dearly.

Many days later, as the deceitful Amalekite lay slain at David's feet, that little song had caused another casualty. The opportunist was hoping he'd find favor with David by claiming he had taken the life of Saul. He was dead wrong.

David poured out his love for Jonathan and, in spite of all the years the mad king's jealousy had cost him, for Saul. He wrote the lament that appears in 2 Samuel 1:19–27. Look at some of David's words of grief:

> *O mountains of Gilboa,*
>> *may you have neither dew nor rain,*
>> *nor fields that yield offerings of grain.*
> *For there the shield of the mighty was defiled,*
>
> . . . .
>
> *Saul and Jonathan—*
>> *in life they were loved and gracious,*
>> *and in death they were not parted.*
> *They were swifter than eagles,*
>> *they were stronger than lions.*
>
> . . . .

I grieve for you, Jonathan my brother;
     you were very dear to me.
Your love for me was wonderful,
     more wonderful than that of women. (2 Sam. 1:21, 23, 26)

In David's song of lament, his words suddenly turned from the refrain of the assembly to the grief of a single heart: "I grieve for you, Jonathan my brother." The Hebrew word for *brother* in this verse was `ach`. It meant "a brother, near relative. `Ach` is any person or thing which is similar to another. It is generally a term of affection."[11] One was a shepherd; the other, a prince, yet they were "one in spirit" (1 Sam. 18:1). They were brothers.

David called his friend's love "wonderful." David distinguished the sacrificial nature of this friendship from anything else anyone had ever demonstrated to him. So determined was Jonathan that David be king, a position Jonathan stood to inherit, that he committed his entire life to that end. David found it "astonishing."

I know what it's like to lose a best friend. My buddy and I were absolutely inseparable. We dressed alike, cut our hair alike, shared a locker, and had endless sleepovers. I had lots of boyfriends as a teenager, but I only had one best friend. Her name was Dodie. One day she dropped by the house to pick me up for a bite to eat. My parents would not let me go because we were preparing to leave town. Dodie never came back. Within half an hour, I heard the blood-curdling siren of an ambulance. I can hardly talk about it even today. I still visit her grave. I still ache for our friendship.

David grieved the tragic loss of life that took place on Mount Gilboa. His thoughts must have been consumed with how differently he wished it had all happened.

Not coincidentally, the next chapter begins with the words "In the course of time, David. . . ." We share a moment of his grief when we see the words "In the course of time." Some things just take "the course of time."

Chapter 25

SETTLING DOWN

2 Samuel 2

David also took the men who were with him, each with his family,
and they settled in Hebron and its towns. Then the men of Judah
came to Hebron and there they anointed David king over the
house of Judah. (2 Sam. 2:3–4)

At least fifteen years had passed since Samuel went to the home of Jesse
and anointed the young shepherd. As chapter 2 unfolds, David is thirty
years old. Let's see what has transpired "in the course of time."

How greatly we could profit if we would take to heart David's example in the first verse of 2 Samuel 2. He inquired of God before he took a
single step in his inevitable journey to the throne.

> *David inquired of the Lord. "Shall I go up to one of the towns of*
> *Judah?" he asked.*
>
> *The Lord said, "Go up."*
>
> *David asked, "Where shall I go?"*
>
> *"To Hebron," the Lord answered. (2 Sam. 2:1)*

Did you notice that David kept asking until he had a specific answer from God? He did not want general directions. He wanted God's exact will for his life. David wasn't interested in simply getting to the throne. He wanted to get to the throne God's way.

Can you identify times when you acted because of a hunch rather than the confirmed will of God? I certainly have! At times I have asked God's direction, then assumed my first hunch was His will for my life. I'm learning to be more patient and to allow God to be more specific if He wishes. No matter how long we may wait for direction, we are wise to ask before we advance. We do well to imitate Moses who said, "If your Presence does not go with us, do not send us up from here" (Exod. 33:15).

God is not going to speak to us from the clouds, nor can we toss the Urim and Thummim, but we have something they did not have: His written and completed Word. God will speak specifically to us through Scripture if we learn how to listen. God has taught me a method that never fails. It may take time but it always works. The method I use consists of four general steps:

1. I acknowledge my specific need for direction. Example: "Lord, I have been asked to serve on the pastor's council. I need to know whether this is Your will for my life at this time." I almost always write my question in a journal so that I can keep a record of God's activity in the matter.

2. I continue to pray daily and study His Word.

3. I ask Him to help me recognize His answer. He usually helps me recognize His answer by bringing His Word and the Holy Spirit He has placed within me into agreement over the matter. In other words, I resist reading into my situation everything God's Word says. I specifically ask Him to confirm with His Word and His Spirit what He desires to apply to my life. One or two weeks later I might be studying a particular passage of Scripture and His Holy Spirit will draw my attention to it and remind me of my question. The Holy Spirit almost seems to say, "Look, Beth, that's it!"

4. I ask for a confirmation if I have any doubt.

What if the Holy Spirit still hasn't given me an answer when the deadline comes? I usually assume the answer is no.

God instructed David to go to Hebron, a region rich in biblical history. It has been occupied almost continually since around 3300 B.C. Hebron is located in the hill country of Judah about nineteen miles to the south of the city of Jerusalem. Some very important people and events are connected with Hebron.

Abraham settled in Hebron and built an altar to God (Gen. 13:18). There God spoke to Abram through three visitors and told him Sarah would bear a child (Gen. 18:1–15). Joshua gave Hebron to Caleb as his inheritance (Josh. 14:13). God chose to write some rich history on the map of Hebron, not the least of it in the life of David. Second Samuel 2:3 says, "David . . . with his family . . . settled in Hebron." Settled. Nice word, isn't it? One that extends the invitation to rest awhile and put down a few roots.

David had been on the move constantly for years. God had probably been his only comfort. After settling in Hebron, "the men of Judah came . . . and there they anointed David king over the house of Judah" (2 Sam. 2:4). What a significant moment in the life of our subject! At last, his private anointing years earlier became public! He was anointed king over "the house of Judah," his first step to reigning as king over the entire nation of Israel.

From the moment David became king over the house of Judah, he began his official works of diplomacy. He sent word to the men of Jabesh Gilead expressing his appreciation for their "kindness to Saul" (2 Sam. 2:5) and pledged his favor to them. But not all could be accomplished by words of diplomacy and pledges of protection. The entire nation of Israel would ultimately have to be under his authority. Much like Joshua, the land was to be David's, but he had to take some of it by force.

Chapter 26

THINGS THAT BRING CHANGE

2 Samuel 3

Abner said to David, "Let me go at once and assemble all Israel for my lord the king, so that they may make a compact with you, and that you may rule over all that your heart desires." (2 Sam. 3:21)

The "house of Judah" anointed David as their king, but the other tribes continued to recognize the family line of Saul as king. Abner, Saul's general, installed Saul's son Ish-Bosheth as king. You may have been surprised to see him identified as one of Saul's sons. He is not listed as one of Saul's sons in the beginning of Saul's reign in 1 Samuel 14:49, but he (also known as Esh-Baal) appears in a final list of sons in 1 Chronicles 8:33, indicating that he was born after Saul became king. We are told that he reigned for only two years. We will learn how his authority came to a sudden end.

Although this kingdom was given to David by God, David would have to take it from the old aristocracy. We will consider the overthrow that enabled David to reign over all Israel.

The pacifist in me would like to skip the bloody details of the civil war in Israel; the Bible teacher in me knows we shouldn't. Old regimes rarely crumble without bloodshed. Rich history was written on the pages of 2 Samuel depicting the end of an old regime and the beginning of the new. Just like America's history, Israel's history was often written in blood.

The first of many battles in the civil war occurred at Gibeon. The results of the battle were to affect David for years to come. Abner commanded the army of Israel. Joab, along with his brothers Abishai and Asahel, commanded the men of Judah. Joab's troops routed those of Abner. Asahel, Joab's baby brother, was fleet of foot. He chased the battle-hardened Abner. Abner tried to talk Asahel out of the pursuit, but without success. Finally, Abner struck Asahel with the butt of his spear, merely trying to stop the youth, but the blow killed Asahel and launched a bitter blood-feud.

The civil war in Israel lasted a long time. "David grew stronger and stronger, while the house of Saul grew weaker and weaker" (2 Sam. 3:1).

We see a fact sadly reflective of human life. Through their behavior, parents teach children to repeat the family sins. Jealousy proved the undoing of Saul. Now his son became jealous and suspicious of someone who had been on his side. Ish-Bosheth accused his general, Abner, of sleeping with one of Saul's concubines. The Bible offers no evidence to support Ish-Bosheth's accusation of Abner, but we do know the end result. The soldier completely transferred his loyalties to David. Abner sent a message to David saying, "Make an agreement with me, and I will help you bring all Israel over to you" (2 Sam. 3:12).

David greeted the offer with a demand, for the return of his first wife Michal. The demand resulted in a heart-wrenching side story. Michal had been married for many years to Paltiel. When the soldiers took her away, Paltiel followed behind her weeping until Abner finally forced him to turn back (2 Sam. 3:15–16).

God does not tell us David's motive for wanting Michal to return to him. He certainly did not lack for female companionship. Maybe he was indignant because he won her fair and square. Maybe he wanted everything back that was rightfully his. Maybe he used her to demonstrate his political and military power. Maybe he loved her. Clearly Paltiel loved her. Whatever David's motives might have been, these events mark a crucial change in Israel—and in David's career.

Since Ish-Bosheth gave the order to return Michal to David, he must have been a party to the agreement. I wonder how different the future might have been for the remaining son of Saul if bitterness had not intervened, but remember Joab and his little brother Asahel?

Abner conferred with the leaders of Israel and arranged for a peaceful transfer of power to King David. Abner even met with the leaders of Benjamin, Saul's tribe. Then he traveled to Hebron to meet with David. Shortly after Abner left David's presence, Joab returned from a raid. When he learned Abner had been there, he secretly sent for Abner and murdered the commander of the armies of Saul.

Though we may not feel a deep bond with Abner as with the noble Jonathan, his murder still saddens me. In all that we read about him, Abner acted with honor. He deserved better. Joab, on the other hand, was a vengeful and murderous man. We would wonder why David put up with Joab's evil but for two facts. First, we learn in 1 Chronicles 2:13–17 that Joab was David's nephew. Second, David doubtless felt that he owed Joab loyalty because they had weathered the fugitive years together. Sometimes justice is more important than loyalty or lineage. In my opinion, David should have opted for justice.

David ordered and led in public mourning for Abner. His grief demonstrated that he had not participated in the murder, so the leaders of Israel proceeded to accept him as king. But the repercussions of the murder continued.

Since Abner was dead, two of Ish-Bosheth's junior officers took it upon themselves to kill Saul's heir. They would have done well to consider what David did to a certain Amalekite. They brought the severed head of Ish-Bosheth to David.

This time we don't have to wonder about the time frame of David's reply. He responded that since he killed the Amalekite, "should I not now demand his blood from your hand and rid the earth of you!" (2 Sam. 4:11).

So at last the stage was set. The anointing from the now long-dead Samuel was about to reach fruition. David was about to become the king of all Israel.

I hope you have been reading the Scriptures along with this story of David. If so, I'm sure you noticed David's additional wives as you read chapter 3. According to Deuteronomy 17:17, David's heart was certain to be led astray. Remember, polygamy was an extremely common practice among eastern kings. However common, the nation of Israel had been told not to "imitate the detestable ways of the nations" (Deut. 18:9). David's actions were acceptable to men during this ancient era, but they were not acceptable to God. The consequences of David's actions would eventually begin to catch up with him. Until then, we have many others to consider.

PART VI

A Man after God's Own Heart

Psalm 18

[David] sang to the LORD the words of this song when the LORD delivered him from the hand of all his enemies and from the hand of Saul. He said:

1 I love you, O LORD, my strength.

2 The LORD is my rock, my fortress and my deliverer;
    my God is my rock, in whom I take refuge.
    He is my shield and the horn of my salvation, my stronghold.

3 I call to the LORD, who is worthy of praise,
    and I am saved from my enemies.

4 The cords of death entangled me;
    the torrents of destruction overwhelmed me.

5 The cords of the grave coiled around me;
    the snares of death confronted me.

6 In my distress I called to the LORD;
    I cried to my God for help.
    From his temple he heard my voice;
    my cry came before him, into his ears.

. . . .

19 He brought me out into a spacious place;
    he rescued me because he delighted in me.

Chapter 27

THE SHEPHERD KING

2 Samuel 5

The Lord said to you, "You will shepherd my people Israel,
and you will become their ruler." (2 Sam. 5:2)

What an exciting day! We are about to see David experience the fulfill-ment of God's promise! As we witness a tremendous pivot in his life, we can assume his introspective mind was swirling with many things, filling him with all sorts of emotions.

In 2 Samuel 5, all the tribes of Israel came to David and acclaimed him as king. The chapter gives some key numbers for the life of David: He was thirty years old when he became king. He ruled for forty years. He reigned seven and one-half years over Judah from Hebron. He ruled all Israel from Jerusalem for thirty-three years. He waited a long time for the fulfillment of 1 Samuel 16.

God didn't choose the person Samuel expected. He chose a shepherd boy. Consider a few reasons why. Look again to 2 Samuel 5:2 when the Lord said, "You will shepherd my people Israel, and you will become their ruler." God called David not in spite of the fact that he was a com-mon shepherd but because he was a shepherd!

Now that David was recognized as king, his days of struggle should be over, right? No! His next obstacle was the most fortified city in the land.

Since the Israelites first arrived in the promised land, Jebus, the city of the Jebusites, had been one key reason the country was divided into Judah in the south and Israel in the north. The city overlooked the main inland route from north to south. With the Philistines in possession of the coastal plain, the inland route provided the only alternative for trade between the tribes.

Up to the time of David, the Israelites had been unable to dislodge the Jebusites from their city. You probably know the city better by another name: "David captured the fortress of Zion, the City of David" (2 Sam. 5:7).

For the first time the tribes of Israel would be truly united into a nation, a mighty nation as long as it remained faithful to God. "Hiram king of Tyre sent messengers to David, along with cedar logs and carpenters and stonemasons, and they built a palace for David" (2 Sam. 5:11).

I love 2 Samuel 5:12: "David knew that the LORD had established him as king over Israel and had exalted his kingdom for the sake of his people Israel." David knew! Many things must have confused David in his previous fifteen years. So many things he did not know:

- Why had God chosen him?
- Why did Saul turn on him?
- Why did Jonathan have to die?
- When would God's promise of the kingdom ever be fulfilled?

David did not know how he would ever live to be king. But when God handed over the most fortified city in all Israel to David and placed favor in the heart of the king of Tyre toward him, David knew the Lord had established him!

You may be going through a confusing time. You may not know how God is going to use a situation in your life or why certain things have happened to you. But you can be encouraged and strengthened by recalling what you know about God in the midst of uncertainties.

In confusing times, recounting what we do know refreshes us. David still had many unanswered questions. He would never know for sure why God allowed certain things to happen, but he knew God had done exactly what He promised. You may never know why or how, but you can always know who is faithful.

We learn two additional facts in 2 Samuel 5. First, we read that "after he left Hebron, David took more concubines and wives in Jerusalem, and more sons and daughters were born to him" (v. 13). Second, the Philistines did not take the news of a united Israel lightly. When they learned David had become king, they came in search of him (v. 17).

Strangely, David had come so far, yet he was back where he started. The hand that wrapped around his weapon as he waited for God's signal to overcome the Philistines looked far different from the hand that had searched for a smooth stone many years before. The first time he ever used his hands in battle was against the Philistines. Now he stood against them once more. To a man on the run, the Philistines had been a temporary refuge. They had taken advantage of his homeless estate by enjoying his strength. To a king on his rightful throne, they were clearly an enemy once more. Perhaps God inspired David to write the words of Psalm 144:1-2 on this very day.

> *Praise be to the LORD my Rock,*
>> *who trains my hands for war,*
>> *my fingers for battle.*
> *He is my loving God and my fortress,*
>> *my stronghold and my deliverer,*
> *my shield, in whom I take refuge,*
>> *who subdues peoples under me.* (Ps. 144:1-2)

God trained David for war, and only God could give him success. Note the names David called God: "my Rock, my loving God, my fortress, my stronghold, my deliverer, my shield, my refuge, the one who trains my hands and who subdues peoples under me." For all of David's needs, his God had a name. We, too, can know God by a name for every need.

David knew without a doubt that God had given him the victory and subdued the people under his leadership. He still didn't know why. He simply knew Who. When David captured the fortress of Zion, the City of David, he must have thought, *You have been to me what these walls have been to this city. No other excuse exists for my safety or my success. You are my fortress.* The names David called his God fell from the lips of experience, from things he knew. Sometimes we stand to learn the most about God from the situations we understand the least.

We began our study with a shepherd-boy. Now we see a shepherd-king. He was still guarding the sheep with "integrity of heart" and "skillful hands" (Ps. 78:72)—hands prepared for war yet still for the same purpose: the protection of sheep. Same shepherd, different sheep. God's sheep.

"You will shepherd my people Israel, and you will become their ruler" (2 Sam. 5:2).

MOURNING TO DANCING

2 Samuel 6

David, wearing a linen ephod, danced before the Lord with all his might,
while he and the entire house of Israel brought up the ark of the Lord with
shouts and the sound of trumpets. (2 Sam. 6:14–15)

Now that David had conquered Jerusalem and defeated the Philistines, what was he to do? In 2 Samuel 6, David set out with thirty thousand men to an even more important work: they were going to bring the ark of God to Jerusalem. Unfortunately, we learn something in verse 3 that can only spell disaster: "They set the ark of God on a new cart" (2 Sam. 6:3).

According to the regulations for kings of Israel, they were to personally hand copy the Law of God, so that they would know every line. How then could David have set out to transport the ark in a wagon? God was extremely specific about every detail of the construction and treatment of the ark. According to Exodus 25:10–16 and Numbers 4:5, 15, the ark was to be transported only by the priests using poles through the rings on the ark. The poles were to be carried on their shoulders.

God masterfully designed the transportation of His glory to literally rest on the shoulders of His revering priests, not on the backs of beasts.

David's actions not only disregarded the Lord's instructions, they included a greater insult. Do you remember when the Philistines captured the ark? After they had suffered seven months of devastation, the Philistines loaded the ark on a cart pulled by two cows. Now David imitated the actions of the Philistines rather than obey the commands of God.

Sure enough, while "David and the whole house of Israel were celebrating with all their might before the LORD" (v. 5), at the threshing floor of Nacon, Uzzah reached out to stabilize the ark, and God struck him dead (vv. 6–7).

Imagine becoming emotionally geared for a great celebration only to greet disaster instead. Uzzah's death would have been shocking under the most somber of circumstances, but can you imagine the shock in the midst of such celebration? David must have felt as if he jumped off an emotional cliff.

Surely all of us have experienced an unexpected, uninvited emotional dive. I have a friend who was left standing at the altar on her wedding day. I have another friend who was told he was being considered for a promotion, but when his boss called him into his office, he was laid off instead. Still others have joyfully expected a baby and miscarried. Devastation is always heartbreaking. Devastation that should have been celebration is almost more than we can take.

David felt two emotions: anger and fear. Note that he felt anger and fear toward God, yet Scripture calls him "a man after God's own heart." I think one reason David remained a man after God's own heart was his unwillingness to turn from God, even when he felt negative emotions. David allowed his anger and fear to motivate him to seek more insight into the heart of God.

We need to follow David's example by allowing our questions and confusion to motivate us to seek God. At first consideration, the account of Uzzah and the ark is hard to swallow. God almost seems mean-spirited.

In times like these, we find out whether we have based our faith on who God is or on what He does. Because His ways are higher than our ways, we cannot always comprehend what God is doing or why He makes certain decisions. When we sift His apparent activity through the standard of who He is, the fog begins to clear.

God is not telling us He is harsh in 2 Samuel 6. He's telling us He is holy. The words represent a big difference, although sometimes our limited understanding leads us to confuse them.

We have difficulty understanding how sacred the ark of the covenant was because we have the advantage of living after the incarnation of Christ. Think with me about the meaning of the ark. We can compare it only to Christ Himself, the Word made flesh to dwell among us! Once man and woman were cast from the garden of Eden, God began His ministry of reconciliation, ultimately fulfilled on the Cross. Hundreds of years followed man's expulsion with no direct invitation for mankind to come and fellowship with God. At last Exodus 25:8 gives the revolutionary words God said to Moses: "Then have them make a sanctuary for me, and I will dwell among them."

What music to starving ears! In the innermost place in this "sanctuary," God commanded them to build the ark of the covenant according to very specific directions. Then He said, "There, above the cover between the two cherubim that are over the ark of the Testimony, I will meet with you" (Exod. 25:22). The awesomeness, the holiness, the majesty of God dwelled right there, between the cherubim on that sacred ark! Until God was incarnate among men many centuries later in the person of Jesus Christ, the ark was the sacred center of God's glory and presence. To treat the ark inappropriately was to treat God inappropriately, not just because of what it was, but because of who God is. Based on who God is, I believe we can draw some conclusions about what He was doing when He killed Uzzah.

God was setting ground rules for a new regime. He was ushering in a new kingdom with a new king He had chosen to represent His heart. God had dealt with the disrespect of man through many judges as well as the reign of a selfish king. With a new day dawning, God was demanding a new reverence.

God wanted His children to be different from the world. The Philistines might transport the ark on an oxcart, but God's people would not. How careful we must be not to think that God is less holy because others seem to get away with irreverence! We are sometimes tempted to measure our respect for God by the lack of respect surrounding us. The godless, however, are not our standard. God is. Through the pen of King David, God told us to "praise him according to his excellent greatness," not according to public opinion (Ps. 150:2, KJV).

God wanted His kingdom to be established on His Word. The Israelites failed to consult God's designated commands for the ark's transportation. At the time David's kingdom was established, David certainly had access to the "Books of Moses," the first five books of the Bible.

God was teaching the relationship between blessing and reverence. After the death of Uzzah, David left the ark at the home of Obed-Edom. God greatly blessed that household. In the process, God demonstrated the relationship between reverence and blessing. God desires His presence and His glory to be a blessing, but reverence for Him is the necessary channel.

Hard lessons learned well undoubtedly usher in a fresh respect and new freedom. As strange as this statement may seem, the more we learn about and fear God, the more freedom we have to worship Him! We'll see this principle at work in David's life as we continue the next portion of 2 Samuel 6.

David reacted to the death of Uzzah with anger and fear. His attitude changed once he discovered that God had blessed the household of

Obed-Edom. He again went down to get the ark, but this time his methods showed a change of attitude. This time the priests carried the ark. With every six steps they offered sacrifices, and David "danced before the LORD with all his might" (2 Sam. 6:14).

The success of the second attempt to transport the ark demonstrates the following points:

1. *All worship is based on sacrifice.* Just as our bold approach to the throne of grace could only have followed Christ's shed blood on Calvary, David's bold approach that day in Jerusalem could only have acceptably followed the shed blood of sacrifice. David was not free to worship acceptably until sacrifice had paved the way.

2. *Worship with abandon is an intimate experience.* We see David almost oblivious to everyone around him, totally liberated in the spirit, dancing through the streets of Jerusalem "with all his might" (v. 14)! Oh, I love this scene! Centuries later, a group of disciples were stunned when Mary of Bethany poured the fragrance of abandoned worship on Christ's feet (John 12:1–8). Completely abandoned worship is often misunderstood.

Sadly we see the legacy of Saul bear more bitter fruit in this chapter of rejoicing. Remember that jealousy destroyed Saul and his son Ish-Bosheth? Now his daughter, David's wife Michal, looked out the window and saw David dancing through the streets of Jerusalem. We can imagine that she could have been filled with either of at least two emotions: she could have been filled with pride, honored by her husband and God; instead she burned with jealousy. "When she saw King David leaping and dancing before the LORD, she despised him in her heart" (2 Sam. 6:16).

David went home to "bless his household," but he was met with ridicule and condemnation (v. 20). He did not allow Michal to quench his spirit. He responded to her with the words, "It was before the LORD" (v. 21). You can almost hear him say, "How dare you! My worship was not for you; it was for the Lord!" Her scolding must have stung his heart. You can sense his reaction from the text, yet he resolved, "I will celebrate before the LORD." He seemed to be saying, "Whether or not my family does, whether or not my friends do, whether or not this nation does, I will celebrate!"

What a slice of life we see in this episode. We've gone from anger to rejoicing, devastation to celebration. We would miss a certain blessing if we did not conclude with David's words in Psalm 30:11–12:

> *You turned my wailing into dancing;*
>> *you removed my sackcloth and clothed me with joy,*
> *that my heart may sing to you and not be silent.*
>> *O LORD my God, I will give you thanks forever.*
> (Ps. 30:11–12)

I'm not sure we will ever be fully released to "dance" before the Lord until we've learned to wail. You'll never know the experience of being clothed with joy until you've allowed Him to remove your sackcloth. Like David, you may be angry at God for taking someone's life you cared for deeply. Perhaps you are still hurt and confused. We have no idea whether David ever fully understood Uzzah's death. We just know he was willing to wait, to study, to hear God's Word, and to approach Him again. Then came indescribable celebration. He may not have understood more about Uzzah's death, but he understood more about God, which made his loss more tolerable. God is not harsh; He is holy. He is not selfish; He is sovereign. He is not unfeeling; He is all-knowing. Like David, we need to come to know Him, and respect Him; and, like David, we will love Him more.

Chapter 29

HUMBLE BEGINNINGS

2 Samuel 7:1–16

Wherever I have moved with all the Israelites, did I ever say to any of their rulers whom I commanded to shepherd my people Israel, "Why have you not built me a house of cedar?" (2 Sam. 7:7)

Now that David sat on the promised throne, let's consider some of the virtues of God's chosen king. With the confetti swept from the streets, the merchants back to work, and the children back in class, after what seemed like an endless struggle, "the king was settled in his palace and the LORD had given him rest from all his enemies around him" (2 Sam. 7:1). In the resulting peace, we get another glimpse of David's character.

Have you ever noticed how the body rests more readily than the mind? We may seize the opportunity to put our feet up for awhile, but the mind stays in overdrive. I think David had a little difficulty getting his mind to rest. Certain thoughts occurred to David "after . . . the LORD had given him rest."

We've all experienced a sudden bout of sober realization, times when we are horror-struck by our own audacity. This was one of those times in the life of David. Life was calm. Enemies were subdued. Perhaps he was taking a load off, perched on his throne, when suddenly his eyes were unveiled to the splendor around him. The one who found refuge in a cave was now throned in a magnificent palace. He must have looked around and thought, *What's wrong with this picture?* He responded with shock: "Here I am, living in a palace of cedar, while the ark of God remains in a tent" (2 Sam. 7:2).

Perhaps several virtues could be noted in David's sudden reaction to his surroundings, but let's not miss the virtue of humility so present in his life at this point. He summoned the prophet Nathan as if lightning would strike if he didn't.

Nathan initially told David to go ahead with his plan to build a house for the Lord, but that night God spoke to Nathan. His words were recorded in 2 Samuel 7:5–16. In that passage God issued several wonderful and significant promises. Some were to David personally. Others were to the nation of Israel as a whole, and several were to David's "offspring."

> *The LORD declares to you that the LORD himself will establish a house for you: When your days are over and you rest with your fathers, I will raise up your offspring to succeed you, who will come from your own body, and I will establish his kingdom. He is the one who will build a house for my Name, and I will establish the throne of his kingdom forever. I will be his father, and he will be my son. . . . Your house and your kingdom will endure forever before me; your throne will be established forever.* (2 Sam. 7:11–14, 16)

These promises capture a wonderful moment between God and His chosen king. We get a fresh glimpse of their highly reciprocal relationship and behold the elements of their everlasting covenant!

The prophet Nathan emerged as a new figure in Israel's history. God sovereignly raised prophets to serve as His voice to Israel. God apparently never intended for civil leaders to have absolute and unquestioned authority. They were to listen to the voice of God through His Word and through His prophets. All persons have someone to whom they must ultimately answer—parents and children alike; employees and employers alike; kings and kingdoms alike.

Samuel was God's prophet through whom He spoke to King Saul. Elijah and Elisha were God's prophets through many years during the Jewish monarchy. Prophets are called to issue the Word and will of God, not necessarily the message leaders want to hear. Nathan served as the prophet in the royal court of David.

King David sought the counsel of Nathan and in doing so revealed another important virtue: accountability. David did not consider himself to be above reproach or the need for advice. The statement David made to Nathan assumed the question, "What am I to do about the ark?" His sudden sense of audacity drew him to accountability.

Sometimes even a fellow believer can offer wrong advice. We are wise to make sure a fellow believer's advice agrees with God's Word.

Nathan's initial response to David was mistaken. "Whatever you have in mind, go ahead and do it, for the Lord is with you" (v. 3). God taught both the king and his prophet a gentle lesson on making assumptions. Perhaps we would be wise to heed as well. God was teaching an important lesson through each man.

To David, God said, "Don't assume that every bright and noble idea in a godly man's mind is of Me." Good ideas and God's ideas are often completely different.

To Nathan, God said, "Don't assume that a leader I have chosen is always right." The Lord can be "with" a man while a man can make a decision "without" God.

We will discover a primary reason why God wanted to dissuade Nathan from thinking David's actions were always right. God was preparing Nathan in advance for a time when he would have to confront and rebuke David. Thankfully, at this point, the hearts of both men were right toward God. Their motive was right even if their move was wrong.

God's message to His new king was so rich. He began with a gentle rebuke, "Are you the one to build me a house to dwell in?" (v. 5). In other words, "David, did I tell you to do that?" God reminded David that He is fully capable of appointing a servant for specific tasks. If we are seeking Him through prayer and Bible study, we will not likely miss His appointments. We need to wait on Him even when we have a great plan.

Waiting on the Lord brings at least two wonderful results, spelled out in Isaiah 40:31: "They that wait upon the LORD shall renew their strength; they shall mount up with wings as eagles; they shall run, and not be weary; and they shall walk, and not faint" (KJV).

When we wait on God, He gives supernatural strength and accomplishes the inconceivable! Did you notice that God gave David the initial vision for the project (the temple), but his offspring was to build it? God can entrust a vision or an idea to us that may be ours to pray about and prepare for but never to participate in directly.

As I read God's gentle rebuke to Nathan and David, I saw another wonderful principle at work. God said, "I have not dwelt in a house from the day I brought the Israelites up out of Egypt to this day. I have been moving from place to place with a tent as my dwelling" (2 Sam. 7:6). God seemed to be saying, "As long as my people are on the move, I'm on the move! You can't tie me down as long as my people are mobile!"

Isn't He wonderful? The "tent" to which God was referring was the Old Testament tabernacle designed by God to move with the people! That's God's way. You can't leave home without Him. The New Testament says it this way: "The Word became flesh and made his dwelling among us" (John 1:14).

The Greek word for *dwelling* was *skenoo*. It means "to encamp, pitch a tent . . . to tabernacle."[12] Once more, God was pitching a tent so He could be where His people were, so that one day they could be where He was. Praise His name!

The climactic point in God's message to David came in verse 11. Allow me to paraphrase: "David, you won't build a house for Me. I'm going to build a house for you!" What overwhelming words! We want to do so many things for God, then they suddenly pale in comparison to the realization of all He wants to do for us! Romans 8:32 says, "He who did not spare his own Son, but gave him up for us all—how will he not also, along with him, graciously give us all things?"

David discovered what we will often discover: You can't outgive God. God drew His message to a close by issuing what is often called the Davidic Covenant. He issued His promise in the form of a declaration (vv. 11–16). Notice that the blessings and cursings of God on David's son might be conditional (v. 14), but God's kingdom covenant was completely unconditional. The covenant rested on God's faithfulness, not man's.

Interestingly, many years later David reflected on an additional reason why God did not choose for him to build the temple. In 1 Chronicles 28:3, David said: "God said to me, 'You are not to build a house for my Name, because you are a warrior and have shed blood.'" God chose to have His temple built during a reign characterized by peace. I am touched by the mercy of God toward his beloved David. He did not snatch the privilege from him in judgment. Rather, He allowed David's son to receive the honor.

What could be better than being appointed to do a marvelous task for God? For me, it would be for my child to do a marvelous task for God!! I would happily forfeit participation in the great things of God for my children to inherit the opportunity!

Chapter 30

COMPULSORY PRAISE

2 Samuel 7:17–29

*How great you are, O Sovereign Lord! There is no one like you, and there is
no God but you, as we have heard with our own ears. (2 Sam. 7:22)*

Have you experienced a time when you were so overwhelmed with both
the person of God and His actions in your life that you simply had to
praise Him? Imagine for a moment the emotions coursing through
David. After all the years of struggle, he found himself seated on the
throne in Jerusalem with rest from his enemies all around. Then Nathan
the prophet delivered the message that God would bless not only David
but also his children. He must have been overwhelmed. No wonder he
"went in and sat before the LORD" (2 Sam. 7:18) and poured out his
heart. In a wonderful and expressive portion of Scripture, 2 Samuel
7:18–29 records David's response to the promises of God.

> *Then King David went in and sat before the LORD, and he said:
> "Who am I, O Sovereign LORD, and what is my family, that you
> have brought me this far? And as if this were not enough in your
> sight, O Sovereign LORD, you have also spoken about the future
> of the house of your servant. Is this your usual way of dealing
> with man, O Sovereign LORD?"* (2 Sam. 7:18–19)

We have looked at the personality of David from many different angles, with many more to go. Few Scriptures allow us to dive into the depth of his passionate soul more deeply than this prayer. While others were prone to wander, he was prone to worship.

> *What more can David say to you? For you know your servant,*
> *O Sovereign LORD. For the sake of your word and according to*
> *your will, you have done this great thing and made it known to*
> *your servant.*
>
> *How great you are, O Sovereign LORD! There is no one like you,*
> *and there is no God but you, as we have heard with our own ears.*
> (2 Sam. 7:20–22)

Have you ever responded like David? Have you experienced a time when someone told you something you knew was an answer from God, and you wanted to run as fast as you could and sit before Him? Moments like those represent an indescribable intimacy in your relationship with God. When those moments occur, you can't even explain how you feel. You can only go and sit before Him.

When I am overwhelmed by something God has done for me or said to me, I often find that I have to sit a moment and wait for my heart to write words on my lips. Sometimes I weep for awhile before I can begin to speak. David might have done the same thing. So intimate were the words God spoke to him through Nathan that he left the messenger's presence and went straight to the One who sent the message.

"Who am I, O Sovereign LORD, and what is my family, that you have brought me this far?" I have asked the same question more times than I can count, but not for the reasons you might assume. Yes, for reasons I will never understand, God has given me opportunities for ministry in this season of my life, and I praise Him for that. Yet the moments that most often move me are extremely intimate and private. Because they are so personal, I will probably never share in a testimony some of the most wonderful things God has done for me. What David was feeling was not about grand positions; it was about personal petitions. We each have countless opportunities to be overwhelmed at the goodness of God on our behalf.

After saying, "Who am I . . . that you have brought me this far?" David said, "And as if this were not enough in your sight, O Sovereign LORD, you have also . . ." (v. 19). How like God to keep giving and giving! David was stunned by God's words of prophecy over his family. What more precious promise could God have given David than to assure him He would remain with his offspring long after David was gone? What peace we can have in knowing God will bless our children! As if David was suddenly overcome, he broke out in compulsory praises! "How great you are, O Sovereign LORD!" (v. 22).

Every now and then we enjoy a moment void of doubt and full of mystery, when we're overwhelmed with humility yet stunned with possibility. Moments when we realize with every one of our senses that God stands alone. "No one—no mate, no child, no preacher, no teacher, no ruler, no principality—no one is like You." Nothing is quite like suddenly realizing that nothing is like Him.

Chapter 31

A VIRTUOUS MAN

2 Samuel 8

*David reigned over all Israel, doing what was just and right
for all his people. (2 Sam. 8:15)*

This chapter undoubtedly represents the zenith of David's career. God
had given him success. David had it all: fame, fortune, power, and position. For just a little while, David handled the unabashed blessings of
God with brilliant integrity. Up until now we've seen David's virtues presented as subtle themes in the shadow of God's own. In 2 Samuel 8, God
directly pinpointed David's character, allowing him to take a moment in
the spotlight. We can glean the following virtues from this chapter:

1. *David showed a spirit of cooperation.* In 2 Samuel 7:10–11, God
promised David that He would give the nation of Israel rest from her
enemies. Second Samuel 8:1 tells us that "in the course of time, David
defeated the Philistines and subdued them." David did not sit on the
throne and simply wait for God to fulfill His promise. He obeyed God's
beckoning to the battlefield to participate in the victory!

When God assures us of a promise, He desires for us to respond by
cooperating in the fulfillment of that promise. Sometimes that means
battle; at other times God directs us to sit still and wait. Wisdom involves
learning to know the difference. Whether God tells us to sit, stand, or
move, He calls us to respond with a spirit of cooperation.

2. *David kept a spirit of hope even through a violent event.* When David defeated his enemies, he did not annihilate them and simply leave the nations destroyed. When he defeated the Moabites, he allowed one-third of them to live (2 Sam. 8:2).

King David lived in a harsh and cruel time. That he would kill two-thirds of the people naturally offends our modern sensibilities—until we compare his actions with the standard of his day. "Normal" behavior would have called for complete destruction of the Moabites. What we remarkably do see is that David had a concern for the spiritual welfare of non-Jews. Both Psalms 9 and 22 spoke of God's message reaching the nations:

> *Sing praises to the LORD, enthroned in Zion;*
> *proclaim among the nations what he has done.* (Ps. 9:11)

> *All the ends of the earth*
> *will remember and turn to the LORD.* (Ps. 22:27)

David's concern was a giant step forward for a man of his day. He left a remnant and exhibited hope for the nations to bend their knees to the King of all kings. I believe David's God-given motive was to bring the other nations to a place of obedience to God rather than to obliterate them.

3. *David had a literal dedication to God.* At this point David had never confused the source of his strength. Any return from his feats he immediately dedicated to the Lord. Second Samuel 8:11 tells us that King David dedicated all the articles of silver and gold from all the nations he conquered. If he was praised for his successes, he quickly gave the praise to God. If he was exalted for his successes, he lifted the name of God even higher. When he was surrounded by splendor, he wanted God to have something more splendid. When he returned with gold, silver, and bronze, he dedicated them immediately to the Lord.

4. *David displayed a concern for justice and righteousness.* The definitive verse of 2 Samuel 8 says, "David reigned over all Israel, doing what was just and right for all his people" (v. 15). The verse describes the moment when David most clearly and completely fulfilled his calling! When God called David a man after His own heart, He meant it literally. For a season, the kingdom of David reflected the kingdom of the supreme King of all kings. These were the glory days of David's kingdom. God had given him the keys to the kingdom: justice and righteousness—keys to a kingdom that will never end.

5. *David employed a wisdom for administration.* He knew that growth meant a greater need for administration. As the eighth chapter concludes, we see one of the first orders of business: the delegation of authority and responsibility. You may not find verses 16–18 exciting, but they record an essential step in David's kingdom.

> *Joab son of Zeruiah was over the army; Jehoshaphat son of Ahilud was recorder; Zadok son of Ahitub and Ahimelech son of Abiathar were priests; Seraiah was secretary; Benaiah son of Jehoiada was over the Kerethites and Pelethites; and David's sons were royal advisers.* (2 Sam. 8:16–18)

David had obviously learned an important lesson in his initial leadership of the distressed, indebted, and discontented (1 Sam. 22:2). A leader needs help! A good administrator knows when and how to delegate.

In this chapter, we see David as a man after God's own heart more than ever before in our study. We've seen Christ's own heart illustrated over and over. No one was more humble. No one held himself more accountable to God. No one revealed a greater heart for worship. No one had such a depth of cooperation with God. In all these ways David provides a picture of Jesus. Christ dedicated His every treasure to God, His Father, and will return for us when the Father nods. He will rule in justice and righteousness. As Chief Administrator, He will delegate the responsibilities of the kingdom to the faithful on earth. The characteristics God saw and loved so much in David are those most like His Son. God has one specific bent toward partiality: He loves anything that reminds Him of His only begotten Son. To be more like Christ is to be a man or woman after God's own heart.

Chapter 32

ROOM IN THE PALACE

2 Samuel 9

David asked, "Is there anyone still left of the house of Saul to whom I can show kindness for Jonathan's sake?" (2 Sam. 9:1)

Don't you love God's Word? How I praise Him that His Word is not just a book of rules and regulations, do's and don'ts. The Bible is a book of the heart! Realize God's Word reflects God's ways as you read a story like we're about to read. His heart must be so tender.

In 2 Samuel 8 we saw the spotlight on the zenith of David's reign. God gave unparalleled success. David was famous throughout the land, both hailed and feared for being the foremost example of God's power on earth. Now we travel from his public feats to his private feelings.

David knew well the feeling of loneliness. He must have looked around at the kingdom and thought of the man who first planned to share it. He missed Jonathan, and in spite of all Saul did, I believe he still loved Saul.

You hear David's loneliness at the top as he said, "Is there anyone still left of the house of Saul to whom I can show kindness for Jonathan's sake?" David had conquered kingdoms and subdued enemies. He had servants at his beck and call. All was momentarily quiet and peaceful—and he missed his best friend. God had fulfilled Jonathan's wish and given David everything, but Jonathan wasn't there to share it with him. David sought the next best thing. Ziba, a servant of the house of Saul, told him about Jonathan's one remaining son named Mephibosheth.

The Bible first mentions Mephibosheth in 2 Samuel 4. The boy was still a small child when news came of Saul and Jonathan's death. The nurse dropped Mephibosheth, resulting in his being crippled in both feet. Ziba's choice of words is interesting. "There is still a son of Jonathan; he is crippled in both feet" (v. 3). Physical deformity was a great source of shame in the ancient world. Ziba's choice of words and timing intimates he might have suspected the son's handicap to disqualify him from anything the king sought. If so, David surprised the servant.

David immediately commanded that Mephibosheth be brought to the court. When he arrived, David said,

> *"I will surely show you kindness for the sake of your father Jonathan. I will restore to you all the land that belonged to your grandfather Saul, and you will always eat at my table."*
>
> *Mephibosheth bowed down and said, "What is your servant, that you should notice a dead dog like me?"* (2 Sam. 9:7–8)

Picturing the scene brings me to tears. Imagine the king sitting on the throne, surrounded by splendor. His brightly adorned servants open the door, and before him stands a crippled man. The Word says, "When Mephibosheth son of Jonathan, the son of Saul, came to David, he bowed down to pay him honor" (v. 6). With crippled legs he crept before the king, then he bowed before him! Can you imagine the difficulty for a handicapped man to get down on his knees, press his forehead to the floor, as was the custom, then rise up? Mephibosheth was obviously humbled. "What is your servant, that you should notice a dead dog like me?" (v. 8).

How amazed Mephibosheth must have been. Possibly he feared that David had summoned him for punishment. Remember that his uncle Ish-Bosheth had been at war with David. Whatever he hoped or feared, he probably had no idea what he was about to receive.

The story of Mephibosheth reminds me of another story in Luke 15. We call that the parable of the prodigal son, but we would do better to call it the parable of the loving father. Like the father in the parable and like our heavenly Father, David was just seeking someone to bless and love.

> *Then the king summoned Ziba, Saul's servant, and said to him, "I have given your master's grandson everything that belonged to Saul and his family. You and your sons and your servants are to farm the land for him and bring in the crops, so that your master's grandson may be provided for. And Mephibosheth, grandson of your master, will always eat at my table."* (2 Sam. 9:9–10)

I see two wonderful pictures in the story of Mephibosheth. First, I see an image of myself. Like Jonathan's son, apart from Christ I am broken, outcast, and crippled in both feet. I could never even crawl into God's presence, but in Christ I put my feet under His table as His child.

Have you ever felt like a Mephibosheth? Surely everyone who ever accepted Christ as Savior has crept before Him, crippled from the fall of sin, overcome by our unworthiness against the backdrop of His Majesty's brilliance.

The second picture in the story is God Himself. In the encounter of Mephibosheth and the king, we see several characteristics of the Father. Consider the following virtues of God.

1. *David displayed God's loving-kindness.* David searched for someone of the house of Saul to whom he could show God's kindness, not his

own (v. 3)! The Lord is, first of all, kind. Compassionate. He desires to deal with us first in mercy. If we refuse to accept His mercy, He often deals with us in the way He must; but He is above all kind. As a man after God's own heart, David was tender. His heart was full of loving-kindness, and he was eager to pour it out on a willing vessel.

2. *David initiated the relationship.* "Where is he?" David inquired. Then he summoned Mephibosheth immediately. Note that Mephibosheth did not seek David. David sought Mephibosheth! David was the king! What could he possibly have needed? He had everything! But he wanted someone to whom he could show God's kindness. God is always the initiator of the relationship, always looking for someone who will receive His loving-kindness!

3. *David completely accepted Mephibosheth.* He did not hesitate when Ziba informed him of Mephibosheth's handicap. In the Old Testament, people considered physical imperfection to be shameful, but David summoned Mephibosheth exactly as he was. How reflective of the heart of God! Many people wait until they can get their act together before they approach God. If only they could understand that God calls them just the way they are; then He empowers them to get their act together!

4. *David displayed God's calming spirit.* As Mephibosheth practically came crawling before the king, David exclaimed, "Mephibosheth!" He knew him by name . . . just as Christ knows us (John 10:3). David's next words were, "Don't be afraid" (v. 7). How many times have we seen those words come from the precious lips of our Lord: "It is I. Don't be afraid."

- To the twelve as He sent them forth: "Don't be afraid" (Matt. 10:31).
- To a bunch of scaredy-cats in a storm: "Don't be afraid" (Matt. 14:27)

⁑ To Peter, James, and John overcome by His glory: "Don't be afraid!" (Matt. 17:7).

⁑ To the father of a dying child: "Don't be afraid" (Mark 5:36).

How very Christlike David was in this moment.

5. *David delighted in restoration.* "I will restore to you all the land that belonged to your grandfather" (v. 7). David's first desire was to restore Mephibosheth. He had been so hurt by the fall. He had lived with such shame. The king could hardly wait to see Mephibosheth's shame removed and his life restored. David knew about restoration. He penned the words, "He restores my soul" (Ps. 23:3). Perhaps the most grateful response we could ever offer God for our restoration is to help another be restored. I was nearly overcome when I looked up the name *Mephibosheth* and found that it means, "shame destroyer" or "image breaker."[13] What a precious portrait of our Savior! He has been my shame destroyer and my image breaker!

6. *David had a desire for another son.* Mephibosheth came stooped as a servant before the king. The king came before Mephibosheth to make him a son. He was family—invited to sit at the king's table to partake of his fellowship as one of his own! Imagine the sight when he first limped to the table set with sumptuous delights, surrounded by festive activity, and sat down, resting his crippled legs at the king's table. Hallelujah! We are like Mephibosheth! No matter how many sons the Father has, He still wants more to conform into the image of His first and only begotten. "How great is the love the Father has lavished on us, that we should be called children of God! And that is what we are!" (1 John 3:1).

That's us, all right. One day, when we sit down to the ultimate wedding feast, the lame will be healed, the blind will see, the restored will leap and skip with ecstatic joy! We will be surrounded by the ministering servants of heaven! He is a God of loving-kindness. He's just searching for someone with whom to share it. Not just the moment when we first bow before Him and acknowledge that He is king, but every single time we sit at His table. Joint heirs. Sons. Daughters. He is the shame destroyer. The lover of the lame.

I would never have learned to walk with God on healthy feet had I never experienced sitting at His table as a cripple. My emotional and spiritual healing has come from approaching God in my handicapped state and believing I was His child and worthy of His love.

Chapter 33

SHUNNED SYMPATHY

2 Samuel 10

In the course of time, the king of the Ammonites died, and his son
Hanun succeeded him as king. David thought, "I will show kindness
to Hanun son of Nahash, just as his father showed kindness to me."
So David sent a delegation to express his sympathy to Hanun
concerning his father. (2 Sam. 10:1–2)

With chapter 10 of 2 Samuel we mark the end of the golden period of
David's reign. In the next chapter we will see him commit the sin that
will dog the rest of his life, so let's enjoy these final unblemished examples of his character.

When Nahash the king of the Ammonites died, David demonstrated
a remarkable degree of sympathy for the suffering. David knew better
than anyone that a crown did not make a person void of feelings and
oblivious to losses. Even though Saul was not his father and had often
treated him with malice, David had grieved his death. Likewise, Hanun
was assuming the throne of the Ammonites but at the cost of his father's
life.

David believed in showing kindness. We saw an example of David's
kindness with Mephibosheth. He attempted such an act toward the
incumbent king of Ammon, desiring to express heartfelt sympathy.

David was exhibiting the character of God as he extended sympathy to someone who had experienced loss. You can depend on a sympathetic God in your need. David knew the disappointment of reaching out to others for sympathy and not receiving it, but he learned from his experience that God is always compassionate and sympathetic.

David penned each of the following verses. See how he described the sympathetic heart of God.

> *As a father has compassion on his children,*
>> *so the LORD has compassion on those who fear him.*
> (Ps. 103:13)

> *The LORD is gracious and righteous;*
>> *our God is full of compassion.*
> . . . .
> *Precious in the sight of the LORD*
>> *is the death of his saints.* (Ps. 116:5, 15)

> *The LORD is good to all;*
>> *he has compassion on all he has made.* (Ps. 145:9)

God is always sympathetic, but His sympathy is not always accepted. David experienced something similar as Hanun rejected his extension of sympathy. The Ammonite nobles led Hanun to believe that David had sinister motives for sending his men. They attempted to make the new king feel foolish for trusting David's motives. "Do you think David is honoring your father by sending men to you to express sympathy?" (2 Sam. 10:3). A possible paraphrase might be, "Are you some kind of gullible idiot?" They said David was spying out Hanun's kingdom for conquest.

Following his advisers' counsel, Hanun humiliated David's men by cutting off half their garments and beards. He was symbolically making them half the men they were. I see an important similarity between David's rejected sympathies, expressed by the humiliation of his delegates, and God's rejected sympathies, expressed by humanity's rejection of Christ. God's most glorious extension of sympathy to a dying world was Christ, His Son.

God sent Christ as the delegate of His sympathy to the misery of men. Christ was also met by those who stirred up misunderstanding among the people, just like the Ammonite nobles. These people in Christ's day were called Pharisees. Ultimately, His message of sympathy was rejected by the very ones to whom it was first extended, and Christ hung on a cross in complete humiliation. For those who have received Him, Christ remains our sympathizer, ever ready to lead us to a door of escape from temptation or a door of mercy when temptation has turned to participation.

We saw David's character reflect God's sympathy. We now turn to another aspect of God's character: the king's fierce protectiveness toward his own. David sent messengers to meet the men so they would not have to be publicly humiliated. He made provision for them to stay in Jericho until their beards had grown because he knew a shaved beard was considered an insult. In effect, he threw a cloak around their exposed bodies and formed a plan to spare their dignity. I'm not sure we can understand what this kind of humiliation meant to a Hebrew. The thought of being exposed in such a heartless manner would be humiliating to anyone, but to a Hebrew such humiliation was virtually a fate worse than death. They were a very modest people. Their enemy had preyed on one of their worst nightmares. David fiercely protected the dignity of his men. God is even more protective of us.

Finally, in this incident, we see David reflect God's vengeance toward the enemies of his people and the mockers of his mercy. David did not just formulate a plan to spare the dignity of his men. He took on their enemy himself. God also takes on our enemies when we've been shamed.

Observe how the following verses show God's defensiveness toward those who hurt or shame His children:

> *O LORD, you took up my case;*
> > *you redeemed my life.* (Lam. 3:58)

> *If anyone causes one of these little ones who believe in me to sin, it*
> *would be better for him to have a large millstone hung around his*
> *neck and to be drowned in the depths of the sea.* (Matt. 18:6)

Let me assure you, God can take on your enemy with far more power and might than you could ever muster. When someone persecutes you, your Father takes the persecution very personally, especially when you are persecuted for obeying Him, as David's men were. The battle is the Lord's!

God has extended His mercy to every single member of the human race. He sent His Delegate of sympathy for our sin problem to hang on a cross as the Divine Remedy. Those who reject His mercy and mock His motives will be punished sooner or later if they do not repent. Pray today for your enemies! Pray they will accept God's Delegate of mercy toward them!

Do you see that any one of us could be a man or woman after God's own heart? God is looking for qualities that remind Him of His Son, the object of His most supreme affections. These qualities are developed in us at no small cost, just as they were in the life of David; but the pleasure of God is profoundly, indescribably worth it!

Let's recap the virtues we've noted in these chapters of 2 Samuel. David was humble, accountable, and worshipful. He was cooperative, hopeful, dedicated, and just. He was a righteous king and an effective administrator. He was an initiator of relationships: kind, loving, accepting, restoring, and welcoming. He was sympathetic, protective, and defensive against the wrongs done to his people. We've seen David at his best, exhibiting the characteristics of the Holy Spirit within him. His heart was patterned after his God's. For a time, he was the greatest king who ever lived—the apple of God's eye.

PART VII

THE WAGES OF SIN

Psalm 51

When the prophet Nathan came to him after David had committed adultery with Bathsheba.

1 Have mercy on me, O God,
      according to your unfailing love;
    according to your great compassion
      blot out my transgressions.
2 Wash away all my iniquity
      and cleanse me from my sin.
3 For I know my transgressions,
      and my sin is always before me.

. . . .

7 Cleanse me with hyssop, and I will be clean;
      wash me, and I will be whiter than snow.
8 Let me hear joy and gladness;
      let the bones you have crushed rejoice.
9 Hide your face from my sins
      and blot out all my iniquity.
10 Create in me a pure heart, O God,
      and renew a steadfast spirit within me.
11 Do not cast me from your presence
      or take your Holy Spirit from me.
12 Restore to me the joy of your salvation
      and grant me a willing spirit, to sustain me.

Chapter 34

UP ON A ROOFTOP

2 Samuel 11:1–10

One evening David got up from his bed and walked around on the roof of
the palace. From the roof he saw a woman bathing. The woman was very
beautiful, and David sent someone to find out about her. (2 Sam. 11:2–3)

The study of David intrigues me for many reasons. He, of all the characters
in the Old Testament, may best prefigure Christ and the gospel message. In
chapters 7 through 10, we scaled the heights of David's reign and the breadth
of his character, but the qualities of God's character only comprise one side
of the gospel. We are about to encounter the dark side—human sin.

David painfully proved the depths to which one can fall after reaching such heights. The contrast between these consecutive seasons of
David's life is staggering. Against God's warning, David multiplied wives
and grew dangerously accustomed to having all he wanted. We will soon
discover the outcome of his eroding self-control.

Through many chapters of Scripture we've seen the qualities of
David extolled. Now in two short verses we see him tumble headlong
into the pit of sin. Join me as we step out on the roof of an ancient
Hebrew home to catch a fresh breath of spring air.

After Hanun shamed the men David sent to bear his sympathies,
the Ammonite king knew he was in trouble, so he formed an alliance

with the Arameans (Syrians). In chapter 10, Joab only began the job of punishing Hanun. David's general thoroughly defeated the Arameans, but then the season for warfare was past. Joab returned the army to Israel, pending the coming spring when he would resume the campaign against the Ammonites. In that context, hear the first words of chapter 11: "In the spring, at the time when kings go off to war, David sent Joab out with the king's men and the whole Israelite army" (2 Sam. 11:1). The first sign of trouble appears when David began to shirk his duty.

You probably know the story that follows. One night David couldn't sleep. He went for a walk on the roof of the palace. From there he saw a beautiful woman bathing. He sent a messenger to find out about her. The messenger told him two facts, either of which should have stopped him cold. He said her name was Bathsheba the wife of Uriah the Hittite, one of David's soldiers. David disregarded common decency. He sent for her. They committed adultery. She went home. Time passed. She realized that she was pregnant.

Few things frighten me more than this testimony of David's life. We too could be persons of character and integrity, and, without apparent warning, destroy our ministries and ourselves through the choice to gratify our sudden lusts. Like David, a few short verses could record the story of our downfall.

As you consider this story, don't be drawn into their sin by romantic—and false—notions. We cannot afford to justify their behavior through sympathy. In our culture we justify immoral behavior with the excuse that two people were "in love." Even if two people are emotionally entangled, don't call self-gratification and breaking promises to God and others love. David and Bathsheba didn't even have that flimsy excuse. They were not in love. They simply chose to act in a dishonorable and destructive way. We could speculate that he was intoxicated by her beauty mixed with an opportunity to display his power. She may have been enamored with his wealth and prestige.

We cannot lend this scene the sympathies we are tempted to offer "victims" of passion in romance novels. The trashy romance we're reading about today is down in the bottom of the barrel, down there with all the sticky stuff, where the stench is—the place we find ourselves when the line between wanting and getting erodes.

We may wish we could get everything we want—until we look at David and Bathsheba. The gap between wanting and getting is where we must flex the muscle of self-control to protect ourselves. David had risen to a position where his every wish was someone else's command. He had ceased to hear a very important word—one without which integrity cannot be maintained. The word *no*.

David was probably like most of us. He could say no rather easily to some things, but he had great difficulty with others. The difficulty was obviously regulated by how badly he wanted what he shouldn't have. In the midst of all his integrity in the other areas of his life, "David took more concubines and wives in Jerusalem" (2 Sam. 5:13). Obviously he lacked self-control in the area of sexual lust.

In Deuteronomy 17:17, God clearly stated the consequences of multiplying wives: the king "must not take many wives, or his heart will be led astray." Just as God warned, David's heart had gone astray. Suddenly the heart that had been so much like God's had wandered to an abyss of no resemblance. David didn't guard his heart, and it began to lie to him.

David, the man of God, the Lord's anointed, the one who enjoyed God's complete provision, took what did not belong to him and cast himself headlong into scandal. He believed his own cheating heart. We do not have the luxury of considering the events between David and Bathsheba a rarity. Unfortunately, many people of God allow their hearts to wander and fall into adultery. The threatened institution of marriage in our society, inside the church and out, beckons us to confront the actions of King David. His actions can teach us not only how adultery can happen but how it can be avoided or prevented. How can we safeguard ourselves against falling to the same kinds of temptations? Let's consider a few places David went wrong.

1. *He was in the wrong place at the wrong time.* Notice the very first phrases of verse 1: "In the spring, at the time when kings go off to war." David had once been a very effective administrator and delegator; however, he had exceeded the wise bounds of delegation and left himself with little responsibility and idle hands. David handed to Joab a baton he should have kept for himself. David should have been leading his troops just as the other kings were leading theirs. He was obviously restless. Second Samuel 11:2 says, "David got up from his bed." Sadly, David had delegated so much responsibility that he left himself open to boredom and temptation.

2. *He failed to protect himself with a network of accountability.* At one time he had been sensitive to the thought of offending God. He sought the counsel of prophets and allowed himself to be held accountable. We've reached a season in David's life when he was answering to no one, apparently not even God. All of us need to be surrounded by people who are invited to hold us accountable and question the questionable.

We discussed the matter of accountability in our previous unit; we are now seeing some of the repercussions of living without it. No one questioned David's actions, yet they knew he was wrong. We don't need those kinds of associates, do we? I want people in my life who love me enough to offend me if necessary and help me not to fall.

David grew accustomed to wanting and getting. What a dangerous habit! This time, he went too far. He took something belonging to someone else, and no one called his hand on it. But God held him accountable!

3. *He was lonely.* He allowed himself to be placed so high on the throne that he found himself all alone. The words of 2 Samuel 9:1 hint at David's loneliness and lack of peers as he cried, "Is there anyone still left of the house of Saul to whom I can show kindness for Jonathan's sake?" Dave Edwards, a well-known Christian speaker, once said, "All rebellion begins in isolation."

How can we avoid making the same kind of mistake? The following three precautions will keep us from being trapped in sin as a result of loneliness:

1. Be careful to fulfill the responsibilities God has given.
2. Deliberately set up a network of accountability partners.
3. Avoid lengthy periods of isolation, if possible.

We could add a fourth precaution. Be aware of the progressive nature of sin. For the remainder of this lesson, we will allow our attention to focus on this fourth safeguard. I believe we have all experienced the progression of sin. Reread 2 Samuel 11:1–5 and note three progressive areas of sin.

Step 1: He sinned in thought. First of all, David saw the woman bathing and concluded she was very beautiful. Sight turned into desire. The seed of sin was first sown in his mind as he tarried on the rooftop, just as the seed of sin is first sown in our minds.

Step 2: He sinned in word. If we do not confess and repent the sin of the mind, it virtually always gives birth to the next stage. The meditation of David's mind turned into the conversation of his mouth. God knows that our meditations (the focus of our thoughts, what we think and rethink) will ultimately turn into conversations. That's why He tells us to meditate on Him and His Word!

Think how often sin not squelched in the mind makes its way to the mouth. If we begin thinking about adultery and do not allow God to halt the thoughts, we'll start talking about it in one form or another, just as

David did. The talking invariably draws us closer to action. Temptations rarely go from the mind to the deed. The second stop is usually the mouth.

David's method certainly wasn't subtle. He saw Bathsheba and allowed wrong desires (the participation of his mind), then he summoned someone and expressed his interest (the participation of his mouth). These two steps enticed a third.

Step 3: He sinned in deed. David flirted with adultery in thought and word, stopping at neither venue to repent and ask God for help. Action followed. David committed adultery and set in motion a hurricane of repercussions.

For years I've approached my time of confession and repentance by categorizing my sins according to the three areas we've addressed. In my prayer time, I ask God to bring to my mind any sins of thought, word, or deed. Virtually everything will fall into one of those three categories. Through David's example I realized how often the three areas can unite as participants in grievous sin.

If wrong thoughts give way to wrong words, often giving way to wrong actions, we must learn to allow God to halt sin in the place where it begins—the thought life! We are wise to aggressively confess the sins of our thoughts! The sins of our thought lives are so numerous that their familiarity tends to make them less noticeable. Jealous thoughts, sudden lusts, quick criticisms, and harsh judgments may be fueled in our minds without any regard toward them as sin.

A heightened awareness of wrong thoughts will work greatly to our advantage. Getting in the habit of confessing sin in the thought life is not to remind us constantly what wretches we are, but to remind us what victors we are! Confessing wrong thoughts stops sin in the first stages, before it comes out of our mouths and then directs our actions. If I allow God to halt sin before it takes one step out of the mind into word or deed, the only person hurt will be me. Once sin progresses from the mind to the mouth and deeds, we've involved others, and the repercussions and chastisements escalate.

Unchecked thoughts will usually progress. Our minds can't be "fairly pure." Purity comes with a radical attitude toward the thought life. God was looking out for our best interest when He commanded us to love Him with our whole minds!

I encourage you to let the following Scriptures become staples in your prayer time to guide you through purity of thought, word, and deed before God.

Regarding thoughts:

> *Search me, O God, and know my heart;*
>> *test me and know my anxious thoughts.*
> *See if there is any offensive way in me,*
>> *and lead me in the way everlasting.* (Ps. 139:23–24)

Regarding words:

> *May the words of my mouth and the meditation of my heart*
>> *be pleasing in your sight,*
>> *O LORD, my Rock and my Redeemer.* (Ps. 19:14)

Regarding deeds:

> *LORD, who may dwell in your sanctuary?*
>> *Who may live on your holy hill?*
> *He whose walk is blameless*
>> *and who does what is righteous,*
> *who speaks the truth from his heart.* (Ps. 15:1–2)

Copy those words of Scripture. Memorize them. Let them guide your confession daily.

None of us is beyond the sin of adultery. Two kinds of people are in greatest danger: those who think they could never be tempted and those who are presently being tempted. May we cast ourselves on the mercy of God and find help in our time of trouble. Big trouble.

Chapter 35

CONTRASTS IN CHARACTER

2 Samuel 11:11–27

Uriah said to David, "The ark and Israel and Judah are staying in tents, and my master Joab and my lord's men are camped in the open fields. How could I go to my house to eat and drink and lie with my wife? As surely as you live, I will not do such a thing!" (2 Sam. 11:11)

We saw David's sin begin in his thought life and end up in the conception of an innocent child with another man's wife. We may see the greatest evidence of his faraway heart in the way he reacted to the news of Bathsheba's pregnancy.

When David heard the news that Bathsheba was pregnant, he immediately tried to cover up his sin. He sent for her husband, Uriah, so he would have intercourse with her and thus think the baby was his. David's initial conversation with Uriah was at best disingenuous but, more accurately, was despicable.

When Uriah came to him, David asked him how Joab was, how the soldiers were and how the war was going. Then David said to Uriah, "Go down to your house and wash your feet." So Uriah left the palace, and a gift from the king was sent after him. (2 Sam. 11:7–8)

Have you ever felt someone was faking an interest in you for an ulterior motive? Most of us know the sting of such behavior. The Scripture gives no hint that Uriah recognized the dishonesty of his king. To the contrary, Uriah's honor spoiled David's plan. Uriah refused to go home to his wife when his comrades were in the field. If only his commander in chief had acted with such honor.

Uriah's honor put David on the spot. The king had an opportunity to confess his sin or to cover it with still more evil. He chose the latter.

We have seen that Joab was a man of flawed character. He trusted God in matters of battle, but he apparently had no compunctions about murder. Note that when Joab murdered Abner, David clearly and publicly disavowed his actions, but now David found Joab's talents useful. In one of the great betrayals of history, David wrote orders for Joab to have Uriah killed in battle: "Put Uriah in the front line where the fighting is fiercest. Then withdraw from him so he will be struck down and die" (2 Sam. 11:15). David gave the orders to Uriah to deliver to Joab. Thus Bathsheba's husband trustingly carried his own death warrant to his executioner.

I grieve to think how loyal Uriah must have felt when the troops around him in battle deserted him to die. I wonder if, in the last moments, he guessed that "good" King David and the wife to whom he had pledged his love were complicit in his death. One thing I know and David certainly should have known: the God of righteousness will not allow such behavior to stand.

As if the one who once knew God so well could forget, David waited for Bathsheba's mourning to be over. Then he added her to his stable of wives, and she bore him a son.

You may be familiar with these passages, but did you find yourself secretly hoping the story had changed this time? Imagine how the Father's heart is wounded when we behave so unlike one of His children. He was no doubt grief-stricken by David's sin, even though He saw it coming. Considering the events we've read, David's heart was obviously further away from God than we imagined. If David were accused of a faraway heart and tried in a court of law, how much evidence would there be to convict him? As members of the jury—not the judge—consider four evidences of David's faraway heart.

1. *David resisted many opportunities to repent of his sin and lessen the charges against himself.* Most of us have been carried away by an overwhelming and sudden craving of the flesh, but we've often cried out for help before sin was heaped on sin. Other times, we've thrown ourselves into a revolving door of sin, just like David, and continued in a destructive cycle.

Why do you think David didn't stop and repent? You might consider the answer from a personal standpoint by asking yourself, "Why have I not at times stopped and repented in the earlier stages of sin?"

After David committed the act of adultery, even though the consequences of the pregnancy were already at work, he could have fallen on his face before God, repented, asked for mercy, and begged God to help clean up the mess he had made. Throughout his encounters with Uriah, he had many opportunities to consider his actions and recant. He didn't.

David was a man with God's Spirit in him! You can be assured the Spirit was doing His job of conviction! Sadly, David had quenched the Spirit to such a degree that he was able to resist conviction repeatedly. Little should frighten us more than realizing the Holy Spirit's conviction has grown so faint we hardly sense it. We are dangerously far away when we can sin with little conviction. We should run home to the Father as quickly as we can!

2. *David was unmoved by Uriah's integrity.* David's faraway heart was unaffected by an encounter with authentic integrity. Psalm 78:72 says David once shepherded his people "with integrity of heart." Uriah's integrity should have spurred such a sense of loss in David that he could not bear to remain so far from the Father. Unfortunately, when people

have moved this far away from God, someone else's righteous behavior often only serves to make them angry and send them further into denial. While they recognize their faults, at that point the pull of sin is often stronger than the desire to set things right.

David surely recognized integrity. For most of his life, his character had been replete with it! When I confront godly character, I never fail to think, *I want to reflect character like him, Lord!* or, *Please, God, make me an example like her!*

3. *David tried to cover his own sin.* Have you ever gotten tangled in a web of sin while you tried to cover the first one? Most of us have tried to cover our sin at one time or another!

In Psalm 32:1 David reminded us that the blessed person is the one "whose transgressions are forgiven, / whose sins are covered." How sad that he learned the lesson through such bitter experience.

The word *covered* in the Hebrew is *kasah,* and it means "to cover, conceal, hide; to clothe; . . . to forgive; to keep secret; to hide oneself, wrap oneself up."[14] When we try desperately to cover up our sinful ways, we are bound for disaster as sin perpetuates. Only through repentance will God "cover" us and "clothe" us with His loving forgiveness. Only when we run to Him in the nakedness of our sin will He wrap us up with "garments of salvation" and a "robe of righteousness" (Isa. 61:10). David was trying to cover his tracks. God wanted to cover his sins. The latter means life. The former means death—to something or someone.

4. *David involved many others in his sin.* Apparently, David never stopped to consider the position in which he was placing others. We, too, can become so self-absorbed that we do not care what we are asking from others. We can be unmoved by the compromises of others on our behalf. Intense selfishness accompanies a faraway heart.

In David's selfishness, he involved a servant in his plans; he invited Bathsheba to a season of guilt and grief; he attempted to entice Uriah to compromise his values; he involved Joab in his sin; and he had Uriah killed. Most importantly "the thing David had done displeased the LORD" (2 Sam. 11:27). Still he did not repent. We may rightly conclude that David had ample evidence to convict him of a faraway heart. The results were tragic.

In my research for *A Heart Like His,* I found a section out of a worn, yellowed book called *The Making of a Man of God* by Alan Redpath. I want to vow never to forget the words I found there. I hope you'll spend some moments in prayer after you read it. Thank you for staying true to God's Word even when it paints pictures that aren't pretty. God's Word is always for our good.

> *David was called "a man after God's own heart." That was the caliber of the man, the height to which he had risen. He had become king of all Israel, and he had defeated all his enemies. He had risen now to the peak of his life and career—when suddenly the devil tripped him up.*
>
> *Oh, from what heights of blessing it is possible for a man to fall! To what depths of sin a man can descend, even with all that spiritual background! The higher the pinnacle of blessing, authority, and publicity he has attained by grace, the deeper and more staggering can be his collapse. There is never a day in any man's life but that he is dependent upon the grace of God for power and the blood of Jesus for cleansing.*[15]

Amen. Pray for yourself, then pray for someone you know who is being used by God.

Chapter 36

YOU ARE THE MAN!!!

2 Samuel 12:1–13

David burned with anger against the man and said to Nathan,
"As surely as the Lord lives, the man who did this deserves to die!
He must pay for that lamb four times over, because he did such a
thing and had no pity." Then Nathan said to David, "You are the man!"
(2 Sam. 12:5–7)

Chapter 11 ended with some very solemn, hair-raising words: "But the thing David had done displeased the LORD" (2 Sam. 11:27). We now begin to assess the cost of a few moments of carnal pleasure.

This chapter is difficult and painful. The scene unfolds with Nathan sent to confront David's sin. We can take a lesson already. We need to be careful not to confront for any other reason than sin. We need to resist selfappointed confrontation with a fallen brother. Galatians 6:1 records one of those reasons: "watch yourself, or you also may be tempted."

Nathan was God's man for this job, but he still needed the protection and leadership of God as he confronted the powerful, persuasive king. He probably dreaded his appointment like the plague, but he was obedient to the will of God. Virtually a year had passed since David's initial sin with Bathsheba. We know the baby had already been born, but we do not know exactly how old he was. Why was the time so important? Because David had shown no sign of repentance!

David appeared to be moving on with his life as if nothing had happened, but how do you suppose his sin affected his relationship with God? Had he simply picked up with God where he had been? Hardly! Most of us have had seasons of unrepentance when we outwardly attempt to go on with life as if we had not sinned against God. However, our unwillingness to repent has internal effects.

David wrote exactly how he felt during his season of unrepentance. Take a moment to look at what David was going through during the course of that year, as recorded for us in Psalm 32.

> *When I kept silent,*
>> *my bones wasted away*
>> *through my groaning all day long.*
> *For day and night*
>> *your hand was heavy upon me;*
> *my strength was sapped*
>> *as in the heat of summer.*
> *Then I acknowledged my sin to you*
>> *and did not cover up my iniquity.*
> *I said, "I will confess*
>> *my transgressions to the LORD"—*
> *and you forgave*
>> *the guilt of my sin. (Ps. 32:3–5)*

I believe Psalm 32:3–5 describes a malady we might call *sin sickness*. I know what it's like to be sin sick. During periods when I refused to repent, I felt sapped of strength and sick all over. I groaned in my sin. Thankfully, the seasons of my sin and rebellion were the most miserable periods of my life, worse than any uninvited suffering I've ever experienced.

God graciously forgave me once I repented, and He forgot my sin, but I am thankful He did not allow me to forget. Have you ever noticed God helps us to forgive ourselves, but He does not make us forget our sins?

Psalm 32:3–5 teaches us an important truth. Spiritual illness (unrepentance) can lead to emotional illness (groaning all day, heaviness all night) and physical illness (bones wasted away, strength sapped). Please do not misunderstand. Certainly not all emotional or physical illness is caused by an unrepentant heart, but a continued refusal to repent can take a serious emotional and physical toll. I know. I've been there.

When the prophet Nathan confronted David, he used a method any good preacher might have used. He used an illustration familiar to his hearer, and then drove the illustration home with the Word of God. His method struck an immediate chord with David.

> [Nathan] said, "There were two men in a certain town, one rich and the other poor. The rich man had a very large number of sheep and cattle, but the poor man had nothing except one little ewe lamb he had bought. He raised it, and it grew up with him and his children. It shared his food, drank from his cup and even slept in his arms. It was like a daughter to him.
>
> "Now a traveler came to the rich man, but the rich man refrained from taking one of his own sheep or cattle to prepare a meal for the traveler who had come to him. Instead, he took the ewe lamb that belonged to the poor man and prepared it for the one who had come to him." (2 Sam. 12:1–5)

Have you noticed how the further we wander outside of God's will, the more we judge others and the less we show mercy?

David burned with anger against the man and said to Nathan,
"As surely as the LORD lives, the man who did this deserves to die!
He must pay for that lamb four times over, because he did such a
thing and had no pity."

Then Nathan said to David, "You are the man!"
(2 Sam. 12:5–7)

David was ready to fine the man "four times over" and kill him—until he found out he was the man! What was God trying to accomplish? I believe He wanted David to recognize the grace of God in the midst of the grave consequences of his sin. God wanted David to recognize that he deserved to die. Bathsheba also deserved death, according to Hebrew law. So did Joab for setting up another person's death. God allowed David to sit as judge over his own life and pronounce a death sentence on himself so his heavenly Father could grant him the undeserved gift of life. No doubt, David never forgot that moment.

God rebuked David through the prophet Nathan by saying in effect, "I anointed you, delivered you, gave you Saul's kingdom and all that belonged to him. If you had needed more, I would have given it. But you didn't ask me for things I longed to give to you. Instead you took something that wasn't yours." Nathan went on to tell David that because of his sin, God said: "The sword will never depart from your house, because you despised me and took the wife of Uriah the Hittite to be your own" (2 Sam. 12:10).

David, through his behavior, wounded the heart of God by despising His Word. The Hebrew word for *despised* is *bazah*, which means "to disesteem . . . to scorn."[16] David's disesteem cost him dearly. As the chosen king of Israel, the man revered for having the hand of God on him, David was the most well-known, highly feared figure in the entire world. Through him God was teaching the nation Israel and the heathen nations about Himself. David's heinous, progressive sin did a terrible thing. The King James Version put it this way: "By this deed thou hast given great occasion to the enemies of the LORD to blaspheme" (v. 14).

The original word for *blaspheme* is *na'ats,* and it means "to revile, scorn, despise, reject; to condemn, to deride."[17] Listen to the rest of the definition, and consider just how serious this cycle of sin was in the life of the chosen king of God's holy nation: "It contains the idea of disdain for one who formerly received favorable attention and then rebelled." What other nations had seen in David caused them to cast their eyes on David's God. Though many had not turned to the God of Israel, He had captured their attention and respect. David's sin caused the nations to lose their respect for God.

God was teaching the way to the Messiah through His chosen king. Through David's victories, God taught something of Himself. Now, through David's failures, God would teach the very foundation of all salvation—God will forgive the sinner, but He will still judge the sin.

Because of David's sin, God said "the sword will never depart from your house." Ominous and predictive words indeed.

Chapter 37

PAINFUL PLEAS

2 Samuel 12:13–31

Then David comforted his wife Bathsheba, and he went to her and lay with
her. She gave birth to a son, and they named him Solomon.
The Lord loved him. (2 Sam. 12:24)

We continue to see David during the most difficult season of his life. We
find some of the events hard to study, but they overflow with vital life lessons. The nuggets of gold we will dig from the painful caverns of the coming
chapters will captivate us until the winds of victory blow in our faces once
again. Pause right now and ask God to tender your heart to His Word.

Nathan delivered a harsh word concerning the child born to David
and Bathsheba.

> *Then David said to Nathan, "I have sinned against the LORD."*
>
> *Nathan replied, "The LORD has taken away your sin. You are*
> *not going to die. But because by doing this you have made the*
> *enemies of the LORD show utter contempt, the son born to you*
> *will die." (2 Sam. 12:13–14)*

Nathan had hardly turned the doorknob to leave before David's child
fell ill. David had been warned that his son would die, and still he "pleaded

with God for the child" (v. 16) for seven days. David refused to eat. He spent the nights lying on the ground. When the child died, the servants were terrified. They thought David might kill himself. So they were afraid to tell him the child had died. They were stunned when David received the news. He got up, washed his face, changed clothes, and went into the house of the Lord and worshiped. Then he went home and ate.

David's servants were mystified by his behavior. They asked him why he wept when the child was ill but worshiped when the child died. David's reply has brought comfort to bereaved parents across the centuries.

> He answered, "While the child was still alive, I fasted and wept. I thought, 'Who knows? The LORD may be gracious to me and let the child live.' But now that he is dead, why should I fast? Can I bring him back again? I will go to him, but he will not return to me." (2 Sam. 12:22–23)

Did David waste his time pleading with God over the life of the child? After all, God's message through Nathan was painfully clear. As we attempt to determine whether or not David's efforts were wasted, we get to peek at just a little of the intense intimacy David shared with God. When he fell on his face before God, the prodigal returned home to the place he belonged. He was bankrupt in soul, demoralized, and terrified, but he was back. Too many months had passed since he had last entered the indescribable place of God's presence, but he still recognized the Father.

Through David's crisis, he was reminded of all he knew of God's ways. David did not plead with God out of ignorance or naïveté but out of his intimate knowledge of God. God does indeed hear our prayers and reserves the right to relent if the change does not compromise an eternal necessity.

David knew something about his God that we need to realize as well. God did not create humanity in His own image to be unaffected by Him.

More than any other creature, we are products, not of His head, but of His heart. Numerous times in Scripture God responds to the needs of His people with the words, "I have heard your cry." I would despair of life if I believed God is unaffected by our cries. The God of Scripture is One who feels.

Unlike us, God is never compromised by His feelings, but He is touched by the things of the heart. When David heard that he would live but his child would die, he probably begged God to allow him to die instead. Can you imagine God's being unaffected by a parent's painful pleas? You may be thinking, *But, Beth, God did not do what David asked. David's prayers didn't change a thing. Where is grace? Where is mercy? What changed?* Let's consider a few of the things that changed.

1. *David's painful pleas forced him back to a crucial place of depending on God.* Somewhere along the line, David had mistaken the power of God as his own. He had so often been told he could do anything, he started to believe it. God demands that we depend on Him because only He can keep us safe. When we depend on Him, He takes care of us. When we seek security in other places, He is obligated to turn us back toward home. When we refuse the less painful nudgings of the Holy Spirit, we risk more drastic measures. Tragedy caused David to depend on God. God's judgment seems harsh until we reconsider David's many transgressions. He multiplied wives and concubines, took another man's wife, took the man's life—all with no willingness to repent.

Don't conclude that the loss of a child must be chastisement on sinful parents. God is not mean-spirited. Remember, David was the king of God's holy nation and had continued to rebel against God in spite of the Holy Spirit's urgings.

2. *David's pleas would satisfy his spirit in the many months of mourning to come.* As he grieved the loss, he needed to know he had done everything he could to prevent the child's death. David did not want his child to die because he did not ask God (see James 4:2).

3. David's pleas ultimately ensured his survival through the tragedy he and his wife would suffer. David's pleas returned him to intimacy with God. The return positioned him to make it through such loss with victory. David's restored relationship to God enabled him to comfort his grieving wife. When tragedy hits, if we cast ourselves on the Savior and rely on Him for the very breath we draw, we will one day get up again. We will even have the strength to comfort another mourner. Perhaps most difficult to fathom, we will have the strength to return to worship.

I'm glad Scripture does not record the scene when David first returned to public worship. The moment belonged to God and David alone. I cannot hold back the tears as I imagine how quickly David's words turned to sobs. I can picture him standing there acknowledging through wails of grief his God's sovereignty and loving-kindness.

Have you ever returned to the Lord in worship after a painful loss that you believe He could have stopped? If so, you may view your return to worship as one of the most difficult and painful experiences of life. I suspect David would concur, but his return restored his sanity. His rediscovered relationship with God became the pillar to hold him up through the painful repercussions of his sins.

4. David's pleas touched the heart of God to respond. God loved this man—just as He loves us. The one He loves He must discipline (Heb. 12:6). But does God's heart ache as He disciplines? I believe the answer is yes. Beautiful evidence of the Father's tender heart toward David emerges in this tragic account. God could not give David what he asked because He had to perform an eternal work and teach an eternal lesson. But He did something else: "Then David comforted his wife Bathsheba, and he went to her and lay with her. She gave birth to a son, and they named him Solomon. The LORD loved him; and because the LORD loved him, he sent word through Nathan the prophet to name him Jedidiah" (2 Sam. 12:24–25).

Out of grace God removed the curse on the sinful union of David and Bathsheba. Their union had been wrong. Their motive was wrong. Even when David found out Bathsheba was pregnant, he tried to manipulate a way for her to stay out of his life. But now we see them drawn together by terrible tragedy. God removed the curse of their marriage and brought a child from their union. *Jedidiah* means "beloved of the Lord."

"The Lord loved him." God loves you. His chastisements can be painful, but God never turns His back on us. He will discipline us, but He will not forsake us. He will always seek to draw us back to a place where He can bless us once more.

Chapter 38

NO RELIEF LIKE REPENTANCE

Psalm 51

Cleanse me with hyssop, and I will be clean;
wash me, and I will be whiter than snow.
Let me hear joy and gladness;
let the bones you have crushed rejoice." (Ps. 51:7–8)

Somewhere between confronting sin and restoring fellowship must come the bridge between those two vital works—contrite confession. We have the blueprint for the bridge of confession fresh from the heart of a grieving king. Psalm 51 will be a fitting conclusion to our study of the infamous transgressions of David. The note in the NIV specifies the psalm as written by David "when the prophet Nathan came to him after David had committed adultery with Bathsheba." From your Bible I encourage you to read the first thirteen verses of the psalm, aloud if you can get to a private place. Seek to feel the passion in David's heart as he wrote the words.

This psalm invites the vilest of sinners to drink from the fountains of forgiveness. Consider these specific phrases from each of the first thirteen verses. Then join me in the following observations.

Verse 1: "Have mercy on me, O God." So great was David's need for cleansing, so urgent his plea, that he began his prayer with no introduction and no high praises.

David understood experientially the teaching of Isaiah 59:2:

> *Your iniquities have separated*
> *you from your God;*
> *your sins have hidden his face from you,*
> *so that he will not hear.* (Isa. 59:2)

He recognized that until he had expressed repentance, words would be wasted.

"According to your unfailing love; / according to your great compassion." David knew his God was complex and multifaceted. In his history with God, David had called on His sovereignty, His might, His deliverance, His intervention. But at this moment, David called on the God of love and compassion. Only on the basis of covenant love could David dare ask for mercy.

Verse 2: "Wash away all my iniquity / and cleanse me from my sin." Don't miss the most important emphasis in this statement: the word *all*. What a wonderful word! The mercy of God is enough to cover all our sins. Few things in life are as fresh and thrilling to me as that moment when I know God has heard my repentant cry and I am completely clean.

Are you able to accept that all your confessed and rejected sins have been completely forgiven? If not, what do you think holds you back from accepting God's complete forgiveness?

Verse 3: "For I know my transgressions." The words prove David could not ignore his sins! Are you in David's position right now? Are you carrying the weight of past sin? Is the guilt and remorse more than you can bear? Do you have a sin you can't seem to give up? You can't live with it, but can't bring yourself to live without it? Satan screams, "To give it up will be far more painful than living with the guilt!" Refuse to hear another of Satan's lies. The freedom of Christ is worth the surrender of absolutely anything! Relief, not remorse, awaits the repentant!

If you are afraid to give up something you know is wrong for you, tell God about it! Confess your fears and let Him encourage you and fill you with His Word! If you are struggling, write a prayer to Him. Express your feelings and ask for His help.

Verse 4: "Against you, you only, have I sinned." For those of us who have known God and experienced the presence of God, the biggest heartbreak over sin comes with the realization that we have offended Him. God takes our sin personally. When we leave sin unconfessed, we scoff at the Cross.

A man who lived many centuries before David also had an opportunity to sleep with another man's wife. In Joseph's case the other woman was Potiphar's wife. He responded to her with the words we should always ask ourselves in time of temptation: "How then could I do such a wicked thing and sin against God?" (Gen. 39:9).

Verse 5: "Surely I was sinful at birth." David recognized something of the depth of his inclination to sin. With a fresh sense of shock he seemed to be saying, "Sin is as much a part of me as the flesh and blood that makes up my body. It's my heritage! Oh, God, have mercy on me!"

Verse 6: "Surely you desire truth in the inner parts." God is our one and only source of transforming truth. Deep inside in the secret places we are most vulnerable to lies.

Virtually every external sin results from the internal practice of believing a deceitful heart. Only God can sow truth in our hearts; only we can let Him. God can always be trusted to tell us the truth, but sometimes we don't want to hear the truth.

Jesus said the truth would set us free (John 8:32). Have you ever found truth to be painful but liberating?

"You teach me wisdom in the inmost place." The inmost place is where experience turns into wisdom! Wisdom is knowledge applied. Head knowledge alone is useless on the battlefield. Knowledge stamped on the heart makes one wise.

Verse 7: "Cleanse me with hyssop." For the people of the Old Testament, hyssop carried a powerful ritual and symbolic message. It first appears in Scripture on the night of the first Passover. Moses instructed them to use hyssop to put blood on the doorpost. Hyssop was always connected to cleansing from sin.

"Wash me, and I will be whiter than snow." When I feel weighed down by sin and guilt, I feel spiritually dingy and dirty. The image of snow speaks volumes to me at those times. As a freshly forgiven sinner, I am whiter than snow! I am cleansed and forgiven and absolutely purified of sin.

Satan lies to you. He tries to convince you that you are covered by guilty stains even when you repented long ago. Let God sow truth in your inner parts. Know the Truth so you can recognize a lie.

Verse 8: "Let the bones you have crushed rejoice." This line is perhaps my favorite in Psalm 51. I know exactly what the psalmist was talking about. Do you? David mixes the pain of confessing and turning from sin with the pleasure of restored fellowship. God sometimes uses circumstances and discipline to figuratively break our legs from continuing on the path of sin. Only the repentant know what it's like to dance with joy and gladness on broken legs!

Verse 9: "Hide your face from my sins." With a sudden realization of his own depravity, David could not bear for God to look. He was filled with shame, Satan's signature of approval. Allowing God to open our eyes to sin is not only painful but also embarrassing! Once we look, we don't want God to look. We must accept the fact that He's already seen our sin, still loves us, and wants to forgive us.

Verse 10: "Create in me a pure heart." The Hebrew word for *create* is *bara.* Also used in Genesis 1:1, the word "refers only to an activity which can be performed by God" and describes "entirely new productions."[18] David was admitting his need for something only God could do. Pure hearts never come naturally. In fact, a pure human heart is perhaps God's most creative work.

Verse 11: "Do not . . . take your Holy Spirit from me." To David, the removal of God's Spirit was a fate worse than death. He said in verse 4, "You are . . . justified when you judge." When we compare his plea in verse 11, he seems to be saying, "Do whatever you must, just don't take your Holy Spirit from me!"

Verse 12: "Restore to me the joy of your salvation." Most of us have borrowed these precious words from time to time. Sometimes our prayers seem to go unanswered because, in our misery, we beg for our joy to be restored without the obedience of fully turning from our sin. In John 15:10, Jesus said, "If you obey my commands, you will remain in my love, just as I have obeyed my Father's commands and remain in his love." Only then did He continue, saying, "I have told you this so that my joy may be in you and that your joy may be complete" (John 15:11).

Nothing equals the moment you begin to sense the return of the joy of His salvation, but we must have the willing spirit to cooperate in His marvelous work!

Verse 13: "Then I will teach transgressors your ways, / and sinners will turn back to you." What happens after God has created a pure heart in a repentant sinner, renewed his spirit, and restored the joy of His salvation? No more willing and effective evangelist and teacher exists than one who has been humbled, cleansed, renewed, and restored! God will never have to goad this person to witness. His or her life will have eternal impact.

Thank you, merciful God, for the words you placed in the heart and on the pen of a broken king. Thank you most of all for forgiveness. May we never be able to resist.

As a repentant sinner who has experienced the misery of broken fellowship with God and reveled in the freshness of forgiveness, I would like to conclude with two verses that mean the world to me. Read them aloud if you have the opportunity. May they be a blessing to you too.

> *Who is a God like you,*
> > *who pardons sin and forgives the transgression*
> > *of the remnant of his inheritance?*
> *You do not stay angry forever*
> > *but delight to show mercy.*
> *You will again have compassion on us;*
> > *you will tread our sins underfoot*
> > *and hurl all our iniquities into the depths of the sea.*
> (Mic. 7:18–19)

David's entire purpose in writing Psalm 51 was to ask for mercy. Did God grant his request? I have a hunch that He was delighted to.

Chapter 39

FAMILY SECRETS

2 Samuel 13

In the course of time, Amnon son of David fell in love with Tamar, the beautiful sister of Absalom son of David. (2 Sam. 13:1)

Sin never fails to bring painful repercussions. We will now see Nathan's prophecy regarding David's sin begin to find fulfillment. Turmoil will escalate within the private quarters of the palace, and David's responses will reveal that he was a far more effective king than father.

If you already know what's coming, you know Amnon's actions were inexcusable, but can you imagine the confusing messages David's children received as they grew up? They had siblings, half siblings, and siblings born to David's concubines. They grew up in a household saturated by sexual excess and lacking any example of parental restraint. We can't and must not excuse Amnon, but we can certainly understand.

These verses are replete with tragedy. The focus of this corruption was a beautiful young virgin daughter of the king, Tamar, no doubt awaiting the man she trusted God would one day bring her. Tamar's brother was Absalom, and their half brother was named Amnon. Amnon was infatuated with Tamar. I believe he was used to getting whatever he wanted, with the result that he became obsessed with the one thing he could not have—his half sister.

The events in chapter 13 are scandalous even by today's standards and as painful as the horrid descriptions of rapes we read in a big city news-paper. Amnon wanted Tamar. On the advice of his shrewd cousin Jonadab, Amnon pretended to be sick. He asked his father David to send Tamar to care for him. Then he raped her.

> "Don't, my brother!" she said to him. "Don't force me. Such a thing should not be done in Israel! Don't do this wicked thing. What about me? Where could I get rid of my disgrace? And what about you? You would be like one of the wicked fools in Israel. Please speak to the king; he will not keep me from being married to you." But he refused to listen to her, and since he was stronger than she, he raped her. (2 Sam. 13:12)

Those who have experienced the trauma of rape know the injury doesn't end with the event. The actions and reactions of others multiply the pain. In this case Amnon quickly added to the hurt.

> Then Amnon hated her with intense hatred. In fact, he hated her more than he had loved her. Amnon said to her, "Get up and get out!"
>
> "No!" she said to him. "Sending me away would be a greater wrong than what you have already done to me."
>
> But he refused to listen to her. He called his personal servant and said, "Get this woman out of here and bolt the door after her." So his servant put her out and bolted the door after her. She was wearing a richly ornamented robe, for this was the kind of garment the virgin daughters of the king wore. Tamar put ashes on her head and tore the ornamented robe she was wearing. She put her hand on her head and went away, weeping aloud as she went. (2 Sam. 13:15–19)

The tragic irony of her dress touches my heart. The richly orna-
mented robe was her cloak of dignity and honor. She ripped the fabric of
her robe as surely as Amnon had ripped the fabric of her honor. His
crime against her was heinous. I am acutely aware that many who read
these words have been victims of rape. I deeply desire to handle this subject with tenderness and reverence. I have asked God to pour His Spirit
through me so that I will be untrue to neither Him nor you.

First we need to assign appropriate responsibility. All wrong, fault,
and blame for the rape belongs to the perpetrator—Amnon. Strangely,
but typically, Tamar also fell victim to all three men surrounding this
event. Consider Amnon, Absalom, and David's roles in Tamar's life.

Amnon. He was David's firstborn. Ironically, his name meant "trustworthy" and "faithful."[19] Obviously, he was neither. We see the immediate evidence of a father's influence on his son. Amnon had watched his
father take one wife after another in a nation where polygamy was forbid-
den. As far as Amnon could see, his father never wanted anything
he did not ultimately get. It is interesting that, in our first introductions to
them, both Bathsheba and Tamar were described as beautiful
(2 Sam. 11:2; 13:1).

Like his father, Amnon saw something beautiful and determined to
have it. He gave no consideration to the other party involved. Only his
lust mattered. He literally became sin-sick to the point of stopping at
nothing to satisfy his appetite. Tamar pled with him to spare her disgrace and his reputation, but "he refused to listen."

I found one of the most sickening moments in the tragic events to
be Amnon's immediate reaction. After the rape, Amnon hated her with
intense hatred.

We humans often practice a kind of blame shifting. When we have
done something sinful and shameful, we blame our actions on someone
else—often the victim of our behavior. Did you notice that Amnon

"called his personal servant"? Amnon knew that servants talk. He did everything possible to increase Tamar's feeling of shame and disgrace.

The story of another cast-out woman appears in Genesis 16. Abram and Sarai could not have children, so Sarai used her handmaid Hagar to bear a child. Then when Hagar conceived she began to taunt Sarai, and Sarai had her cast out.

God did not ignore Hagar's pain. In her rejection she discovered that God is El Roi—the God who sees (Gen. 16:13). Surely God was just as faithful to Tamar as she mourned before Him, completely innocent of any sin. He did not look away for an instant. Tamar lived the rest of her life in desolation, but ultimately God will replace her tattered robe and cover her with finest white linen, and she will stand before Him once again the virgin daughter of a king.

We can also be assured that God will deal appropriately with Amnon. We see no sign of repentance. When he sees the face of the Righteous Judge, he may utter words like those in Revelation 6:16: "They called to the mountains and rocks, 'Fall on us and hide us from the face of him who sits on the throne and from the wrath of the Lamb!' "

Absalom. Both Absalom and David reacted inappropriately toward Tamar and the crime she suffered. Absalom obviously discovered his sister in extreme distress. He guessed the nature of the crime against her from the tearing of the virgin's robe. No one can doubt Absalom's love for his sister, but his reaction to her could only have added further injury. Countless victims of rape and molestation have been hurt by similar advice. Absalom told her to "be quiet" and not "take this thing to heart" (v. 20).

Perhaps you have been the victim of shame in some way. If so, I offer you company today. I've been there too. When I was a small child, someone my parents should have been able to trust caused great pain and suffering by crimes against me. Friends and family members of victims often ask me what they can possibly say to their hurting loved one. I know from my own experience that the most important thing anyone can say to a victim of a shame-breeding crime is, "I am so sorry. I love you, and I support you." We often think we need to come up with answers when another has been hurt. Sometimes the words of comforters are well-meaning but hurtful.

Simple words like "I love you" and "I support you" work best for those of us who are not counselors. In case you've been a victim of shame and no one has ever said these words before: I am so sorry.

Absalom's advice to Tamar was to keep the secret and pretend nothing happened. Unfortunately, he took his own advice. He never said a word to Amnon, either good or bad. But his hatred for him would finally cause him to lose control. You see, overwhelming feelings cannot be stuffed. They invariably turn inward, take the person prisoner, then often force a breakout with tragic consequences.

Have you experienced a time in your life when you had to remain silent on an overwhelming issue? If so, what emotions did your silence evoke in you?

Look at David's own words in Psalm 39:1–3 as he described an attempt to keep his mouth shut when he was overwhelmed with emotion.

> But when I was silent and still,
>   not even saying anything good,
>   my anguish increased.
> My heart grew hot within me,
>   and as I meditated, the fire burned;
>   then I spoke with my tongue. (Ps. 39:2–3)

David's next words in Psalm 39:4 were "Show me, O LORD." Pour out your heart to God when emotions threaten to overtake you, and ask Him what to do next. He will provide positive outlets for painful emotions.

Absalom was wrong to tell Tamar to be quiet and not take it to heart. The shame was crushing her to pieces. He minimized the significance of the terrible crime against her. She was invited to live with him, but she was not invited to be honest with him. She was left desolate—like the living dead.

David. Absalom's immediate assumption of Amnon's guilt speaks volumes. Amnon's lack of character was common knowledge. David should have dealt with Amnon before disaster struck. Then after the crime, David still refused to do anything. If only David had applied the wisdom of Psalm 39 to this tragedy, things would have been so different!

How did David react? We see just one description: "He was furious" (2 Sam. 13:21). What did he do about the crime? Absolutely nothing.

Why didn't David take control of his family tragedy? I believe the enemy may have been working on David just as he works on us when we really blow it. His own complicity and sin blinded him to the need of Tamar to find release for the fire of hurt and shame that burned in her. Satan uses sin and failure so effectively against us that even after sincere repentance we often remain completely disabled. He whispers all sorts of questions in our ears like, "How dare you expect obedience from your children after what you've done? How dare you walk into church again? You hypocrite!"

Two wrongs don't make a right! If we blow it as a parent, spouse, servant, employee, or leader, we should fall before God in complete repentance and ask Him what we must do to cooperate with restoration. Then we should follow Him in utmost obedience to His precepts. Restoration does not mean you can no longer stand for the truth because you fell. Restoration means you must stand!

Micah 7:8–9 are two of my favorite verses.

> *Do not gloat over me, my enemy!*
> *Though I have fallen, I will rise.*
> *Though I sit in darkness,*
> *the LORD will be my light.*

Because I have sinned against him,
      I will bear the LORD's wrath,
until he pleads my case
      and establishes my right.
He will bring me out into the light;
      I will see his righteousness. (Mic. 7:8–9)

David allowed his own failure to disable him to lead his household in justice and righteousness. He had been forgiven by God, but he had not chosen to live like a forgiven person. He allowed his own sense of guilt to handicap him as a parent.

David and his family would have been better off had he never fallen at all, but he could not change the past. He could, however, learn from his mistakes, become zealous for righteousness in his life and household, and affect the present with God on his side.

"Be ye angry, and sin not" (Eph. 4:26, KJV) does not mean "be angry and do nothing." God created anger. It energizes us to respond when something is wrong. David needed to channel his anger and respond to the crime committed in his household. No weaker house exists than one that lacks appropriate authority. Lack of authority is a breeding ground for untold recklessness and sin. Just ask Tamar.

I pray you will continue to allow God to bring you victory in vulnerable areas. God is faithful. He has miraculously escorted many women just like Tamar through their grief. I can't explain it, but I've seen it with my own eyes. Hallelujah! That's my God.

Chapter 40

Bring Home the Banished

2 Samuel 14

Like water spilled on the ground, which cannot be recovered, so we must die.
But God does not take away life; instead, he devises ways so that a
banished person may not remain estranged from him. (2 Sam. 14:14)

Two years had passed since Amnon's crime against Tamar. Two years with bitterness multiplying in Absalom's heart. That's the nature of bitterness. It never stays in its cage. Absalom must have watched and waited to see if his father would call Amnon to account for his crime. His father didn't.

Absalom waited for an opportunity. He devised an elaborate scheme to summon Amnon to his house. The time of sheep shearing was a festive occasion with huge family celebrations. Absalom seized the opportunity, counting on his father to continue in distancing himself from family obligations and celebrations. When David refused to come, Absalom requested Amnon's presence in his place, assuming no one would be suspicious. Customarily, the oldest son represented his father in the father's absence.

David may have been suspicious since he questioned Absalom's choice, but he apparently concluded no grounds existed to refuse Amnon the right to attend the celebration. David sent Amnon and the rest of his sons—never to see his eldest again.

> *Absalom ordered his men, "Listen! When Amnon is in high spirits from drinking wine and I say to you, 'Strike Amnon down,' then kill him. Don't be afraid. Have not I given you this order? Be strong and brave." So Absalom's men did to Amnon what Absalom had ordered. Then all the king's sons got up, mounted their mules and fled.* (2 Sam. 13:28–29)

Absalom did not take the sword to Amnon himself, but like his father, involved subordinates in the crime. Irony rings from the mouth of a coward who shoves others into action with the words, "Be strong and brave" (v. 28).

Cousin Jonadab reared his ugly head again. A messenger came to David with the erroneous report that Absalom had killed all the king's sons. Jonadab quickly assured David that only Amnon was dead. He would never have known Absalom's plans had he not become his confidant. I wonder if he ever told Absalom that he was the one who devised the scheme against Tamar in the first place. Not likely.

After ordering Amnon's death, Absalom fled to the king of Geshur. The tragedy ends with one son dead, one son missing, and one father grief-stricken. David had two responses toward Absalom after Amnon's death: he mourned for him and longed for him. How odd. Remember when David became furious over Amnon's sin but did nothing? He had the appropriate feelings but inappropriate actions. Once again David feels the right thing and does the wrong thing.

After a time Joab grew weary of seeing David mope and do nothing. Anyone who studies the life of Joab will see that the general was no fan of doing nothing. He had obviously witnessed David's irresponsibility toward Absalom for as long as he could. He devised a plan to capture

David's attention. Through a concocted story of a woman and her prodigal son, Joab convinced David to summon Absalom. I believe Joab used this method because he had seen God use a similar approach through the prophet Nathan once before (2 Sam. 12:1–7).

David granted Joab's request and allowed him to summon Absalom. Joab was so thrilled, he "fell with his face to the ground . . . and he blessed the king" (2 Sam 14:22). He joyfully hastened to bring the young man home, no doubt picturing the emotional but wonderful reunion of father and son. He brought Absalom back to Jerusalem, bracing himself and his charge for the glorious reunion. He was met with these words from the king: "He must go to his own house; he must not see my face" (v. 24).

Often David's heart and actions showed us a picture of Christ. In this case he shows the opposite. I am very grateful God will not call us to the heavenly Jerusalem and say, "She must not see my face." I've waited all my life to see His beautiful face!

David did not respond like the father of the prodigal son in Christ's parable—the father who searched the horizon daily for his wandering son to come home. That father, who represents our heavenly Father, caught a glimpse of his son in the distance and "ran to his son, threw his arms around him and kissed him" (Luke 15:20).

Some things in life are do-overs. God sometimes gives us a second chance to do something right. Some chances never come back around. The chance for David and Absalom to be genuinely reunited in their hearts would not come again. By the time David finally received Absalom, his son's heart was cold.

Have you noticed what children will do to get their parent's attention? Absalom proved an extreme example. He sent for Joab to send him to David, but Joab refused to come. So Absalom told his servants, "Joab's field is next to mine, and he has barley there. Go and set it on fire." This time Joab got the message. He delivered Absalom's message: "I want to see the king's face, and if I am guilty of anything, let him put me to death" (2 Sam. 14:30–32). David had a last chance. Sadly, he blew it. He summoned Absalom. Absalom bowed down with his face to the ground, and David kissed his son.

Do you find yourself like me, wishing God had told you more about their reunion? I believe God didn't tell us any more about it because there was nothing more to tell. Nothing else happened. The scene had all the right ingredients: Absalom bowing down; the king kissing his son. Only one thing was missing—the heart. The actions of David and his son were generated by custom, not emotion. Fearing his son would do something more than set Joab's field on fire, David summoned Absalom to appease him, not accept him. Absalom sought his father's face to force David to look him in the eye, not to beg forgiveness like the prodigal.

This father and son could have shared the blame for their separation, but David did nothing to bring about reconciliation. God is never in the wrong when He and one of His children are separated; yet He devises ways so that the banished person may not remain estranged from Him. Never underestimate the significance of timing when it comes to mending. You may not get another chance.

What in the world was David doing? His heart was often far too complex for us to risk conjecture, yet one thing was obvious: again he refused to take action regarding his family. Without more knowledge of David's story, we could still predict more pain would follow.

PART VIII

THE UNRELENTING SWORD

Psalm 3

When he fled from his son Absalom.

1 *O LORD, how many are my foes!*
     How many rise up against me!

2 *Many are saying of me,*
     "God will not deliver him."

3 *But you are a shield around me, O LORD;*
     you bestow glory on me and lift up my head.

4 *To the LORD I cry aloud,*
     and he answers me from his holy hill.

Selah

5 *I lie down and sleep;*
     I wake again, because the LORD sustains me.

6 *I will not fear the tens of thousands*
     drawn up against me on every side.

7 *Arise, O LORD!*
     Deliver me, O my God!
     Strike all my enemies on the jaw;
     break the teeth of the wicked.

8 *From the LORD comes deliverance.*
     May your blessing be on your people.

Selah

Chapter 41

AN ABANDONED THRONE

2 Samuel 15

Then the king said to Zadok, "Take the ark of God back into the city. If
I find favor in the Lord's eyes, he will bring me back and let me
see it and his dwelling place again." (2 Sam. 15:25)

King David and Absalom finally saw each other face-to-face. Sadly, however, their reunion was too little, too late. We now see evidence of Absalom's deep dissatisfaction about his encounter with his father. Their meeting did nothing but fuel his bitterness. The relationship between David and Absalom teaches us an important object lesson: reuniting and reconciliation can be two very different things.

Many previously separated couples have returned to one another to live under the same roof for the sake of the children, finances, religious convictions, or the family business. They may live together the rest of their lives without healing or dealing with the problems. Reuniting is one thing; reconciliation is another. One difference is the presence or absence of misery. We'll see this principle work itself out in the life of David and Absalom.

Absalom was dissatisfied by his meeting with his father. Possibly he suffered from the same thing many adults suffer from today. When

Absalom was a child, his daddy was his hero. He was strong and smart. He was his son's idol. David had plenty of shortcomings, but the boy could not see them until one day an emotional bombshell hit home—exploding in the bedroom of Amnon.

Although people got mad, no one cleaned up the mess. Lives continued to be torn by the shrapnel no one ever swept away. David did not—perhaps could not—live up to Absalom's expectations. The results were devastating. The revenge Absalom had taken on Amnon's life was not enough. The fact that his father still called him a son was not enough. He still cried out for vengeance and was determined his father would pay.

Obviously, Absalom tried everything he knew—good and bad—to get his father's attention. He could not get to David through his home, so he determined to get to him through the throne.

Absalom began a very deliberate campaign to win the hearts of the people. Each morning he arrived with a chariot and an entourage of men and horses. He looked impressive as he stood at the gate of the city. When anyone entered the city with a complaint, Absalom proclaimed that if he were appointed judge, anyone with a complaint would get justice. He was quite an effective politician. I wouldn't be surprised if he even kissed a few babies.

Absalom proved a patient and diligent schemer. He continued to work through every step of his plan for four years, waiting for the right moment to attempt to overthrow the father he now hated.

Absalom spent two years waiting for David to punish Amnon, three years in hiding after killing his brother, two years in Jerusalem waiting for David to receive him, and four years working his devious plan of vengeance against his father. Unforgiveness and retaliation stole eleven years of his life! Eleven years is a long time for anyone to seethe, for anyone to harbor bitterness.

Has anger or bitterness stolen years of your life? God tells us to forgive those who hurt us, but He never qualifies the command by saying forgive only when someone asks for your forgiveness. He simply says forgive (Luke 6:37). Christ set the perfect example in Luke 23:34. From the cross He cried, "Father forgive them, for they do not know what they are doing." Those crucifying Jesus had not realized what they were doing. They had not asked forgiveness. Rather, they were gambling over His clothes. I believe Christ asked God to forgive them not to let His persecutors off the hook, but for Christ to disavow bitterness. He chose to continue His painful destiny with the love of the Father, not unforgiveness.

David never asked for forgiveness. He never took his rightful place of authority over family events. David made plenty of mistakes, but Absalom did not have to follow suit. He could have called on the mercy of God and forgiven David for failing him, even if his father never admitted how wrongly he had handled his family. God would have held David responsible, and Absalom would have been free. Instead, he locked himself in the prison of bitterness where character eroded in the darkness of his soul. We often resist forgiveness by saying, "It's too difficult to forgive." Forgiveness may be excruciating for a moment, but anger and bitterness are excruciating for a lifetime.

Often, the people who hurt us don't realize the magnitude of their actions. The people who mocked and crucified Christ had no idea they were dealing with the fullness of the Godhead bodily! The man who hurt me when I was a small child had no idea how much I would suffer for decades to come. Can we muster the courage to say regarding those who hurt us, "God forgive them and help me to forgive them"?

When we harbor bitterness and refuse to forgive, we become our own persecutors. While we blame the other person, we really continue to injure ourselves.

Those who hurt us often have no idea how deeply we will suffer. If we follow Christ's example, we will be free. We can save ourselves a lot of heartache! Learning to forgive even if no one takes responsibility for his

214 A Heart Like His

or her actions will save us from the kind of misery that ultimately destroyed Absalom.

Finally, after waiting and scheming, Absalom went to Hebron to initiate his rebellion. He sent messengers throughout Israel to say, "As soon as you hear the sound of the trumpets, then say, 'Absalom is king in Hebron'" (2 Sam. 15:10).

Ahithophel was a highly respected adviser and Bathsheba's grandfather, thicker than blood with David. Ahithophel's counsel was more valuable than many troops. Absalom may have been miserable, but he was not dumb. Absalom won Ahithophel over to his side, "and so the conspiracy gained strength" (2 Sam. 15:12). If Absalom's plan had been a chess game, stealing Ahithophel was checkmate.

When David heard of the rebellion, the warrior king did a remarkable thing. He packed up, abandoned Jerusalem, and ran (2 Sam. 15:14).

Is this the same David God anointed as His chosen king? The one who conquered the giant? The one God prospered like no other? Did he not know that God gave him the kingdom, and only He could take it away? How could he run from his throne?

David found himself right in the middle of a cycle of self-appointed failure. Stricken with grief and dressed for mourning, he and his loyal followers trudged the Mount of Olives where people once worshiped God.

There on the Mount of Olives, continuing up to the summit, an amazing thing happened: "David prayed" (v. 31). Little by little, things began to happen. David had run from his throne practically hopeless. But somewhere on top of that mountain, David got down on his knees and prayed. See his prayer for yourself. God had him write it down. It's Psalm 3.

> 1 *O LORD, how many are my foes!*
>   *How many rise up against me!*
> 2 *Many are saying of me,*
>   *"God will not deliver him."*

3 But you are a shield around me, O LORD;

  you bestow glory on me and lift up my head.

4 To the LORD I cry aloud,

  and he answers me from his holy hill.

5 I lie down and sleep;

  I wake again, because the LORD sustains me.

6 I will not fear the tens of thousands

  drawn up against me on every side.

7 Arise, O LORD!

  Deliver me, O my God!

  Strike all my enemies on the jaw;

  break the teeth of the wicked.

8 From the LORD comes deliverance.

  May your blessing be on your people.

God did not answer every one of those requests immediately, but He returned enough strength to David for him to begin walking in faith instead of fear. On the Mount of Olives, David confronted the Spirit of God who had grown accustomed to being honored there.

Many years later Jesus trudged that same path and found strength to walk on to a cross. I wonder if Christ thought of David when He prayed on that same mountain. One thing is certain: as He sat on the Mount of Olives on the eve of His crucifixion, He was thinking about us. You don't have to climb a mountain to find strength to fulfill your God-given calling. He's as close as a whisper. He's as close as a prayer.

Chapter 42

TRAITORS AND FRIENDS

2 Samuel 16–17

Absalom and all the men of Israel said, "The advice of Hushai the
Arkite is better than that of Ahithophel." For the Lord had determined
to frustrate the good advice of Ahithophel in order to bring
disaster on Absalom. (2 Sam. 17:14)

The conflict between David and Absalom rekindled old supporters of
Saul who were still nursing grudges against David. Have you ever noticed
that mean-spirited people will kick a person when he's down? David had
seemed invincible; yet the moment he appeared vulnerable, opportun-
ists descended on him like vultures.

As David fled, he met Ziba, the steward of Mephibosheth, with
donkeys loaded with provisions for the fleeing troops. David certainly
needed the help, but Ziba's motives were less than pure.

> *The king then asked, "Where is your master's grandson?"*
>
> *Ziba said to him, "He is staying in Jerusalem, because he thinks,*
> *'Today the house of Israel will give me back my grandfather's*
> *kingdom.'"*

Then the king said to Ziba, "All that belonged to Mephibosheth
is now yours."

"I humbly bow," Ziba said. "May I find favor in your eyes, my
lord the king." (2 Sam. 16:3–4)

David had no reason to disbelieve Ziba. If Absalom, his own flesh
and blood, could betray him, why not the adult son he adopted? David
had suffered so much betrayal, he assumed no one was beyond turning
on him. In fact, however, Ziba lied to David. The steward had abandoned his crippled master in Jerusalem in order to swindle him out of
his property.

Can you remember ever feeling like someone took advantage of you at
a time when you were vulnerable? Nothing makes us as vulnerable as family problems. Personal difficulties may cause us to lack discernment. David
told Ziba he would give him everything Mephibosheth owned without
confirming Ziba's claims. David's vulnerability caused him to believe the
worst and respond with haste rather than prudence. We are wise to be
careful about the decisions and assumptions we make when we are stressed.
We will tend to react rather than respond. When pain is acute, we often
can't discriminate properly between good and bad decisions.

I can't think of a situation when godly advice is more valuable than
in times of great vulnerability. David could have used a little advice
before he gave Mephibosheth's belongings to Ziba. Unfortunately,
Ahithophel, his head counselor, was unavailable. He was busy advising
Absalom! No wonder David was vulnerable!

On the heels of Ziba's claims about Mephibosheth, David encountered a profane, violent man by the name of Shimei. He began to curse
David and throw stones at the deposed king. The stones hit him, yet I
have a feeling the words hurt more than the stones. The man's actions
were wrong, but David feared his words might be right. When Abishai
wanted to kill Shimei, David forbade it because the Lord may have told

him to curse. He said, "It may be that the LORD will see my distress and repay me with good for the cursing I am receiving today" (2 Sam. 16:12).

Through all his ups and downs, victories and failures, we've never seen David walk through this kind of humiliation.

Jesus also walked the road of humiliation as He went to the cross. People spat on Him and slapped Him in the face. Unlike David, He was completely innocent. He could have summoned the armies of heaven or ordered the earth to quake, yet He "for the joy set before him endured the cross, scorning its shame, and sat down at the right hand of the throne of God" (Heb. 12:2).

Like Christ, we could be in the middle of God's will and find ourselves on a path of humiliation. Or like David, we could suffer the further humiliation of knowing we chose our own path. God is still merciful to meet us on the humiliating paths of our lives whether or not we chose them through rebellion.

Consider the timing of Shimei's attack—just as David was regaining a shred of strength! Just when Satan suspects we are regaining a spark of hope, he hastens to greet us with discouragement and rejection. Notice David's response to Abishai's request to avenge David's persecution: "My son, who is of my own flesh, is trying to take my life. How much more, then, this Benjamite! Leave him alone" (v. 11). David might have been saying: "My own beloved son has rejected me. There is nothing anyone can do to injure me any more deeply. Let him go ahead. Maybe I deserve it."

I want to express something to you that I hope you'll receive with your whole heart: We can still cry out to God for help even when we think we're getting what we deserve! God comes to us even when our pain is self-inflicted. Times of humiliation and persecution do not have to be permanent injuries.

Few experiences are more exhausting than keeping your head up through the unjust attacks, but all journeys have an end. Finally, "The king and all the people with him arrived at their destination exhausted. And there he refreshed himself" (v. 14).

How can you refresh yourself when you've been down a rocky path? One way is to appreciate the support you do receive.

David's friend Hushai the Arkite risked his life by defecting to Absalom and then giving him bad advice to offset the wise counsel of Ahithophel. Ahithophel encouraged Absalom to pursue David and kill him. Hushai convinced him to wait and consolidate his hold on the nation first. Thus Hushai saved David's life in the early days of the rebellion.

The priests Zadok and Abiathar risked their lives and those of their sons to send messages to David. They warned him not to stop before crossing the Jordan and not to stay with the troops lest Absalom follow Ahithophel's advice.

Sometimes when we're down, it's hard to see how many people have come to our aid. We're often so focused on our circumstances that we don't realize how many people God has sent to encourage us in some way. At times I've cried out, "God, please help me get through this difficult time!" or "Please help me meet this deadline!" I am often humbled as He opens my eyes to all He's done and says to my heart, "I was the One who sent Mary Helen to your house with home-baked cookies. I was the One who told Nancy to send you a note of encouragement. I was the One who gave you that good laugh. I've been there all along."

God was there all along for David too. We will have missed the turning point of the conflict between David and Absalom if we miss the importance of God's "frustrating" Ahithophel's advice. After Absalom decided not to follow Ahithophel's counsel, the counselor went home and killed himself. Absalom's decision led to David's upper hand in the battle for the kingdom. Ahithophel was a traitor to his king. Note several parallels between David's betrayer and Christ's betrayer many centuries later. Ahithophel and Judas had several things in common:

❧   Both were chosen members of a very important cabinet. A factor that certainly separates King David from the King of Kings is that Christ knew Judas would betray Him, yet Jesus loved him and treated him like His other disciples.

❧   Both betrayed their masters and went with the crowd. In their own ways, both Ahithophel and Judas defected from what they believed to be a losing team to sign up with the obvious winners. We're so tempted to think numbers mean power. What a lesson to be learned! Don't let the enemy make you think you're on a losing team. Remember, looks can be very deceiving. Ahithophel would testify from the grave if he could! Don't let Satan tempt you to betray the One who promised victory because it looks like the bigger team is winning. When the final judgment comes and the few who took the narrow road oppose the masses who followed the wide, safety will not be in numbers.

❧   The last parallel I'd like to draw between Ahithophel and Judas is their tragic end. Both hung themselves when things went wrong.

I'd like to consider one last question. Why did Ahithophel betray David while Hushai remained faithful? Hushai risked exposure and death by entering the household of the enemy. He helped buy time for his king by "counseling" and deceiving Absalom so that David could strengthen his forces. Why did he respond so differently to a leader who appeared to be on his way out? First Chronicles 27:33 offers a beautiful explanation: "Ahithophel was the king's counselor. Hushai the Arkite was the king's friend."

You and I have a "friend who sticks closer than a brother" (Prov. 18:24) for "greater love has no one than this, that he lay down his life for his friends" (John 15:13). No matter what happens, no matter who rejects you or humiliates you, God will never betray you. Stay faithful, believer. You are on the winning team. The King of all kings will return and take His rightful throne.

Chapter 43

IF ONLY

2 Samuel 18

As he [David] went, he said: "O my son Absalom! My son, my son
Absalom! If only I had died instead of you—O Absalom, my son, my son!"
(2 Sam. 18:33)

In David and Absalom we watched an emotional match involving two opponents torn between love and hate. Now we will see one go down tragically. We can't change the story. We can only agree to be changed through it.

We saw that David won the battle of the counselors. Now came the battle of blood and bone. Absalom drew up his army to fight his father. David sent forth his army to fight the men of Absalom, but he gave each of his commanders, in the hearing of their troops, the same command. "Be gentle with the young man Absalom for my sake" (2 Sam. 18:5).

Imagine how demoralizing David's behavior must have been for the men who were risking their lives for him. Small wonder how Joab responded. He had had enough of David's behavior.

The battle took place in the forest of Ephraim with twenty thousand casualties. Absalom rode his mule under a tree and caught his head in the branches. A soldier brought word to Joab that Absalom was "hanging around" in the area. The soldier feared harming Absalom because of David's words, but Joab hurried to kill the king's son. "He took three javelins in his hand and plunged them into Absalom's heart while Absalom was still alive in the oak tree. And ten of Joab's armor-bearers surrounded Absalom, struck him and killed him" (2 Sam. 18:14).

The final words in the account of Absalom ring with irony. They took his body, threw it into a pit, and piled a heap of rocks over him (v. 17). The irony comes from the fact that "Absalom had taken a pillar and erected it in the King's Valley as a monument to himself" (2 Sam. 18:18).

At one time Absalom was a handsome and compassionate man. He loved his sister deeply, grieving the shame Amnon had heaped on her. He made a place for his desolate sister in his own home. He named his daughter Tamar in her honor. He tried to do the right things for Tamar, but he ended up doing all the wrong things for himself.

My oldest daughter Amanda has always been relatively easy to discipline. When she was a little girl and misbehaved, all I had to do was walk toward the drawer that held a flimsy plastic spatula and she would sweetly say, "I feel better!" Though she could not state the situation clearly, she chose to respond to discipline in the least painful way: "I feel better."

One day a good friend of mine grabbed that same spatula and swatted her little boy for repeatedly disobeying her. The son wasn't hurt, but he was as mad as a hornet. Amanda stood right next to him while his mother paddled him and continued to ask, "Do you feel better?" If looks could kill, my precious angel would have been dead! He finally screamed, "No, I not feel better!"

Those words could apply to Absalom. He didn't feel better after Amnon was in the grave. He didn't feel better when David let him return to Jerusalem without punishment. He didn't feel better after he was summoned to the king's quarters and reunited with his father. And after stealing the hearts of his father's people, he still didn't feel any better. Absalom ultimately possessed as little self-control as the brother he despised. His lack of self-control finally killed him.

Another figure came to my mind as I thought about Absalom's tragic end. His name was Samson, and he also lived outside the restraints of self-control all of his adult life. He finally went too far, but he didn't realize he was caught until it was too late. "He . . . thought, 'I'll go out as before and shake myself free.' But he did not know that the LORD had left him" (Judg. 16:20).

We can only shake ourselves free so many times. If we keep flirting with disaster, we're finally going to get trapped. Whatever the issue, unrestrained passions will ultimately catch up with us. Samson learned the hard way. So did Absalom. Can you imagine the thoughts going through the head of that beautiful but troubled young man as he struggled to set himself free? The picture of his death was the picture of his life: the noose of bitterness choking the captive's cry. In the end, those close enough to hear him choking no longer cared.

Like departing words on a tombstone, we read Absalom's eulogy in verse 18: "Absalom had taken a pillar and erected it in the King's Valley as a monument to himself." At first glance, the verse seems to fit the chapter like a square peg in a round hole. At second glance, the passage relates perfectly to the verse before it.

The people of Israel often set up stones as a memorial of a never-to-be-forgotten event. The pile of stones taught lessons—either good or bad. The rocks over the body of Absalom did not just keep wild animals away; it served as a traitor's reminder.

I see great irony in the fact that the record of Absalom's grave and the account of the monument he erected to himself appear together in Scripture. The verses demonstrate that Absalom's death as a traitor remains far more memorable than his self-absorbed life. Through bitterness, Absalom's heart became as hard and cold as the pillar he raised. Even though David committed many sins and was unfair to others, his heart did not grow cold.

After Absalom's death, word reached the waiting David. He cried out, "O Absalom, my son, my son!" The words send chills up a parent's spine, don't they? Suddenly, a heart of tragically suppressed love exploded. Tears he should have cried long ago poured from his eyes. Words he should have said the moment he first saw his prodigal finally burst from his lips: "My son, O, my son!" He did not speak about him. He spoke right to him, as if his voice would carry to the depths of the pit where the body lay.

"If only I had died instead of you!"

Death would have been far easier than life without him. What grieving parent hasn't cried those same words? Felt those same emotions? And where was God when David lost his son? Where was He when a king's own countrymen pierced his son? Where was He when the blood poured forth? The same place He was when He lost His own Son.

Chapter 44

CROSSING THE JORDAN

2 Samuel 19

He won over the hearts of all the men of Judah as though they
were one man. They sent word to the king, "Return, you and all your men."
(2 Sam. 19:14)

After the defeat and death of Absalom, David returned to the throne where he belonged. No one would hand him his rightful throne. He would take back his kingdom with exhausting tenacity. We will see a long season of conflict and crisis take its toll on David, but we will also encounter the heroes God raised to aid him. Years of turmoil and final exhaustion did not extinguish David's praises to his God. David will lead us to a fresh discovery of God's mercy in peculiar circumstances.

We saw the tragic death of the young prince Absalom and the broken heart of the aging King David. The son's body grew cold, and the father's grief nearly consumed him. Divided loyalties left God's chosen nation in an upheaval.

Grief over Absalom was crippling and consuming David. Once again Joab stepped in. He went to David and said: "Today you have humiliated all your men, who have just saved your life. . . . You have made it clear today that the commanders and their men mean nothing to you. I see that you would be pleased if Absalom were alive today and all of us were dead." He warned that unless David started acting like a king everyone would desert him (2 Sam. 19:5–7).

The next time I suffer a painful loss, remind me not to call someone like Joab for a sympathetic ear. Nothing is more natural than grieving a devastating loss, but David was met by immediate condemnation from Joab.

I think a pretty good rule for comforting a grieving friend is to offer hugs and say little. Joab did not confront King David as a friend however. He approached him as commander over the king's armies. He had the best interests of his soldiers in mind and not the emotional well-being of a mourning father. He had seen many lives stolen in battle. If we give Joab the benefit of the doubt, we could see a shred of humanity in his desire to see David cease mourning. If we don't, we can assume his resistance to David's grief showed his guilt for having disobeyed David's order to spare Absalom's life. Joab was the same man who thrust the javelins into Absalom's heart.

Even though Joab's heart was wrong, David concluded his advice was right. He returned to the business of the kingdom. David also realized that his army had fought for him, and he could not have them return in shame. The eighth verse tells us he got up and took his seat in the gateway. The words represented a pivotal moment—the king became accessible once more. David was back—in his heart—if not yet on his throne. "He won over the hearts of all the men of Judah as though they were one man" (v. 14).

God's holy nation would not officially split into a Northern Kingdom (Israel) and a Southern Kingdom (Judah) until after the death of Solomon, but the tribe of Judah already functioned in many ways as a separate people. David realized the tribes of Israel were in a quandary because they had alienated their king and pledged allegiance to a leader who was now dead. David responded by appealing to his own tribe, Judah, suggesting they lead the way for Israel in restoring the throne to its rightful king.

David sent word to Zadok and Abiathar, the loyal priests who had stayed in Jerusalem as his spies. He would receive his people back without punishing the general population, but he had every intention of making some changes. Most significantly, David replaced his nephew Joab with another of his nephews, and Joab's cousin, Amasa—who had been Absalom's general.

Apparently David's victory combined with his fair treatment of the defeated won over the hearts of the men of Judah. So they escorted him back across the Jordan to Jerusalem. On the trip, David had encounters that showed his intention to bring peace to the land.

Shimei, the Benjamite who had cursed and stoned David and his men on their retreat from Jerusalem, came and begged forgiveness. Abishai, Joab's brother, asked permission to kill Shimei, but David said there had been enough killing.

Mephibosheth also came to meet the returning David. Mephibosheth obviously had been mourning the king's situation: he "had not taken care of his feet or trimmed his mustache or washed his clothes from the day the king left until the day he returned safely" (2 Sam. 19:24). When David asked about Ziba's story that Mephibosheth allied himself with Absalom, he replied,

Since I your servant am lame, I said, "I will have my donkey saddled and will ride on it, so I can go with the king." But Ziba my servant betrayed me. And he has slandered your servant to my lord the king. My lord the king is like an angel of God; so do whatever pleases you. All my grandfather's descendants deserved nothing but death from my lord the king, but you gave your servant a place among those who sat at your table. So what right do I have to make any more appeals to the king? (2 Sam. 19:26–28)

David responded in a puzzling fashion. He ordered the land be split between Ziba and Mephibosheth. One of two reasons may have been at the heart of David's order. Either David was attempting to end the rivalry as simply as possible, or he was testing Mephibosheth's heart.

David may have been employing some of the same wisdom his son Solomon later applied between two women fighting over a child (1 Kings 3:24–26). When Solomon suggested the child be cut in half and divided between them, the true mother emerged, ready to sacrifice her own position to spare the life of her son. Likewise, Mephibosheth's integrity emerged as he responded, in effect, "Let Ziba have everything as long as I have you back safely."

No doubt, the encounter between David and Mephibosheth was a priceless moment—an example of authentic restoration. Ironically, the son of his own blood was never reconciled to David; but his adopted son escorted him back to his throne, inspired by love and loyalty. I cannot help but notice an astonishing parallel. God's own beloved nation, His chosen ones, His natural descendants, refused to be reconciled to Him through Christ; yet the adopted sons—the church—accepted Him, loved Him, remained loyal to Him, and will escort Him to His rightful throne!

The point where the parallel ends is perhaps the point of greatest celebration. Absalom was never reconciled to his father on this earth, but the apostle Paul suggests that Israel will be reconciled to her God (Rom. 11:25–26). Somehow God intends to heal His wayward people.

This promise does not mean Jews will be saved apart from Christ. Romans 9:6 warns that "not all who are descended from Israel are Israel." But the promises of Scripture encourage me to believe that Israel will one day take her rightful place among the nations. God's natural-born children and the church, His adopted children, will one day gather as His family before the throne of God (see Rom. 8–11).

I will never forget having a family picture taken at Thanksgiving after we had adopted our son, Michael. As I framed the new picture, he jumped up and down and exclaimed, "It's the whole Moore family, and not one of us is missing!" We had covered our house with his pictures, but I never realized how much the family picture taken before he came had bothered him. One day God may take a family portrait in heaven. All of God's children—the natural-born of Israel and the adopted sons and daughters, the church—will be there, and not one of us will be missing.

As David returns, we meet another of those characters I'd like to know better. His name was Barzillai. He was a very old and very wealthy man. When David fled Jerusalem, Barzillai provided him provisions and a place to stay. In verses 31–43, the aging king and his aged benefactor parted. Barzillai resisted David's pleas to come to Jerusalem, preferring to spend his remaining days at home.

We've all seen our sin nature at work in children. They argue over toys, space, companions, and even over work to be done, not because of what they want but because of what someone else may get. The men of Israel and Judah were clearly not far removed from such children. The men of Israel complained that the men of Judah stole the king and brought him across the Jordan. Not to let pettiness go without adding to it, the men of Judah responded that they had transported David because he was their kinsman.

Going home isn't always fun, especially when infighting awaits you. The smoke between Israel and Judah was coming from a fire that had only begun to blaze. The nineteenth chapter of 2 Samuel ends with business as usual. The king crossed the Jordan with an entourage escorting him back to his throne, and before he could dry off his feet, his folks were in a fight. How typical!

Chapter 45

UNFINISHED BUSINESS

2 Samuel 20–21:14

They buried the bones of Saul and his son Jonathan in the tomb of Saul's
father Kish, at Zela in Benjamin, and did everything the king commanded.
After that, God answered prayer in behalf of the land. (2 Sam. 21:14)

In chapter 19, we smelled the smoke of trouble, and now we will see the
fire. David had ample business to settle as he returned to his post.
Reclaiming a kingdom is no small matter! I sincerely hope that you will
find the encounters we are about to consider interesting enough to keep
you focused. Sometimes God speaks in black and white. Other times, as
in the following, He speaks in living color.

When people begin to bicker, they provide an opportunity for slick
troublemakers. In this case his name was Sheba. He sounded a trumpet
and called the Israelites to a rebellion against David. All the men of
Israel followed him.

Once again David was faced with a civil war. He sent Amasa, the
new commanding general, to gather the army of Judah. When Amasa
returned, he found Joab waiting with the army ready to march. Joab
took his cousin Amasa by the beard as if to give him the customary kiss
of greeting and stabbed his rival, leaving him to bleed to death in the
road.

We can't seem to get rid of Joab, can we? We might as well accept him as a permanent figure in our study whether or not we like him. David should have known Joab was not going to clean out his desk and resign peaceably when replaced by Amasa. He killed Abner, Saul's former general. Now he forced his way back into his old position by murdering Amasa. Power was so important to Joab that he did not stop at spilling his own family's blood. I was a little amused over Joab's words in verse 20 of 2 Samuel 20: "Far be it from me to swallow up or destroy!" He probably sold beachfront property in the wilderness as a side job.

Joab meant to cause Amasa's death, but he didn't mean to cause a traffic jam. We may see the first reference to rubbernecking in all of Scripture: "Amasa lay wallowing in his blood in the middle of the road, and the man saw that all the troops came to a halt there" (v. 12).

The army pursued Sheba to the city called Abel Beth Maacah. Joab laid siege to the city and prepared to break down the wall. As the plot thickened, one woman was willing to become more than a spectator to imminent disaster. She negotiated a solution to the problem. The inhabitants tossed the head of Sheba over the wall, and Joab lifted the siege. As a result, an entire city was spared. Let's allow her a moment's glory. We don't even know her name. She wasn't looking for recognition. She was looking for her city's salvation. An entire village could have perished because one person, Sheba, was such a troublemaker.

Do you know of someone who risked involvement in a community need or another's personal need and made a significant difference? I know a woman whose son was openly pursued by a homosexual college professor. Her son could have been easy prey for the shrewd predator. The professor had confused many other young men, but no one was willing to confront him. The woman tried to enlist her husband's support. He did not want to get involved. She tried to enlist her pastor's support. He did not want to get involved. She finally approached the dean of students and an investigation ensued. Many people came forward, and mountains of evidence emerged. The professor never again pursued another young man on that campus. The woman's son is now a devoted husband and father. He credits his mother for having snatched him and others from the jaws of a ferocious lion.

A sobering realization falls on us from our next passage. Many years later, the people of Israel were still suffering the ill effects of a king who was rebellious to God. I once heard a preacher say, "Never forget, God can outwait you. Time is always on His side." That preacher could have been thinking of what happened next in Israel.

> During the reign of David, there was a famine for three succes-
> sive years; so David sought the face of the LORD. The LORD said,
> "It is on account of Saul and his blood-stained house; it is because
> he put the Gibeonites to death." (2 Sam. 21:1)

God was making an important point. He was holding the nation of Israel to an old vow made with the Gibeonites generations prior to David's reign. I think you will find the circumstances of the vow very interesting.

The story appears in Joshua 9. When the Israelites entered Caanan, the Lord sent a great fear of them upon the peoples. Most of the people groups in Palestine joined forces to fight the Israelites, but the people of Gibeon chose a wiser and sneakier course of action. They dressed as if they had come from a distant country to make a treaty with Israel. The elders of Israel did not inquire of the Lord and so were fooled. They made a promise never to destroy the Gibeonites.

Fast forward three hundred years. During his forty-two years as king, Saul sought to destroy the Gibeonites, but God has a long memory— much longer than a few hundred years.

God meant for His people to be good for their word. He still does. Surely one reason He expects His people to be good for their word is so that observers will come to believe He is good for His. Israel had to keep her agreement with the Gibeonites even though they should never have entered the agreement. Saul broke the agreement with the probable aid of his sons and tried to annihilate a people innocent of their father's sins. Ironically, Saul's sons were brought to account for their father's sins.

God considers vows extremely important. Ecclesiastes 5:5–6 says, "It is better not to vow than to make a vow and not fulfill it. Do not let your mouth lead you into sin. And do not protest to the temple messenger, 'My vow was a mistake.'" Countless men and women have broken marriage vows by claiming their marriage was a mistake. Maybe they were like the Israelites who did not inquire of the Lord and were sorry later, but a vow is still a very serious thing. Others have vowed to honor their mates, but although they still live under the same roof, honor moved out long ago. Still others have decided they prefer richer over poorer. We don't live in a society that supports the seriousness of long-term vows, but we live under the heavenly authority who does.

Many young people have taken vows of purity to God through a wonderful program called True Love Waits. I spoke at a youth camp one summer in which several high schoolers came to me individually grieving their broken vows. They asked my advice, and I didn't have to think very long to answer based on what I understand about God and His Word. I explained to them that I have also made promises to God along the way that I have not kept. Rather than continue in disobedience, God desires two responses to broken vows: repent and recommit! Several vows I made to God as a teenager I broke within the first couple of years; but after recommitment, most of those have been kept for decades through the grace of God. Oh yes, I wish I had kept every vow just as I had promised from the very beginning; but I am so thankful to have had the opportunity to recommit my life and try again successfully.

The king summoned the Gibeonites and spoke to them. . . . David asked the Gibeonites, "What shall I do for you? How shall I make amends so that you will bless the LORD's inheritance?"
(2 Sam. 21:2–3)

The Gibeonites made what seemed a horrible request. The very horror of it should remind us how very seriously God takes vows. They wanted pure blood revenge—seven of Saul's male descendants to kill and to expose their bodies to the elements.

I'm sure your stomach turns over as mine does, but again, a vow is a serious matter. The Israelites recommitted themselves to the vow they made with the Gibeonites by satisfying their demands. David gave the Gibeonites what they asked, and the famine ended. The first drops of rain fell from the skies, bringing the sweet smell of water on parched land.

Disasters and times of great loss often also provide times that demonstrate great love and character. Such was the case for Rizpah, the mother of two of the men killed by the Gibeonites.

Rizpah daughter of Aiah took sackcloth and spread it out for herself on a rock. From the beginning of the harvest till the rain poured down from the heavens on the bodies, she did not let the birds of the air touch them by day or the wild animals by night.
(2 Sam. 21:10)

As rain drenched her hair, a grieving mother gathered her sackcloth and returned home. The mental image of a mother guarding her sons' bodies from predators was obviously more than David could shake. The image reawakened old pictures from years past that disturbed him so deeply—the exposed bodies of Saul and his dear friend, Jonathan (1 Sam. 31). Their remains were not where they belonged.

The king had unfinished business left waiting too long. He went and gathered the bones of Saul and Jonathan as well as the men killed by the Gibeonites. David did not send a soldier for their bones. He went for them himself. He gathered them, brought them back, and "they buried the bones of Saul and his son Jonathan in the tomb of Saul's father Kish" (2 Sam. 21:14). Obedience has amazing effects: "After that, God answered prayer in behalf of the land."

Do you happen to have any unfinished business in your life? Old scores that need to be settled Christ's way? Chapters that need to be completed? Ends that need to be rewritten? Books that need to be closed?

Christ has led us to a new form of warfare far more effective than guns and tanks. We have weapons of grace, mercy, love, and the Sword of the Spirit which is the Word of God. Anybody out there need your forgiveness? Your acceptance? Your release? It's time for some old battles to end. Just like the Israelites, we will suffer in ways that seem totally unrelated when we allow matters to continue unsettled and outside the will of God. Rebellion inevitably leads to famine in our relationship to God. A new beginning is as close as the fresh smell of rain.

Chapter 46

THE UNWELCOMED SIGHT OF AN OLD ENEMY

2 Samuel 21:15–22; 23:8–39

Once again there was a battle between the Philistines and Israel. David went down with his men to fight against the Philistines, and he became exhausted. (2 Sam. 21:15)

King David returned to Jerusalem and realized he had to take back his throne—rather than receive it from cheerful givers. The business of politics and inevitable battles must have seemed insurmountable. One last enemy arose before he could take a breath and proclaim a victory. One very familiar enemy. One very persistent enemy. The Philistines were at it again. Again David went to fight them, but this time he became exhausted in battle. One of Goliath's relatives, who dwarfed God's king, said he would kill David.

But Abishai son of Zeruiah came to David's rescue; he struck the Philistine down and killed him. Then David's men swore to him, saying, "Never again will you go out with us to battle, so that the lamp of Israel will not be extinguished." (2 Sam. 21:17)

I am so thankful God chose to tell us David knew about exhaustion in battle! I need to know that others have experienced the weariness of fighting the same old enemy over and over. The word for *exhausted* in Hebrew is *uwph.* The word even sounds like something you might say at a glimpse of an old enemy! *Uwph* means "to cover, to fly, faint, flee away."[20] It is the overwhelming desire to run and hide.

When was the last time you wanted to run and hide? Few things make us want to flee more than the prospect of fighting an old battle. The moment that old enemy reappears, we want to run into the nearest forest and never come out. Have you ever noticed that Satan always chooses just the right time to haunt you through an old enemy? When you haven't had enough rest, when things have been emotional and turbulent, when you've been swinging from one extreme to the other, when you're completely vulnerable—that's when the enemy strikes.

Satan is the counterfeit god of perfect timing. He's watching for just the right moment to pull the rug out from under us, but even that rug is under God's feet. And God always has victory in mind! He will never allow Satan to discourage you without a plan to lead you to victory! We may not always follow Christ to victory, but He is always leading! "Thanks be to God, who always leads us in triumphal procession in Christ and through us spreads everywhere the fragrance of the knowledge of him" (2 Cor. 2:14).

One of the most important truths we can apply from David's ongoing battles with the Philistines is that God will always lead us to victory—but He will lead us His way. God led David to victory through all four of the battles mentioned in 2 Samuel 21:15–22, but He brought the victory to David through someone else.

Just like us, I'm sure David's preference would have been for God to make him the hero and leave others in awe over his great strength. God had other plans. He saved David all right, but He purposely made him dependent on someone else. Several wonderful reasons might exist for the method God used. We may see some of them by looking ahead in Scripture. Second Samuel 23:8–39 contains a list of David's mighty men. For example, Eleazar fought the Philistines by himself. The passage tells us that "he stood his ground and struck down the Philistines till his hand grew tired and froze to the sword" (2 Sam. 23:10).

On another occasion when David was in the stronghold and the Philistine garrison was at Bethlehem, David said he longed for a drink from the well at Bethlehem. "So the three mighty men broke through the Philistine lines, drew water from the well near the gate of Bethlehem and carried it back to David" (2 Sam. 23:16).

God purposely brought victory to David through the courage of others on many occasions. Consider a few reasons why God might have used this method in the life of David.

1. *For the sake of the people.* Israel did not need David to be like a god to them. He could not deal with being put on that kind of pedestal or subjected to that kind of pressure. He was bound to disappoint them. When it comes to hero worship, the line between love and hate is very fine! How many close followers have turned against their leaders? God will never allow any of us to be the only one through whom He appears to be working mightily.

2. *For the sake of King David.* Do you remember what happened when David was so highly exalted on his throne that he became disconnected from his people? Remember how lonely he was for his friend? Remember how isolated he became? Remember what happened when he thought he had risen above the normal duties of a king and stayed behind in the spring when other kings went off to war? That's when the nightmare began! David believed his own press. He came to believe he could not be overtaken. He was wrong. God protected David by not always letting him be the hero. God extended David a wonderful gift. He gave David a few heroes instead—a few men who commanded his respect. He

humbled David and made him depend on them for his life. None of us will escape this important life lesson. God will teach us dependency. God will allow us to become exhausted and force us to receive help.

3. *For the sake of the men he empowered.* People can easily be discouraged if they perceive that God works mightily through others but never works through them. God does not play favorites. Anyone who cries out to Him, He answers. Anyone who surrenders to His call, He uses.

Ministry to the individual is as mighty an act of God as is ministry to the masses. Which is better: a speaker empowered to encourage a thousand believers in their walk, a homemaker praying with a neighbor to receive Christ, a mom singing "Jesus Loves Me" with her preschooler, or a popular Christian artist leading a massive crowd in "Amazing Grace"? They are all mighty works of God. They are all His heroes.

Don't cringe. God has heroes. If you don't believe it, check Hebrews 11. You'll only find part of the list, however, because it just keeps getting longer and longer in heaven. The name of every surrendered person who endures by faith and not by sight is on it. No doubt some of your heroes are on that list. You may be surprised to find your name listed there as well!

Having heroes of the faith is perfectly appropriate for you. In fact, I am saddened at the thought of anyone who cannot name a living hero. We can let one person's failure tempt us to believe no one is genuine. Don't let Satan make you cynical. If you can't name a single hero in the faith, you may have already allowed Satan to sow a seed of cynicism in you. Remember, heroes aren't perfect. They simply live to serve and honor God.

In my neighborhood I have a friend in the faith I admire deeply. She has joyfully ushered more of our neighbors to a place of receiving Christ than anyone I have ever known. She attends a weekly Bible study I teach and is personally responsible for at least fifteen or twenty people attending. If she meets someone who can't afford to buy the Bible study book, she buys it. The latest new members of our Bible study are three women my friend met at a health club. They didn't know how to get to our church. She picked them up and brought them. God's Word is changing their lives—all because of one obedient minister of the gospel. I can hardly hold back the tears as I celebrate her faithfulness with you. She is one of my heroes. And I know she's one of God's.

Through David and Eleazar (whose hand grew tired and froze to the sword) God is reminding us that heroes get tired too. Getting weary is no shame. The shame comes in refusing to accept the victory through another when God supplies a hero. A hero accepts help. Remember, genuine martyrs are never self-appointed.

Our God is so faithful, isn't He? His ways are so much higher than ours. Who would ever have guessed that He could use things like exhaustion to take our minds off ourselves and cause us to esteem another?

Chapter 47

A GREAT
CELEBRATION

2 Samuel 22

He brought me out to a spacious place;
he rescued me because he delighted in me. (2 Sam. 22:20)

Nothing is more appropriate than celebrating a victory God sovereignly and majestically won for us! After all the ups and downs of David's journey, in chapter 22 we get to experience the sheer pleasure of attending a celebration. Anyone who has ever experienced victory in Jesus is invited to attend. Someone else just wouldn't understand. Second Samuel 22:1 tells us: "David sang to the LORD the words of this song when the LORD delivered him from the hand of all his enemies and from the hand of Saul."

Think about what motivated David to sing the words. Sometimes God puts a new song in our mouths—a hymn of praise to our God! Other times, He brings us back to an old song, one which fell from our lips many years ago and has gathered a film of dust only a fresh breath could blow away. No doubt about it, sometimes God wants to hear an old song from a new heart. This was the case for David.

David remembered the words he had sung many years before, after God delivered him from the hand of Saul. I believe his recent victory over the Philistines rekindled the remembrance of his victory over Saul because of several similarities. Both conflicts seemed they would never end. Both conflicts sapped his strength. Both conflicts caused him to rely on another's strength.

Decades wedged their way between the solos of this one song. How different the sound of the same singer's voice—so young and daring when first he sang. Now the voice was old, but suddenly, unexpectedly filled with the passion of a young warrior. I believe the words comprise the testimony of an old man with a fresh passion. Praise God, we need never get too old to experience a young passion! Chapter 22 is a lengthy song of praise. David catalogued the ways God had worked in his life.

> He reached down from on high and took hold of me;
>   he drew me out of deep waters.
> He rescued me from my powerful enemy,
>   from my foes, who were too strong for me.
> (2 Sam. 22:17–18)

You will notice in 2 Samuel 22 that David is serving us a slice of his personal history with God. Are you actively building a history with God? Can you readily say that the two of you have done lots of living together since your salvation? Have you allowed Him to reveal Himself to you in the many experiences of life?

If you are a Christian but you've attempted a life of self- sufficiency, you may not be able to relate to having a close personal relationship with God. Claiming Him personally is the most precious right of any believer! Look at the revolutionary news the risen Lord told Mary Magdalene: "Go . . . to my brothers and tell them, 'I am returning to my Father and your Father, to my God and your God'" (John 20:17). Blessed Calvary, cheated grave that made Christ's God my very own! Glory in the Cross!

The Book of 2 Samuel is not the only place David's words of victory are found. Psalm 18 contains an almost identical set of verses to those God placed in 2 Samuel 22. One of the exceptions is too precious to miss. Verse 1 of Psalm 18 simply declares, "I love you, O LORD, my strength."

"I love you, Lord." No demands. No despair. Just "I love you." The words might seem more fitting as the grand finale rather than the opening line. Their sudden appearance suggests they were words that could not wait. The psalmist considered his delivered state and his Father's stubborn love, and he burst forth with the words: "I love you, LORD."

The One who delivered David from his enemies was no distant deity. He was the object of the psalmist's deepest emotions, the One with whom he shared authentic relationship. David deeply loved God. David was a man after God's own heart because his desire was also the sheer pleasure of the Father. The Father's deepest desire is to be loved—genuinely loved—by His child.

If 2 Samuel 22 and Psalm 18 compel us to see one thing, it is that God is a personal God we each can call our own.

- He is my strength when I am weak.
- He is my rock when I am slipping.
- He is my deliverer when I am trapped.
- He is my fortress when I am crumbling.
- He is my refuge when I am pursued.
- He is my shield when I am exposed.
- He is my Lord when life spins out of control.

A heart that makes Him its own—one that can state, "He is mine"—is a heart that cannot help but love. I love you, Lord.

Chapter 48

A HAND WITHDRAWN

2 Samuel 24

But the king replied to Araunah, "No, I insist on paying you for it.
I will not sacrifice to the Lord my God burnt offerings that cost
me nothing." (2 Sam. 24:24)

Second Samuel 24 gives us an opportunity to do some research into an easily misunderstood event in David's history. Satan always seeks to make us believe that God is unfair or unkind. In this task, the adversary particularly likes to use a few difficult-to-understand events recorded in Scripture. Chapter 24 may be confusing and unsettling to us if we don't keep one thought in mind: We do not know every fact about every event in Scripture. We don't always have the explanations for certain events and acts of God. He is sovereign. He owes us no explanation. He purposes to teach us to walk by faith and not by sight. When Scripture records an event or judgment of God that seems cruel or unfair, we need to do two things.

1. *Acknowledge that His ways are higher than ours.* We do not have all the information or understanding. We have no idea the depth of evil God may have seen in human hearts that necessitated such serious judgment.

2. *Acknowledge what we do know about God.* Anytime you are overwhelmed by what you do not know or understand about God, consider what you do know about Him. Your heart and mind will be quieted, and you will be able to walk in faith.

In 2 Samuel 24, we get a chance to practice using this method so we can deal with these kinds of difficulties in future study.

> *Again the anger of the LORD burned against Israel, and he incited David against them, saying, "Go and take a census of Israel and Judah."*
>
> *So the king said to Joab and the army commanders with him, "Go throughout the tribes of Israel from Dan to Beersheba and enroll the fighting men, so that I may know how many there are."*
> (2 Sam. 24:1–2)

Like David, Joab was a complex man. He could murder his own cousin, yet on other occasions he displayed a steadfast belief in the power and sovereignty of God. For example, when going into battle against two armies at once, Joab said: "Be strong and let us fight bravely for our people and the cities of our God. The LORD will do what is good in his sight" (2 Sam. 10:12). Sometimes Joab also showed himself quite perceptive about David's blunders. When he did, Joab never feared confronting his commander in chief. He said, "Why does my lord the king want to do such a thing?" (2 Sam. 24:3).

In today's vernacular, Joab said, "What are you thinking?"

David refused to listen. He did the military census of Israel, but the action was barely completed when he realized he had made a serious mistake.

> *David was conscience-stricken after he had counted the fighting men, and he said to the LORD, "I have sinned greatly in what*

> *I have done. Now, O LORD, I beg you, take away the guilt of*
> *your servant. I have done a very foolish thing."*
>
> *Before David got up the next morning, the word of the LORD*
> *had come to Gad the prophet, David's seer: "Go and tell David,*
> *'This is what the LORD says: I am giving you three options.*
> *Choose one of them for me to carry out against you.'"*
> (2 Sam. 24:10–12)

God's three options were all dreadful: three years of famine, three months of defeat in war, or three days of plague. David chose to fall into God's hand rather than those of men. In the ensuing three days of plague, seventy thousand Israelites died.

As you can see, we have the perfect opportunity to employ the method of Bible study I suggested—to measure what you don't know or understand by what you do! I see at least two occurrences that Satan could twist to cause doubt or dismay in the reader: (1) God's role in David's sin, and (2) punishment that appears to exceed the crime.

Let's consider the first point. The first verse of chapter 24 says, "[God] incited David against them, saying, 'Go and take a census of Israel and Judah.'" A brief look at this one verse may cause us to wonder why God would ask David to do something and then kill seventy thousand people as a result.

Just as God included four Gospels to tell the story of the incarnate Christ, He recorded many of the occurrences of David's reign in both 2 Samuel and 1 Chronicles. We can better understand passages or events by comparing these "parallel" accounts.

First Chronicles 21:1 sheds a little light on what happened to David. "Satan rose up against Israel and incited David to take a census of Israel" (1 Chron. 21:1).

So who did it? Who enticed David to sin—God or Satan? As we confront something we do not know, consider what we do know. How could the following Scriptures shed light on our understanding of 2 Samuel 24:1 and 1 Chronicles 21:1?

> *When tempted, no one should say, "God is tempting me." For God cannot be tempted by evil, nor does he tempt anyone; but each one is tempted when, by his own evil desire, he is dragged away and enticed.* (James 1:13–14)

> *No temptation has seized you except what is common to man. And God is faithful; he will not let you be tempted beyond what you can bear. But when you are tempted, he will also provide a way out so that you can stand up under it.* (1 Cor. 10:13)

From these two passages we know that God does not tempt us. He may allow us to be tempted to test, prove, or help us to grow; but He is definitely not the tempter. In our temptation He always makes a way of escape.

How do we explain the activity of God in David's sin? His role must have been somewhat like His part in the suffering of Job. Satan insisted that Job was only obedient to God for the rewards God provided. In response, God gave Satan permission to test Job.

God did not tempt Job. In the same way we can be assured that God did not tempt David to sin and then judge him harshly for it. God has no sin, therefore He is incapable of enticing one to sin. He did, however, allow David to be tempted because He saw something in David's heart that needed to be exposed. The *Disciple's Study Bible* suggests that God allowed Satan to tempt David by giving him the idea of a military census, which Joab knew was contrary to faith in God.[21] In light of 1 Corinthians 10:13, Joab's plea was David's "way out."

Now consider the second issue that Satan, as the author of confusion and doubt, may use: the punishment seemed to exceed the crime. If we are not careful to study the text, seventy thousand men seemed to die solely as a result of David's sin. Although David's actions no doubt displeased God and caused judgment, 2 Samuel 24:1 clearly states that the anger of the Lord burned against Israel. Let's apply our method once again. What is the first thing we do not know? We do not know why God's anger burned against Israel. What can we know in order to shed light on Israel's action that angered God?

Based on Deuteronomy, we can conclude that Israel's sin against God angered Him. Deuteronomy 28:1–24 contains the promises of blessing and cursing. In general, God promised blessing for obedience and cursing for disobedience.

We don't know what Israel had done to make God so angry, but we do know that His judgment was consistent with that which He had promised for rebellion against His commands. Somehow Israel had severely disobeyed God. Several scholars suggest God may have been judging Israel for their quickness to desert David, God's sovereign choice, and follow Absalom.

Why, then, was David also wrong? I'd like to suggest three possible reasons David was involved in the anger of God toward Israel.

1. *He deserted the throne God had given him and did not trust God to fight his battles for him.* Earlier, David had trusted God to direct his battles and to fight them for him. This time David ignored God and depended on human resources and wisdom.

2. *He did not stand in the gap and intercede for the sins of his nation.* In Exodus 32–33, God revoked a portion of His judgment on Israel as a direct result of the humility and intercession of Moses. David saw the evil ways of his nation and did not intercede or take any responsibility. David finally arrived at a place to cry out on behalf of the people, but not until the angel threatened his own area.

3. He possessed wrong motives for taking the census. David fell to the temptation of counting his fighting men either out of the sin of pride, distrust, or both. Anyway, as king of Israel, David's heart was wrong toward God. God had proved Himself many times in the life of this king. David had no grounds for pride or distrust.

Based on 2 Samuel 24 and 1 Chronicles 21, David and the people of Israel shared the responsibility for the judgment handed down to them. In the heart of this difficult account of anger and judgment is something vital you must not miss—God's mercy.

> When the angel stretched out his hand to destroy Jerusalem, the LORD was grieved because of the calamity and said to the angel who was afflicting the people, "Enough! Withdraw your hand." The angel of the LORD was then at the threshing floor of Araunah the Jebusite. (2 Sam. 24:16)

God grieved when the angel stretched out his hand to destroy Jerusalem. At the time, the angel was standing at the threshing floor of Araunah the Jebusite. We will see the special significance of this threshing floor and the mercy God poured out at this place.

The prophet Gad told David to build an altar at the site of Araunah's threshing floor. According to 1 Chronicles 21:27–22:1, something else was to happen at the site of the threshing floor. David said, "The house of the LORD God is to be here, and also the altar of burnt offering for Israel" (1 Chron. 22:1).

The exact location of the threshing floor of Araunah the Jebusite was the most vital place in Israel's history. Scripture says God grieved when the angel reached the threshing floor of Araunah the Jebusite and stretched out his hand to destroy Jerusalem. The Hebrew word for "grieve" in this passage is *nacham*. *Nacham* carries the idea of breathing deeply as "a physical display of one's feeling, usually sorrow, compassion, or comfort."[22] The word was used once before in 2 Samuel 12:24, where it meant "being consoled over the death of an infant child."[23]

When the angel of the Lord stretched out his hand at the threshing floor of Araunah the Jebusite, God seemed to cry. He "panted" in grief somewhat like one "being consoled over the death of an infant child." I want to suggest that the primary reason God grieved as if over the death of a child at that exact location was related to an event that took place on that very soil many years before. In Genesis 22, Abraham obeyed God and almost sacrificed his son Isaac—in this very spot.

God did not coincidentally grieve at this exact spot generations later during David's reign, then coincidentally direct an altar, and ultimately the temple of God, to be built there as well. Each occurrence was based on the vivid lesson God taught about substitutionary death at the same location. Look at the similarities!

The altar. God commanded that an altar for sacrifice be built by both Abraham and David—and ultimately by Solomon—on the same spot. Something at that location obviously represented sacrifice and substitution.

The timing. Genesis 22:10–12 tells us that when Abraham reached out his hand and took the knife to slay his son, God intervened and stopped him. God then presented a sacrifice in his place. Consider the timing during David's reign: 1 Chronicles 21:16 tells us "David looked up and saw the angel of the LORD standing between heaven and earth, with a drawn sword in his hand extended over Jerusalem." Of the same event, 2 Samuel 24:16 says, "When the angel stretched out his hand to destroy Jerusalem, the LORD was grieved because of the calamity and said to the angel who was afflicting the people, 'Enough! Withdraw your hand.' The angel of the LORD was then at the threshing floor of Araunah the Jebusite." In both cases, the moment God saw a sword raised to destroy life at this location, He intervened and accepted substitutionary sacrifices. That both of these events happened at the same place and at the moment a sword was being drawn is no accident.

When the angel of the Lord drew his sword at the threshing floor of Araunah the Jebusite, I believe God remembered a father who was willing in obedience to take the life of his dearly loved son. I believe God not only cried over the memory of Abraham and Isaac, but over the gospel they foretold—"For God so loved the world, that he gave his only begotten Son, that whosoever believeth in him should not perish, but have everlasting life" (John 3:16, KJV).

The day that Abraham offered Isaac portrayed the Cross as the ultimate altar of sacrifice and the substitutionary death of the unblemished Lamb as the perfect sacrifice. Many years later, during David's reign, God saw the angel raise his sword over the lives of His people at that same location, and He grieved and said "Enough!" Why? Because when God saw the threshing floor at Mount Moriah, He saw mercy—mercy that would finally be complete on Calvary when God would look on the suffering of His Son and be satisfied (Isa. 53:11). The legacy of sacrifice on Mount Moriah would continue from Abraham to David to Solomon because access to God is forever based on sacrifice and mercy.

As we conclude, we must meditate for a moment on David's words as Araunah offered him the threshing floor free of charge. He said, "I will not sacrifice to the LORD my God burnt offerings that cost me nothing" (2 Sam. 24:24). Mount Moriah did not represent a cheap offering. The sacrifice depicted on that mountain throughout the ages was costly. Abraham's sacrifice cost him dearly. God's sacrifice cost Him severely. The chastened king's sacrifice was costly as well. At the threshing floor of Araunah, the cost of sacrifice was counted—and God wept.

When faced in Scripture with something you don't understand and when God seems cruel, never forget how God identifies Himself. "Then the LORD came down in the cloud and stood there with him and proclaimed his name, the LORD. And he passed in front of Moses, proclaiming, 'The LORD, the LORD, the compassionate and gracious God, slow to anger, abounding in love and faithfulness'" (Exod. 34:5–6).

When you don't know why, a personal history with God will tell you who.

Chapter 49

A New King

1 Kings 1

When King David was old and well advanced in years, he could not keep
warm even when they put covers over him. (1 Kings 1:1)

We now come to the final years of David's life. Our protagonist was old and frail. God made the life of David literally an open book—one that teaches until the very last page. David had mounds of work to do before he could rest. A new king had to be prepared and presented before the people of Israel. Preparations for the temple needed to be made. David often neglected his parental duties, but we will discover him rising to the occasion as father and counselor to the new king.

God graced us with the accounts of David's final years in the beginning of 1 Kings and the ending of 1 Chronicles. We do not know the exact order of events because the books record different activities without an explanation of their joint order. Therefore, we will concentrate on the events and subjects addressed rather than the exact chronological order.

I am saddened by the initial words of 1 Kings: "When King David was old and well advanced in years . . ." The words suggest the inevitable to us. One of the most well-documented lives in history was hastening to an end. Perhaps more difficult to consider are the words that followed: "He could not keep warm even when they put covers over him." Our

David? The one who had killed a lion and a bear? The one who had thundered the ground with the frame of an overgrown Philistine? The one who had made caves his bed and had stolen the spear of a savage king? The one who had conquered nations and called on the might of heaven? I am almost shocked by his sudden mortality. As he lay chilled beneath the weight of heavy blankets, we realize his humanity and his frailty.

By the standards of his day, David was not an extremely old man. He was approaching his death at a far younger age than the patriarchs who preceded him. Perhaps his seventy years of active living could easily compare to one hundred years of simply being alive. He had known virtually every extremity of the human experience—unparalleled success, unabashed rebellion, unashamed mourning, and uninhibited celebration. Life rarely free of extremity can be life rarely free of anxiety. It takes its toll.

Sometimes I feel much of my life has been lived in the extremes. I seem to find myself in the valley or on the mountain as often as in between. At times I've even felt that I was experiencing both! My earthly circumstances would be in the valley while my awareness of God would take me to the mountain. Some years ago God led me to express on paper my responses to the extremities of life. I'd like to share these words with you.

> *Satisfy me not with the lesser of You*
> *Find me no solace in shadows of the True*
> *No ordinary measure of extraordinary means*
> *The depth, the length, the breadth of You*
> *And nothing in between.*
> *Etch these words upon my heart, knowing all the while*
> *No ordinary roadblocks plague extraordinary miles*
> *Your power as my portion, Your glory as my fare*
> *Take me to extremities,*
> *But meet me fully there.*

David lived most of his life in the extremes, but he met God at every venture. I want my life to be like his. I don't want to make the mistakes he made, but I want to meet God at every high, every low, and every stop in between.

David's roller-coaster ride was nearing an end. The psalms prove he had discovered God at every curve. His tumultuous journey left him weak and chilled. The fourth son of David took quick advantage of his father's failing health and followed in the footsteps of his deceased half-brother Absalom.

Adonijah declared himself king. He was the oldest surviving son. Joab and Abiathar the priest threw their support to Adonijah. That he would become the next king seemed a foregone conclusion, but he did not count on Bathsheba warning David about his plan.

After a long absence from Scripture, the prophet Nathan reentered the scene. He joined Bathsheba in the plan to inform David and to put Solomon on the throne. I am touched by his support of David and the union with Bathsheba after acknowledgment of their grave sin. Nathan was the prophet God used to confront the sin between David and Bathsheba. He was also the one who warned Bathsheba about Adonijah's plans, which probably would have resulted in death for her and Solomon. Nathan showed himself to be a true prophet of God. He could both confront sin and lovingly care for sinners.

> Then Nathan asked Bathsheba, Solomon's mother, "Have you not heard that Adonijah, the son of Haggith, has become king without our lord David's knowing it? Now then, let me advise you how you can save your own life and the life of your son Solomon." (1 Kings. 1:11–12)

Nathan knew Bathsheba was the key to restoring decision-making strength to the king. He sent her to inform David. Then he confirmed her words to the king.

Bathsheba bowed low and knelt before the king.

"What is it you want?" the king asked.

She said to him, "My lord, you yourself swore to me your servant
by the LORD your God: 'Solomon your son shall be king after me,
and he will sit on my throne.' But now Adonijah has become
king, and you, my lord the king, do not know about it."
(1 Kings 1:16–18)

Bathsheba captured David's full attention with the threat to Solomon's succession. Then Nathan confirmed Bathsheba's claims. Apparently, Bathsheba stepped out of the room so Nathan could have full access to the king. Then David confirmed his promise to Bathsheba that Solomon was to be his successor.

David could easily have issued the orders without Bathsheba being present, but he summoned his queen so that he could make an oath to her. The words were addressed directly to Bathsheba, intimating to us that this was a matter not only between king and queen but also between husband and wife—father and mother.

The king then took an oath: "As surely as the LORD lives, who
has delivered me out of every trouble, I will surely carry out today
what I swore to you by the LORD, the God of Israel: Solomon
your son shall be king after me, and he will sit on my throne in
my place." (1 Kings 1:29–30)

I wonder if Bathsheba was a sight for David's tired eyes. To the exclusion of all good judgment, she had captivated his attention on a moonlit roof many years before. Now after the passage of decades, I imagine he found her beautiful once more.

Need has a way of breathing fresh life into a soul, if just for a moment. We will see David, who seemed chilled with the onset of death, assume swift control, perform the will of God, and meet the desires of his queen's heart. Whether on his sickbed or on his throne, David was indeed still king.

David's brief refreshment reminds me of someone very dear to me. My family watched helplessly as our mother approached the age of seventy with rapidly failing health. I watched her pace slow dramatically. I resented the various senior adult publications around her house and despised the pain that continued to increase in her body. Then my older sister announced that she was expecting a baby. Mother, the eternal optimist, responded with firm resolve: "Well, I may as well forget getting old. We've got a baby coming. I've got work to do." And work, she did. Eight months later a beautiful red-headed baby boy named Joshua came into our lives. My mother, who just months before was aging rapidly, kept him virtually every weekday of his young life. She didn't just keep him; she rocked him, sang to him, kissed his plump little cheeks, read to him, took pictures of him, called his mom with every new accomplishment, kept a journal about him, and added continually to his adorable vocabulary.

I called my mother right after Joshua's first birthday and almost cried as I said, "Thank you, Mother, for giving him the sweetest gift in all the world—an enormous amount of time and attention." My mother responded with a broken voice, "Are you kidding? He practically brought me back to life."

Mom went to be with Jesus last summer after a long battle with cancer. Joshua is still a young boy now, but I know one thing for sure: We'll see her in him for the rest of his life. All because she was needed once again.

That's what Bathsheba did for David. She called on him for something only he could do, and the need breathed enough life into his soul to finish the task. We will see David live no longer than his last few responsibilities lasted. We will allow his final contributions to God's chosen nation to capture our attentions for the remainder of our journey.

David rose from his bed and formulated a plan to place Solomon on the throne.

> *King David said, "Call in Zadok the priest, Nathan the prophet and Benaiah son of Jehoiada." When they came before the king, he said to them: "Take your lord's servants with you and set Solomon my son on my own mule and take him down to Gihon. There have Zadok the priest and Nathan the prophet anoint him king over Israel. Blow the trumpet and shout, 'Long live King Solomon!' Then you are to go up with him, and he is to come and sit on my throne and reign in my place. I have appointed him ruler over Israel and Judah."* (1 Kings. 1:32–35)

David purposely called three specific men to escort Solomon to his rightful place of authority. Nathan was the primary prophet of the day. Zadok was the priest, and Benaiah was a mighty warrior. For the nation to be strong, all four areas of authority needed to be present: prophet, priest, warrior, and king. Interestingly, our Lord and Savior Jesus Christ will ultimately fill every one of those positions. All authority has been given to Christ (Matt. 28:18)! Under one Head, all nations will finally be unified.

David sent his most trustworthy warrior and his army to protect Solomon. They were to put Solomon on King David's mule and escort him. Customarily, a king rode on a mule to signify his intent to be a servant to the people. The mule was often dressed with a wreath of flowers around its neck or a royal drape over its back.

Solomon surely knew he would one day be king. He knew the time would come, but I wonder if he knew what it would be like. Did a servant girl tell him three VIPs were at the door to speak to him? Or did he hear the bray of the mule? We simply read that Zadok, Nathan, Benaiah, the Kerethites, and the Pelethites went down and put Solomon on King David's mule. Picture the scene as Solomon took the ride of his life!

David specifically commanded the men to escort Solomon to Gihon. Two springs provided Jerusalem's water supply: the En Rogel spring and the Gihon spring. According to 1 Kings 1:9, Adonijah was staging his own coronation at En Rogel.

The Gihon spring was directly east of the city wall. The ancient Hebrew people believed God's glory and authority would come from the east. The Gihon spring did not provide a steady flow, but gushed "out at irregular intervals, twice a day in the dry season to four or five times in the rainy season. Water issues from a crack sixteen feet long in the rock."[24] Even the name was significant. The name *Gihon* comes from a Hebrew word that means "a bursting forth."[25] A new king was bursting on the scene to supply the nation of Israel with security and authority.

Zadok the priest took the horn of oil from the sacred tent and anointed Solomon. Could this have been the same horn tipped by the hand of Samuel over the head of a young shepherd boy? What other horn would have had a place in the sacred tent?

Solomon is not described like Absalom and Adonijah, handsome and obvious choices for a would-be king. God told Samuel, "The LORD does not look at the things man looks at. Man looks at the outward appearance, but the LORD looks at the heart" (1 Sam. 16:7). Solomon may not have been the natural choice in the eyes of men; he was not the oldest of the sons of David. Solomon represented God's divine mercy. He was the embodiment of second chances. He was the innocence that came from guilt. He was God's choice, as history would prove.

I find enormous security in the consistency of God. He is always merciful. Christ Jesus would never have become flesh to dwell among us had it not been for man's scandalous sin. Jesus certainly did not display the image of the king that Israel was expecting, yet He was the embodiment of second chances. He took our guilt on His innocent shoulders and became sin for us so we could become the righteousness of God in Him (2 Cor. 5:21). Why? Because we were God's choice.

> *Then they sounded the trumpet and all the people shouted, "Long live King Solomon!" And all the people went up after him, playing flutes and rejoicing greatly, so that the ground shook with the sound.* (1 Kings 1:39–40)

When David received the news from his royal officials, "the king bowed in worship on his bed and said, 'Praise be to the LORD'" (vv. 47–48).

This verse records the last time God used the word *king* in the Book of 1 Kings in reference to His beloved David. God chose to pen this last reference to King David in a sentence eternally linked to two responses:

1. *Worship.* Too weak to move to the floor, David fell on his face right where he was.

2. *Praise.* "Praise be to the LORD, the God of Israel, who has allowed my eyes to see a successor on my throne today" (v. 48).

David's rule ended just as it officially began. His stiffened body bowed before God on his final day as king, with the same abandon he demonstrated when he danced through the streets of Jerusalem. Was it not he who said, "Bless the LORD, O my soul: and all that is within me, bless his holy name" (Ps. 103:1, KJV).

With all that was within him, he once danced. On that last day as king, he bowed to worship. David's actions were often contradictory, but one consistency he wove throughout his life and reign—he was a man of worship, a man after God's own heart.

I'm thankful David enjoyed a brief reprieve from his sickbed. I was not ready to part with him yet. Were you? Deep within the aging king we can still see glimpses of a heart after God's own. May God deal tenderly with us as we approach our journey's end.

Chapter 50

WHOLEHEARTED DEVOTION

1 Chronicles 28

My son Solomon, acknowledge the God of your father, and serve him with wholehearted devotion and with a willing mind, for the Lord searches every heart and understands every motive behind the thoughts. (1 Chron. 28:9)

Historians generally agree that David lived somewhere between one to two years after Solomon assumed his reign. God allowed David the strength to prepare the new king for public coronation and for an effective beginning.

The first order of business for the new king was the building of a house for the "Name of the LORD" (1 Chron. 22:7). Before he died, the old king gathered the materials and drafted the plans for the work. Whether David made these preparations shortly before or shortly after Solomon's anointing is not clear, based on a comparison of 1 Kings and 1 Chronicles.

The Book of 1 Chronicles records the vivid account of the extensive preparations David made before his death (1 Chron. 22:5). In 1 Chronicles 22:14–16, David shared with Solomon all that had been gathered for the building of the sanctuary and all who had been commissioned to help. I find his words so pertinent and applicable to us today: "Now begin the work, and the LORD be with you" (v. 16). In other words, "I've set aside everything you will need. You have all the materials and all the support your task will require. Now get started." When I was a little girl, I often remember my mother giving her children various instructions that were often received with moans, complaints, and questions. She'd finally say, "I've already told you. Now, get busy." Her words, like David's, were wise and practical. God provides what we need. Now we, like Solomon, need to get busy.

God promised His plans are to prosper us, to give us hope and a future (Jer. 29:11). The Word of God and Christ's indwelling Spirit equip us to fulfill the works preordained for us in God's perfect plan. As my mom would say, "Get busy!"

Some of the most important words ever formed on David's tongue appear in 1 Chronicles 22:19: "Now devote your heart and soul to seeking the LORD your God." The Hebrew word for *devote* is *nathan*. It means "to give, place, add, send forth. *Nathan* indicates . . . fastening something in place."[26] I especially love the idea this wonderful definition expresses in the word *fastening*. David told Solomon and the leaders of Israel to fasten their hearts to seeking the Lord.

David's choice of words challenges us too. To what is your heart fastened? To what is your heart most attached?

In the Book of Matthew, Christ simplified the process of finding our hearts and their attachments. He said, "For where your treasure is, there your heart will be also" (Matt. 6:21). Our hearts are attached to our treasure. So the question becomes, What is our treasure? Little awakens us to a realization of what we've treasured like turmoil and suffering. We find out quickly what our priorities have been.

The aged David had learned a few things about priorities. He knew what he was talking about when he told the leaders of Israel to devote their hearts and souls to seeking the Lord. I don't believe David was only looking out for the nation of Israel. He was also looking out for his son. One of my most heartfelt pleas before the throne of grace is this: *Please surround my children with positive influences. Raise up godly friends for my children!* David knew that little would influence Solomon's success more than being surrounded by leaders whose hearts were devoted to seeking the Lord.

First Chronicles 23–27 document the organization of Solomon's kingdom under the commands of David. These five chapters bridge David's two proclamations and chronicle the appointment of the Levites and priests to serve God in the temple, the singers to lead His praises, and the army to protect the people.

First Chronicles 23:5 tells us David appointed four thousand people to praise the Lord with musical instruments. Can you imagine an orchestra of four thousand? God Himself gave David the words:

> *Praise him with the sounding of the trumpet,*
> *praise him with the harp and lyre,*
> *praise him with tambourine and dancing,*
> *praise him with the strings and flute,*
> *praise him with the clash of cymbals,*
> *praise him with resounding cymbals.*
> *Let everything that has breath praise the LORD.* (Ps. 150:3–6)

> *Four thousand are to praise the LORD with the musical instruments I have provided for that purpose.* (1 Chron. 23:5)

Chapter 28 rings with strong statements from David. He reminded Solomon that God had chosen both him and his task: "Solomon your son is the one who will build my house and my courts, for I have chosen him" (1 Chron. 28:6). He summed up his godly, fatherly advice:

> *You, my son Solomon, acknowledge the God of your father, and serve him with wholehearted devotion and with a willing mind,*

*for the LORD searches every heart and understands every motive
behind the thoughts.* (1 Chron. 28:9)

David's words to Solomon apply to us in every area of potential success. David gave his son three vital directives we would be wise to obey:

1. *Acknowledge God.* Acknowledging God first thing every morning transforms my day. I often begin my day by reconfirming His authority over me and submitting to Him as Lord in advance of my daily circumstances. I try to accept the words of Joshua 24:15 as a personal daily challenge: "Choose for yourselves this day whom you will serve." When I fail to begin my day by settling the matter of authority, I am often in a mess by noon! Remember, any day not surrendered to the Spirit of God will likely be lived in the flesh (Gal. 5:16–17). Spiritual living does not come naturally—sin does. The first step to victory is acknowledging the authority of God in our lives.

2. *Serve Him with wholehearted devotion.* The Hebrew word for "wholehearted" is *shalem* and means "unhewn, untouched stones." In the Old Testament *shalem* often referred to rocks that were uncut.[27] Notice something quite interesting about the temple God commanded Solomon to build. First Kings 6:7 tells us, "In building the temple, only blocks dressed at the quarry were used, and no hammer, chisel or any other iron tool was heard at the temple site while it was being built." Do you see the significance? No stone could be cut in the temple. The uncut stones represented the kind of devotion God was demanding from His nation—*Shalem,* wholehearted devotion, uncut hearts. David was used of God to describe *shalem* perfectly in Psalm 86:11: "Teach me your way, O LORD, / and I will walk in your truth; / give me an undivided heart, / that I may fear your name."

Do you have a divided heart? Or does God have a piece of your heart, but the rest belongs to you? Or someone else? If you've given your heart wholly to God, perhaps you remember a time when your heart was divided. A divided heart places our entire lives in jeopardy. Only God can be totally trusted with our hearts. He doesn't demand our complete devotion to feed His ego, but to provide for our safety. God uses an undivided heart to keep us out of trouble. David learned the price of a divided heart the hard way. He lived with the repercussions for the rest of his life. Let's just take his word for it and surrender now! Never forget, God's commands are for our good.

3. *Serve Him with a willing spirit.* The Hebrew word for "willing" in this reference is *chaphets,* which means "to find pleasure in, take delight in, be pleased with, have an affection for; to desire; to choose; to bend, bow. The main meaning is to feel a strong, positive attraction for something, to like someone or something very much."[28] Do you see what God is saying? He wants us to serve Him and honor Him because we want to! Because it pleases us! Because we choose to! You see, the Lord searches every heart and understands every motive behind the thoughts! Hear the beat of His tender heart as He says, "Choose me because you delight in me!"

Many motives exist for serving God other than pleasure and delight. God wants us to serve Him with a willing spirit, one that would choose no other way. Right now you may be frustrated because serving and knowing God is not your greatest pleasure. You may be able to instantly acknowledge a divided heart. Your question may be, How can I change the way I feel? You can't. But God can. Give Him your heart—your whole heart. Give Him permission to change it. The words of Deuteronomy 30:6 have changed my life and my heart.

> The LORD your God will circumcise your hearts and the hearts of
> your descendants, so that you may love him with all your heart
> and with all your soul, and live. (Deut. 30:6)

I pray daily that God will circumcise my heart to love Him. I know we will never be men and women after God's own heart with halfhearted devotion. A heart wholly devoted to God is a heart like His.

We started this journey with a pair of underlying questions: Why was David a man after God's own heart? And how can I be a man or woman after God's own heart?

Any old heart will do. Any whole heart will do.

PART IX

FINAL YEARS
AND SETTLED FEARS

Psalm 30

For the dedication of the temple. Of David.

1 *I will exalt you, O LORD,*
   for you lifted me out of the depths
   and did not let my enemies gloat over me.
2 *O LORD my God, I called to you for help*
   and you healed me.
3 *O LORD, you brought me up from the grave;*
   you spared me from going down into the pit.

4 *Sing to the LORD, you saints of his;*
   praise his holy name.
5 *For his anger lasts only a moment,*
   but his favor lasts a lifetime;
   weeping may remain for a night,
   but rejoicing comes in the morning.

6 *When I felt secure, I said,*
   "I will never be shaken."
7 *O LORD, when you favored me,*
   you made my mountain stand firm;
   but when you hid your face,
   I was dismayed.

8 *To you, O LORD, I called;*

   to the Lord I cried for mercy:

9 *"What gain is there in my destruction,*

   in my going down into the pit?

   Will the dust praise you?

   Will it proclaim your faithfulness?

10 *Hear, O LORD, and be merciful to me;*

   O LORD, be my help."

11 *You turned my wailing into dancing;*

   you removed my sackcloth and clothed me with joy,

12 *that my heart may sing to you and not be silent.*

   O LORD my God, I will give you thanks forever.

Chapter 51

PRAISES OF THE GREAT ASSEMBLY

1 Chronicles 29:1–24

Yours, O Lord, is the greatness and the power
and the glory and the majesty and the splendor, for everything in
heaven and earth is yours." (1 Chron. 29:11)

We can only imagine the emotions that flooded David's heart as he addressed the assembly for the last time. In the first verse of 1 Chronicles 29, he reminded the people, "My son Solomon, the one whom God has chosen, is young and inexperienced." David was looking at a young man bursting with energy, full of plans, rehearsing promises—a young man childishly confident he would never do certain things and would always do others.

Solomon lacked nothing but age and experience—a lack that probably scared his father half to death. Looking at a son full of dreams, David dared not say, "This will be the most difficult thing you have ever done." He could not explain how lonely Solomon would be at the top, the exhaustion of too much responsibility, the temptation of too much power, the loneliness of too few friends. Chances were good that Solomon would not have understood David anyway. He had too many stars in his eyes and accolades in his ears.

So David looked at the whole assembly and basically said, "Give him a hand. He's going to need it." David began with a challenge concerning the temple. He gave testimony of his sacrificial gift to build the temple. The people followed his example and gave willingly. Two results came from the situation. In what I consider the lesser result, materials were provided for the temple. In the greater result, the people experienced a great outpouring of worship.

Never underestimate the power of a positive example! David could not have motivated the leaders of Israel to give freely and wholeheartedly to the Lord unless he had given. He could have forced them, but the willing spirit God so deeply desired would have been forfeited. David knew their cheerful giving would be motivated by his own; therefore, he had to give more than what belonged to the kingdom. The third verse clearly tells us, "I now give my personal treasures of gold and silver for the temple of my God, over and above everything I have provided for this holy temple."

David gave what was his. What belonged to him. That which was personal. The people overwhelmingly responded. Do you give that which is personal? Does your monetary giving come from your heart, not just your checkbook? Does the giving of your time flow from rejoicing, not resentment? God delights in the giving of your personal treasures—and others are motivated by your example! I love the way the ninth verse captures the electricity of the moment: "The people rejoiced at the willing response of their leaders, for they had given freely and wholeheartedly to the Lord. David the king also rejoiced greatly." What a glorious moment! I can't think of much that spurs the hearts of the people of God like the wholehearted devotion of their leaders. When leadership is sold out to God, the followers become willing to sell out too.

As always, when God's people have right hearts, and God acts, God's people respond with praise.

David praised the LORD in the presence of the whole assembly,
saying,

"Praise be to you, O LORD,
  God of our father Israel,
  from everlasting to everlasting.
Yours, O LORD, is the greatness and the power
  and the glory and the majesty and the splendor,
  for everything in heaven and earth is yours.
Yours, O LORD, is the kingdom;
  you are exalted as head over all.
Wealth and honor come from you;
  you are the ruler of all things.
In your hands are strength and power
  to exalt and give strength to all.
Now, our God, we give you thanks,
  and praise your glorious name." (1 Chron. 29:10–13)

David had a heart to praise God. In the field with his father's sheep, he had praised God. Now, a lifetime later, he still had a heart to praise God.

Then David said to the whole assembly, "Praise the LORD your
God." So they all praised the LORD, the God of their fathers; they
bowed low and fell prostrate before the LORD and the king.
(1 Chron. 29:20)

Passionate hearts and genuine praises are invariably contagious. David's overflow caused a tidal wave of praise. When David called the whole assembly to praise the Lord their God, "they bowed low and fell prostrate before the LORD and the king" (1 Chron. 29:20). Scripture records many instances in which the Hebrew people wandered from

God and rebelled against His perfect plan. Joyfully, the Word of God also records refreshing instances in which they rightly responded to the awesomeness of God. This wonderful chapter chronicles one of those precious moments—a contagion of praise! David and his people were overwhelmed with the privilege of giving: "But who am I, and who are my people, that we should be able to give as generously as this?" (v. 14). The enormity of what they had been able to give represented the enormity of what they had been given. And they fell on their faces.

Surely time stood still in David's mind as the people fell prostrate before the Lord and before the king. Close your eyes for a moment and picture the scene. Keep the picture like a snapshot in your memory. We've waited through more than fifty years of David's life to witness an entire kingdom in unity before God! As we compare verses 9 and 20, we know that David was the one to whom Scripture referred as king. All the people fell before the Lord and His beloved David, God's first choice, a man after His own heart. So there David stood, a man of many years and experiences. His legs trembled with illness and age. His heart blazed with emotion. The streets of the city of God were paved with praises, blanketed with the prostrate bodies of all who called Jehovah their God.

May we never forget the awesome benefits of authentic praise. God desires our praises for many reasons, but I believe among the most vital are these two.

1. *Praise reminds us who He is.* When I am overwhelmed and wonder if God can see me through, He often calls on me to rehearse out loud—before His ears and mine—some of His many virtues:

- His wonders in the lives of those recorded in the Word
- His wonders in my own life
- His wonders in the lives of those I know

I proclaim out loud His greatness and His power and His glory. Then when I consider my need compared to His strength and bounty, I can proclaim with confidence the words of the prophet Jeremiah: "Ah, Sovereign LORD, you have made the heavens and the earth by your great power and outstretched arm. Nothing is too hard for you" (Jer. 32:17).

2. *Praise reminds us who we are.* Praise is an exercise in perspective. Notice David's words in verse 14 of 1 Chronicles 29, "But who am I?" Authentic praise works every time! Things seem to fall right into perspective. I don't believe you can truly praise and worship without ending up with a humbled heart.

Perspective invariably accompanies praise. Hearts prone to praise will keep perspective on the timeless might and power of God. Without an active praise life, our perspective of God gets turned upside down. We become like the people described in Isaiah 29:16:

> *You turn things upside down,*
> *as if the potter were thought to be like the clay!*
> *Shall what is formed say to him who formed it,*
> *"He did not make me"?*
> *Can the pot say of the potter,*
> *"He knows nothing"?* (Isa. 29:16)

A heart far from God tends to think it's in charge, demanding its own way. A faraway heart has lost its perspective. Worst of all, a faraway heart can never be a heart like His, the kind of heart God searches for to show Himself strong (2 Chron. 16:9, KJV)!

Long after we have closed the last page of this study, I pray we will continue to keep our hearts in check. Surely David's life has taught us to watch over our hearts "with all diligence" (Prov. 4:23, NASB).

In light of all we've learned together, I hope you see the extreme importance of watching over your heart and giving it wholly to the One who created you. If so, I encourage you to pray a prayer of commitment, naming specific ways you will commit to keeping your heart in check.

Have courage in your prayer. Ask God to uncover every impurity in your heart as it first develops! Remember, a little discomfort and humiliation in the privacy of your relationship with God is far better than the ultimate exposure of a heart out of control.

Chapter 52

A RESTING PLACE

1 Chronicles 29:25–30

David son of Jesse was king over all Israel. He ruled over Israel forty years—
seven in Hebron and thirty-three in Jerusalem. He died at a good old age,
having enjoyed long life, wealth and honor. His son Solomon succeeded
him as king. (1 Chron. 29:26–28)

How will I ever express to you my gratitude for your desire and discipline to see this lengthy journey through to completion? I approach you with deep emotion, praying the truths we've acquired through these chapters have been sewn into our spirits forever. May the very mention of the psalmist's name spark familiar thoughts and draw portraits in our minds for the rest of our lives. May we remember the heights of his praise and the depths of his sin and be moved appropriately by each.

David has been a worthy subject for study. In the final words of 1 Chronicles: "As for the events of King David's reign, from beginning to end, they are written in the records of Samuel the seer, the records of Nathan the prophet and the records of Gad the seer, together with the details of his reign and power, and the circumstances that surrounded him and Israel and the kingdoms of all the other lands."

Indeed, our God gave no insignificant space to the chronicles of David's life. He was the object of much love and continues to be the object of much learning. May our final look at David be no exception.

In Psalm 69:16, David wrote: "Answer me, O LORD, out of the goodness of your love." As his life came to its end, we see how God graciously answered. In Psalm 51, David begged forgiveness. Solomon was the tangible evidence of David's pardon, for of him Scripture says, "The LORD loved him" (2 Sam. 12:24). Just as the contrite father had asked, the Word says of Solomon, "He prospered and all Israel obeyed him" (1 Chron. 29:23). And, "All the officers and mighty men, as well as all of King David's sons, pledged their submission to King Solomon" (v. 24).

The unrelenting sword was finally at rest. David's house was in order. God had given a weary man strength and helped him prepare a family and a nation for life in his absence. Surely as he bowed on his sickbed, David had prayed the words of Psalm 71:9: "Do not cast me away when I am old; / do not forsake me when my strength is gone."

God did not cast David away. God did not forsake him when he was old. The God whose faithfulness endures to all generations completed the good work He started in a shepherd. Now the work was finally finished. The empty grave pleaded to be filled, the warrior to cease fighting. His thoughts must have been like those of the writer of Psalm 102: "For my days vanish like smoke; / my bones burn like glowing embers. / My heart is blighted and withered like grass; I forget to eat my food. / Because of my loud groaning / I am reduced to skin and bones" (vv. 3–5).

David had no reason to resist death's call. He had lived the length of his days. His throne was filled. It was fitting that his grave be filled as well. He had turned over his crown and joyfully dedicated his personal riches to the building of the temple. He was too old to conquer kingdoms, too sick to fill a sling, too frail to feast on the fatted calf. But that which he treasured most was never so dear to him and never so real. Scholars generally agree that the words of Psalm 71 were written in David's old age as he confronted his hastening death. In verse 14 he wrote, "But as for me, I will always have hope; / I will praise you more and more." David proclaimed a specific hope as the cords of death encompassed him:

> *Though you have made me see troubles, many and bitter,*
> *you will restore my life again;*
> *from the depths of the earth*
> *you will again bring me up.* (Ps. 71:20)

He had hope of the blessed resurrection, just as we do! Not just an empty wish, but an anxious and certain expectation! From his proclamation of hope came Psalm 71:22: "I will praise you with the harp / for your faithfulness, O my God."

I picture the aged king praising God. Once more his fingers wrapped around the strings of his harp, his hands no longer the calloused young hands of a hardy shepherd boy. Bent with age, slowed with time, David's fingers brushed across the strings. His voice, once wavering with adolescence, now wavered with age.

No sweeter voice could be heard than the one that flowed, however unevenly, from the sincere heart of the aged. No longer did David's voice resound with the richness that had once awed a tormented Saul. Resigned to the will of the Father, in perfect harmony with God's plan for his life, he sang a final song of hope. The One who would take him to the depths of the earth would bring him up. So he departed this life with two magnificent treasures: peace with his family and hope in his resurrection.

"Then David rested with his fathers and was buried in the City of David" (1 Kings 2:10). The eyes that had peeked into the heart of God now closed in death. The earthly life of one of the most passionate and controversial figures ever to grace this planet ended. The deadly silence must have lasted only long enough for Bathsheba to place her ear close to his mouth and her hand on his heart. The faint rise and fall of his chest had ceased.

No doubt the silence gave way to wails of grief. Trumpets carried the news. A kind of mourning peculiar to the Hebrew nation filled the days that followed. The very instruments commissioned by David for the dedication of the temple ironically may have first played his funeral dirge. Multitudes heaped ashes on their heads and draped sackcloth on their bodies. After an intense period of national mourning with visits from foreign dignitaries, life continued—just as it has the audacity to do after we've lost a loved one.

Life went on, but forever marked by the life of God's chosen king. God sovereignly chose to chisel David's reign into a kingdom that would last forever.

As we close our study, carefully read the words of Jeremiah and Luke. How certain is the covenant God made with David?

> "'The days are coming,' declares the LORD, 'when I will fulfill the gracious promise I made to the house of Israel and to the house of Judah.
>
> "'In those days and at that time
>   I will make a righteous Branch sprout from David's line;
>   he will do what is just and right in the land.
> In those days Judah will be saved
>   and Jerusalem will live in safety.
> This is the name by which it will be called:
>   The LORD Our Righteousness.'
>
> For this is what the LORD says: 'David will never fail to have a man to sit on the throne of the house of Israel, nor will the priests, who are Levites, ever fail to have a man to stand before me continually to offer burnt offerings, to burn grain offerings and to present sacrifices.'"

The word of the LORD came to Jeremiah: "This is what the LORD says: 'If you can break my covenant with the day and my covenant with the night, so that day and night no longer come at their appointed time, then my covenant with David my servant—and my covenant with the Levites who are priests ministering before me—can be broken and David will no longer have a descendant to reign on his throne.'" (Jer. 33:14–21)

So Joseph also went up from the town of Nazareth in Galilee to Judea, to Bethlehem the town of David, because he belonged to the house and line of David. He went there to register with Mary, who was pledged to be married to him and was expecting a child. While they were there, the time came for the baby to be born, and she gave birth to her firstborn, a son. She wrapped him in cloths and placed him in a manger, because there was no room for them in the inn. (Luke 2:4–7)

He will be great and will be called the Son of the Most High. The Lord God will give him the throne of his father David. (Luke 1:32)

The distant grandson David wrote about in Psalm 110 was no surprise to David. God whispered these truths in his spirit and caused him to write them down for all eternity.

The LORD says to my Lord:
"Sit at my right hand
until I make your enemies
a footstool for your feet." (Ps. 110:1)

Indeed, one unexpected day the clouds will roll back and the King of all kings will burst through the sky. "On that day his feet will stand on the Mount of Olives, east of Jerusalem, and the Mount of Olives will be split in two from east to west. . . . Then the LORD my God will come, and all the holy ones with him. On that day there will be no light, no cold or frost. It will be a unique day, without daytime or nighttime—a day known to the LORD. . . . The LORD will be king over the whole earth. On that day there will be one LORD, and his name the only name" (Zech. 14:4–7, 9).

Christ Jesus will sit on the throne of David in the city of Jerusalem, and hope will give birth to certainty! We will join the one who said, "You turned my wailing into dancing; / you removed my sackcloth and clothed me with joy, / that my heart may sing to you and not be silent. / O LORD my God, I will give you thanks forever" (Ps. 30:11–12). With David, we will sing to One who is worthy!

That day there just might be one who can't seem to stop singing. Oh, yes, I believe David will dance once more down the streets of Jerusalem—this time without an eye to despise him. Oblivious to anyone but God—the focus of his affections, the passion of his heart. David will dance his way to that same familiar throne, but this time it will be occupied by Another. No one above Him. None beside Him. David will see the Lord high and lifted up, and His train will fill the temple. He'll fall before the One who sits upon the throne, take the crown from his own head and cast it at His feet. He'll lift his eyes to the King of all kings and with the passions of an entire nation gathered in one heart, he will cry, "Worthy!"

Surely God the Father will look with great affection upon the pair.

All wrongs made right. All faith now sight.
He'll search the soul of a shepherd boy once more
And perhaps He will remark
How very much he has
A heart like His.

Review Questions

Part I

Psalm 23: Summoned From the Sheepfold

Chapter 1: A Look at the Heart

1. How do you feel when you are the ostracized "little brother"?
2. What skills or experiences in your life might God have planned for His service?
3. Why do you suppose God chose David over his brothers?
4. In what ways do you see the young David foreshadowing the later ministry of Christ?
5. How do you suppose David felt when Samuel anointed him to be king?

Chapter 2: David's Back Story

1. What reason would you use to argue against the practice of polygamy?
2. Have you ever tried to bargain with God? If so, have you kept your commitments?
3. How difficult do you think Hannah's obedience was for her?
4. Who has been your greatest example of faithful obedience?
5. Trusting Eli with Samuel must have seemed almost impossible for Hannah. Has God's way in a situation ever been difficult for you to believe?

Chapter 3: Taking God for Granted

1. In what ways do people today disrespect God?
2. Why did God punish Israel for taking the ark into battle?
3. How could God's afflicting the Philistines be an expression of His grace?
4. What moral would you draw from the experiences with the ark of the covenant?

Chapter 4: Chords of Comfort

1. What do you think it would be like for God to withdraw His Spirit from you?
2. Which trait in David do you value the highest, the artist or the warrior?
3. In which area, artist or warrior, do you need to grow? Do you need greater sensitivity or courage?
4. Which trait of Christ, tenderness or strength, means the most to you? Why?

Chapter 5: The People's Choice

1. How do you suppose Samuel felt when the people rejected his sons?
2. Why do you think Samuel's sons turned out like Eli's sons?
3. Has God ever used something like a "donkey chase" to lead you to encounter Him?
4. What is the difference between godly humility and a poor self-concept?

Chapter 6: The Seeds of Destruction

1. What characteristics of Saul could have led him to greatness?

2. Do you think Saul was a people pleaser, and do you struggle with the same issue?

3. What do you think Saul lacked in his attitude toward God?

4. How do you react to your detractors?

Chapter 7: How to Lose a Kingdom

1. Do you believe God's rejection of Saul was fair? Why or why not?

2. How have you seen the progressive nature of sin as did Saul?

3. Do you ever struggle with the goodness of God in light of some of the harsh stories in the Old Testament?

4. How did Saul's disobedience grow as he continued in rebellion against God?

Chapter 8: A Father Unlike His Son

1. Why do you think Jonathan's character was so different from his father's?

2. What elements of Jonathan's faith could you benefit from?

3. Have you ever made a snap decision without either thinking or praying about it? If so, what were the results?

Chapter 9: One Smooth Stone

1. What does it feel like to "wear Saul's armor"?

2. How does David's experience with his family illustrate Jesus' words: "Only in his hometown and in his own house is a prophet without honor" (Matt. 13:57).

3. What "giants" do you have to face in your life?

4. What is one thing you could do to help develop the practice of measuring your obstacles against God?

Chapter 10: An Amazing Covenant

1. Who in your experience has been your "Jonathan"?
2. How could you become a Jonathan to another person?
3. Which of the three elements of a covenant impresses you most?
4. On what basis could you earn partnership in a covenant?
5. How does a covenant picture the grace of God?

Part II

Psalm 59: A Friendship Made in Heaven

Chapter 11: A Jealous Eye

1. How does anger lead to bad decisions and actions?
2. How does it feel to be the object of someone's unrighteous jealousy?
3. How does it feel to burn with jealousy?
4. What separates godly and ungodly jealousy?

Chapter 12: The Great Escape

1. Have you ever experienced "gale-force, out-of-control" emotions?
2. What encouragement do you get from the fact that Christ knows how it feels to be tempted by feelings (Heb. 4:15; 2:18).
3. What caption would you write if you were reporting on Samuel's encounters with Saul and his men?

Chapter 13: Common Bonds, Uncommon Friends

1. What do you think it means to "love someone as yourself"?
2. Has the Spirit of God ever brought you together with another person for purposes of His kingdom?
3. How would you react if a friend accosted you the way David confronted Jonathan?
4. How easy or difficult is sharing your fears with a friend?

Chapter 14: The Blessed Reminder

1. What might Ahimelech have thought when David appeared at his door?
2. What represents the presence of God to you?
3. What object or event in your life reminds you of the power of God?
4. How has God encouraged you during a time of great stress or discouragement?

Chapter 15: For Crying Out Loud

1. Can you describe a time when you had to "cry out" to the Lord?
2. Have you ever felt like David when he declared: "no one cares for my life"?
3. How do you rehearse your trust in God?
4. What can you do to make your prayer life more specific and personal?

Part III
Psalm 54: Survival Skills and He Who Wills

Chapter 16: The Inhumanity of Humanity

1. Have you felt sympathy for King Saul? If so, how do his actions in chapter 22 affect your attitude?
2. Have you ever known anyone who made him- or herself feel bigger or better by putting others down?
3. Which of the four closing points in the chapter means most to you? Why?

Chapter 17: Count Your Blessings

1. Have you ever reconfirmed what you understood to be God's will?

2. What is the difference between doubting God and doubting that you understood God?

3. What toll does repeated betrayal take on a person?

4. How did David manage to overcome the effects of Saul's betrayal?

Part IV
Psalm 63: In the Desert of Judah

Chapter 18: A Chance for Revenge

1. Can you recount a character lesson God has chiseled into your life during a time of particular challenge or discouragement?

2. How difficult do you think it was for David to offend his followers rather than to offend God?

3. Have you been faced with an opportunity for revenge? If so, did you take the opportunity or not, and what was the outcome?

4. What evidence of David's sensitivity to the Holy Spirit impresses you most?

Chapter 19: A Surly Man and a Smart Woman

1. Under what circumstances do you struggle with the prosperity of the unrighteous and the suffering of the righteous?

2. What do you admire most about Abigail?

3. How do you suppose Abigail's life had been with Nabal?

4. What lesson can you take away from the story of Nabal? Of Abigail? Of David?

5. How do you suppose it felt to be one of many wives in a plural marriage?

Part V
Psalm 56: The Long-Awaited Throne

Chapter 20: A Case of Overkill

1. Have you ever become so discouraged that you made foolish or destructive decisions?
2. David went to great lengths to cover his tracks. Have you ever made a bad situation worse by trying to cover yours?
3. How can we avoid the problem of runaway emotions that lead to destructive actions?

Chapter 21: The Living Dead

1. Have you gone through times when God seemed to be silent?
2. Have you made commitments that you later have found yourself breaking?
3. What do you suppose the witch thought when Samuel appeared?
4. What moral would you write for Saul's quest to know the future?

Chapter 22: Alone with God

1. Why do you think we humans tend to blame ourselves or others when we have experienced a hurt or loss?
2. Have you ever reacted to a perceived threat to your children?
3. How do you find strength in God during times of stress?
4. What has God taught you in the battles He has brought you through?

Chapter 23: The Death of Israel's Giant

1. How do you feel about the death of Saul? Jonathan? The armor-bearer?

2. To whom do you feel gratitude across many years, as the men of Jabesh Gilead did?

3. Has anyone ever blessed you by repaying a kindness in a surprising way?

Chapter 24: A Fallen Friend

1. Why did the man who brought the message assume David would be glad to hear of Saul's death?

2. What do you think motivated the women who sang of Saul's and David's feats?

3. Have you ever lost a dear friend as David lost Jonathan?

4. What actions help you in times of grieving over a great loss?

Chapter 25: Settling Down

1. Do you tend to inquire of God before you act, or do you act and then inquire of God?

2. When you seek God's will, do you seek specific or general directions?

3. What do you do when answers from God do not come quickly?

4. How do you think David felt when he was finally declared king over Judah?

Chapter 26: Things That Bring Change

1. Why do you suppose jealousy so plagued Saul's family?

2. Why do you think David demanded the return of Michal?

3. Do you think David did all that he should have following the death of Abner? Why?

4. Why do you think David was so inconsistent in avenging the death of Ish-Bosheth but not the murder of Abner?

Part VI

Psalm 18: A Man after God's Own Heart

Chapter 27: The Shepherd King

1. David waited half his life to see the fulfillment of the promise to be king. How long have you waited for a promise of God to be fulfilled?
2. By what names has God made Himself known to you?
3. Have you ever reached a goal only to encounter new struggles?
4. What characteristic of God encourages you most in time of stress?

Chapter 28: Mourning to Dancing

1. Why did God insist that the ark be transported as He had commanded?
2. Why do you think God killed Uzzah?
3. What does worship have to do with sacrifice?
4. What do you think it would have been like to be there for the celebration of the return of the ark?
5. How does it feel to have your motives for worship questioned?

Chapter 29: Humble Beginnings

1. Have you ever decided to do something for the Lord without directions from Him? If so, how did your efforts work?
2. Everyone has someone to whom they must answer. To whom are you accountable?
3. How have you learned something about waiting on the Lord?
4. When did you discover that you can't outgive God?

Chapter 30: Compulsory Praise

1. Have you experienced a time when you simply had to praise God? Explain.
2. When was the last time you "ran to sit before the Lord"?
3. What is the greatest cause of praise God has brought into your life?

Chapter 31: A Virtuous Man

1. Which of David's virtues do you most admire? Which would you most like to be part of your life?
2. What do you think most represents a man after God's own heart?
3. In this chapter we saw David at a time when he most fulfilled his calling. At what time have you most fulfilled your calling so far in your life?

Chapter 32: Room in the Palace

1. Have you ever felt loneliness during a time of success?
2. Who would you like to show kindness like David showed Mephibosheth? For whom would you be showing the kindness (who is your Jonathan)?
3. How do you suppose Mephibosheth felt when he was welcomed into David's home?
4. Have you ever been welcomed home as the returning prodigal?

Chapter 33: Shunned Sympathy

1. Why did Hanun's advisors tell him to respond as he did?
2. What is God's attitude toward those who harm or shame His children?
3. What enemies do you need God to deal with rather than trying to deal with them yourself?

Part VII
Psalm 51: The Wages of Sin

Chapter 34: Up on a Rooftop

1. What factors contributed to David's eroding self-control?
2. Why do you suppose David was not in the field with his army?
3. Whose sin was more disgusting, David's or Bathsheba's?
4. What surprises you most about David's plunge into sin?
5. How are you protecting yourself with a network of accountability?

Chapter 35: Contrasts in Character

1. Has sin ever taken you much farther away from God and from honor than you would have thought possible?
2. Why do you think David didn't stop and repent?
3. Have you ever gotten tangled in a web of sin as you tried to cover an earlier sin?
4. What would you say to David if you could intervene in this tragedy-in-progress?

Chapter 36: You Are the Man!!!

1. How much courage did Nathan need to confront David?
2. How do you suppose hiding his sin was affecting David?
3. With what consequences of forgiven sin have you still had to live?

Chapter 37: Painful Pleas

1. Have you ever pled with God as David pled for the child—seemingly without success?
2. What did David learn about God during this time of crisis?
3. Why did God deal so harshly with David?
4. How do you feel about God's loving chastisements?

Chapter 38: No Relief like Repentance

1. When have you felt the relief of restored fellowship with God after a season of sin?
2. What makes repentance difficult for you?
3. Which phrase of Psalm 51 touches you most? Why?
4. What would you say to encourage a friend to humbly repent?

Chapter 39: Family Secrets

1. How did David's sin bear fruit in the lives of his children?
2. Why did Amnon "hate" Tamar more than he had "loved" her?
3. How did Absalom and David add to Tamar's injury?
4. How can you learn to minister better to someone who has suffered a deep, shame-inducing injury like Tamar experienced?

Chapter 40: Bring Home the Banished

1. Do you suppose Absalom's vengeance satisfied anything in his heart?
2. Did Absalom's action in any way restore his sister? How do you suppose Tamar felt about the situation?
3. Why did David refuse to deal with Absalom?

Part VIII
Psalm 3: The Unrelenting Sword

Chapter 41: An Abandoned Throne

1. Why did Absalom come to hate his father so?
2. How does bitterness feel? How does it affect your life?
3. Do you have difficulty forgiving someone who has offended you deeply?
4. Have you had your own "Mount of Olives" crisis of prayer?

Chapter 42: Traitors and Friends

1. Have you ever been surprised by the mean-spiritedness of those who kick you when you are down?
2. Have you ever been amazed by the people who have supported you when you did not expect them to do so?
3. How have you learned to refresh yourself when you've been down a rocky path?
4. Are you more a friend like Hushai or an advisor like Ahithophel?

Chapter 43: If Only

1. What would you write on a tombstone for Absalom?
2. Why did Joab kill Absalom in spite of the king's command?
3. Why did David wait until Absalom was dead to cry out to him?

Chapter 44: Crossing the Jordan

1. How did David respond to those who had participated in the rebellion against him?
2. Why do you think David responded as he did to Mephibosheth?
3. How do you feel about being included in God's family?

Chapter 45: Unfinished Business

1. Why did Joab kill his cousin Amasa?
2. Why did David continue to put up with Joab's murderous ways?
3. How did the woman save Abel Beth Maacah?
4. Do you need to fulfill any old vows from your past?

Chapter 46: The Unwelcomed Sight of an Old Enemy

1. Do you relate in any way to David's experience of exhaustion in battle?

2. How highly did David's men esteem him?

3. How has God protected you by not always allowing you to be the hero?

4. Who are some heros of the faith to you?

Chapter 47: A Great Celebration

1. How do you celebrate the victories God provides?

2. How do you record your personal history with God?

3. What made David's relationship with God so authentic?

Chapter 48: A Hand Withdrawn

1. How has Satan attempted to make you believe God is unfair?

2. What about God's discipline is most difficult for you to understand?

3. How has temptation revealed to you what was in your heart?

4. Why did God prohibit a census of the fighting men of Israel?

5. How did the plague and its end portend the ministry of the Messiah?

Chapter 49: A New King

1. Having walked with David through these many years, how do you feel about his advanced age and infirmity?

2. Why did Nathan ally himself with Bathsheba to save the kingdom for Solomon?

3. Why did David choose the men he did to escort Solomon?

4. What significance was attached to the Gihon spring?

Chapter 50: Wholehearted Devotion

1. How did David assist Solomon to begin his reign?

2. What wise advice did David give Solomon?

3. What did David know about serving God with wholehearted devotion?

4. What motivates your service to God?

Part IX
Psalm 30: Final Years and Settled Fears

Chapter 51: Praises of the Great Assembly

1. How did David motivate his countrymen to give to the Lord?

2. What that is personal to you are you giving to the Lord?

3. What difference does praising God make in your life?

Chapter 52: A Resting Place

1. What that you have learned about David means most to you personally?

2. Why do you now believe David was the man after God's own heart?

ENDNOTES

1. Trent Butler et al., eds., *Holman Bible Dictionary* (Nashville: Holman Bible Publishers, 1991), 774.

2. Warren Baker, general editor, *The Complete Word Study Old Testament* (Chattanooga, Tenn.: AMG Publishers, 1994), 2363.

3. Ibid., 2372.

4. Ibid., 2306.

5. John Dryden, "The Hind and the Panther," *The Poetical Works of John Dryden,* Cambridge Edition, ed. George R. Noyes (Boston: Houghton Mifflin Co., 1909), 236.

6. Baker, 2318.

7. Ibid., 105.

8. James Strong, *Strong's Exhaustive Concordance* (Grand Rapids, Mich.: Baker Book House, 1982), 95.

9. Butler et al., 21.

10. Baker, 106.

11. Baker, 2300.

12. Spiros Zodhiates, general editor, *The Complete Word Study New Testament,* revised ed. (Chattanooga, Tenn.: AMG Publishers, 1993), 1295.

13. Butler et al., 946.

14. Baker, 2326.

15. Alan Redpath, *The Making of a Man of God* (Grand Rapids, Mich.: Fleming H. Revell, 1962), 197.

16. Baker, 19.

17. Ibid., 2337.

18. Ibid., 2306.

19. Butler et al., 45.

20. Baker, 86.

21. *Disciple's Study Bible* (Nashville: Holman Bible Publishers, 1988), 390.

22. Baker, 2339.

23. Ibid., 2340.

24. Butler et al., 553.

25. Ibid.

26. Baker, 2344.

27. Ibid., 2375.

28. Ibid., 2317.

ABOUT THE AUTHORS

BETH MOORE

Beth Moore is a writer and teacher of best-selling Bible studies whose public speaking engagements carry her all over the United States. A dedicated wife to Keith and mother to Amanda and Melissa, Beth is a graduate of Southwest Texas State University, where she met her husband. Beth lives in Houston, Texas, where she teaches a Sunday school class attended by more than two hundred women at First Baptist Church. Beth has written several books and Bible studies, including *A Woman's Heart: God's Dwelling Place, Living Beyond Yourself, Whispers of Hope, To Live Is Christ, Breaking Free, Praying God's Word, Jesus, the One and Only* and *The Beloved Disciple.* She is also the author of an autobiographical collection of poems and vignettes entitled *Things Pondered.* Beth believes her calling is Bible literacy: guiding believers to love and live God's Word.

DALE MCCLESKEY

Dale is the husband of Cheryl and father of Jason and Jodi. He was born in 1952 in Tezuitlan, Mexico, and born again in 1969 in Tinian, Navajo Indian Reservation, New Mexico. He attended Wayland Baptist University and Southwestern Baptist Theological Seminary. Dale served as a pastor for fifteen years in New Mexico before coming to LifeWay Christian Resources in Nashville, Tennessee, as an editor in the Adult Discipleship and Family Department. He has written or contributed to twelve books. His passions are ministry to hurting people and missions, especially among the disadvantaged.

Beth Moore invites you to grow in god's word.

Join Beth Moore in a fascinating journey through Scriptures to learn more about the amazing life and ministry of the Apostle Paul. This eleven-week, video-driven study will help you gain a new appreciation of servanthood and why Paul said, "to live is Christ and to die is gain."

Beth's video and print studies include *A Woman's Heart, A Heart Like His, Breaking Free, To Live is Christ, Jesus, the One and Only,* and *The Beloved Disciple.* Each in-depth discipleship study contains similar print, audio, and video resources. And each offers rich biblical studies to challenge and encourage women to live and to love God's Word.